The Marvelous Riches
of Savoring Christ:
The Letters of Ruth Bryan

With a Preface by the
Rev. A. Moody Stuart

REFORMATION HERITAGE BOOKS
Grand Rapids, Michigan

*For additional Reformed literature, both new and used,
request a free book list from the above address.*

PREFACE.

RUTH BRYAN stands in no need of introduction to the Christian public as a stranger, for the 'happy gleaner' is already well known by the Diaries published under the title of "Handfuls of Purpose." That book, though singularly devoid of all attraction except that of real worth, has been received with so cordial a welcome and so large a circulation, as to induce the Editor to prepare the present volume, which breathes the same spirit, but is marked by a livelier and more interesting character.

These Letters drop down among us from an upper gallery in the house of God, where a few chosen disciples are seeing and hearing Him over whom the Father opens the heavens and announces, "This is my beloved Son." Between them and the crowd of worshippers below there is little intercourse, and but slender sympathy; while they have almost forgotten the multitude outside, and their voice and their writings rarely reach so far. It is scarcely, indeed, out of them that Wisdom commonly chooseth and " sendeth forth her maidens to cry in the highest places of the city : Come eat of my bread, and drink of the wine which I have mingled, forsake the foolish, and live." Yet for themselves they took their place in the lowest room till the King came in and called to them, " Come up hither ;" and, while sitting now at the feet of Jesus, they never forget the miry pit from which they have been drawn, and they are ever humbled anew by being so near to the High and Holy One.

There is in these Letters a savour of Christ at once sweet and rare, with a marvellous richness and variety even in what may seem to some an incessant repetition. They describe themselves in these characteristic words:—" My endless, blissful theme is ever new ; Jesus and His salvation will never wear out. I would never have any sit down satisfied, but still press on after fuller revelations of Jesus ; for there are heights and depths in the

love of Christ of which the most favoured have
no conception, and there are beauties and glories
in His person which none have yet beheld. Oh !
I would have none rest short of the revelation
of His person, though His benefits are all precious.
Things of earth often repeated grow stale, but the
same view of a precious Jesus a thousand times
over is ever new. When Jesus shews Himself
again to us, is He not as a lamb newly slain ;
and is not His sacrifice, as an odour of a sweet
smell, as fragrant as though but just offered without spot unto God ? Oh, yes, He is ever the same
without sameness, and will be to all eternity. The
glories, beauties, and excellences of His person
are infinite ; and from these boundless sources our
finite minds will be feasted for ever and ever."

Ruth Bryan's letters are remarkably like Samuel
Rutherford's ; not rivalling them in depth, and
genius, and sanctified wit sublimed into heavenly
imagery; but closely resembling them in most
winning, unwearied, and gloriously endless eulogy
of the King in His beauty. They are admirably
fitted to allure believers into a nearer fellowship
with the Lord Jesus. Many who are already
standing within holy ground, but only in the

Court of the Gentiles, may be drawn by them to desire a place in the inner sanctuary of Israel, of the peculiar people, of the kingdom of priests ; for they are calculated in no ordinary manner to humble, to elevate, to refresh and enliven the reader. There are few Ruth Bryans in these days, the Church greatly needs more ; and we are therefore thankful to God that she 'being dead yet speaketh.' If her letters are blessed to provoke some to a holy emulation to tread in her heavenly footsteps, this seed-corn now cast into the ground will be reaped in a harvest of joy in the Great Day.

A. M. S.

EDINBURGH, 16*th January* 1865.

MEMOIR.

How is it that our God so long endures this open contempt
of His government and His holy name? Such is the question which will ofttimes occur to the Christian, as passing
through the streets of our towns he notes the ungodliness
that prevails in every form,—profanity, deceit, and drunken-
ness among the poor; mammon-worship and luxury among
the rich. The cities of the plain were swallowed up in a
sudden deluge of wrath—Nineveh and Babylon have perished, and their places are not found; how is it that judgment has not yet fallen upon us, when God is thus provoked
every day? His Word supplies the answer: "As the new
wine is found in the cluster, and one saith, Destroy it not;
for a blessing is in it: so will I do for my servants' sakes,
that I may not destroy them all." [1] "Ye are the salt of the
earth," preserving the mass from utter corruption. Here
and there, amid the turmoil of a world that knows not
God, sometimes in the stately streets, but more often in
the lanes of the cities, lowly believers may be found—
pilgrims where others seek to abide, strangers where others
are at home, dwelling in the world and using it, but not of

[1] Isaiah lxv. 8.

it; breathing a different air, born of another parentage from those around them; leading a life peculiar to themselves, secret in its essence, but manifest in its workings and its fruits. For the sake of these His jewels, which He is gathering, and preparing, and polishing for Himself, does the Lord yet awhile spare the polluted casket in which for a little season they are placed, "shewing mercy unto thousands of them that love Him and keep His commandments."

How strikingly does the comparison, "A lily among thorns," seem exemplified when true believers are seen dwelling amid the worldliness and excitement of town life! The thorns surround but do not choke them, for they are deeply rooted in Christ; the heavenly dew finds its way through all hindrances to their souls, and the graces of the Spirit are shewn forth in a life fragrant with holiness. Such an one was Ruth Bryan, the writer of the letters in this volume, who lived and died in Nottingham. She possessed no outward advantages of appearance or position, and a person less influential in the eyes of the world could hardly be found; yet it might be truly said of her, "As unknown, and yet well known; . . . as poor, yet making many rich; as having nothing, and yet possessing all things." The earthen vessel contained a treasure beyond all price—a wealth of love and light, which, like Gideon's lamps, gleamed all the more brightly for the shattering of the frail pitcher which enclosed it. "Riches of grace" are displayed in her letters, compared with which the best things of this world are but worthless. Some of these are now collected for the first time, in the hope that they may prove as strengthening and comforting to the Church at large, as they were to the friends to whom they were immediately addressed. To these

letters, combined with her personal influence, many trace
their own establishment in grace; the Lord the Spirit
having chosen her to lead them on, from the first feeble
gropings after light, to that view of Christ as their Redeemer, their Substitute, and their near Kinsman, which
was revealed to her with such rare clearness.

Ruth was the child of believing parents. Her father
began life as a tradesman, but gave up business to become
a preacher of the gospel. Her mother was his third wife,
a sensible, stirring woman, full of vigour, but somewhat
deficient, perhaps, in tenderness. Ruth, her only child,
instead of being spoiled, was brought up in habits of
almost Spartan hardihood. Not that she was treated
with undue severity, for her mother never punished her
but once, when she was guilty of some misconduct during
public worship ; but she taught the little girl to discipline
herself, and to despise pain and inconvenience. Ruth used
to tell her friends that when she hurt herself, or suffered
from casual ailments, her mother treated the matter with
the utmost unconcern, and expected the child to do the same.
This, no doubt, seemed hard at the time, but afterwards
Ruth traced the Lord's hand in it, training her the more for
the sevenfold-heated furnace of affliction, through which she
was called upon to pass. She was a good and docile child,
and keenly sensitive to reproof. She herself has mentioned
that once when her mother called her "a wayward child,"
the reproach nearly broke her heart. She was much alone
with her parents, as her half-brothers and sisters were
grown up and gone out into the world while she was yet a
child. Under these circumstances her father judged wisely
in sending her early to a day-school, so that she might mix

with other children without losing the advantage of parental guidance at home.

Her school career was not marked by any special incident. She was known among her companions as a quiet, staid, little girl, who went on her own way and let others alone. They could not help respecting her consistent good conduct, but she was not generally beloved, as she lacked the qualities which win popularity among children. They mistook her natural shyness for closeness or pride, and were chilled by the reserved manner which veiled her, even then, intense feelings. This reserve may have been increased by the consciousness of a want of sympathy on the highest points between her companions and herself, for even thus early the Holy Spirit had begun His work in her heart. There was a shaking among the dry bones—a very strong sense of sin—heart-sin which was continually baffling her efforts to overcome it, and an awful fear of the wrath of God declared against it, while she only believed in a Deliverer, as it were, afar off, not daring yet to claim Him as her own. When this concern was first felt she knew not, for she could never remember the time when she was without it, and this inability to point to any definite season of conversion harassed her more or less in after years. A note in her own Bible marks the text which was used by the Spirit to repel this attack of the enemy,—" So is the kingdom of God, as if a man should cast seed into the ground, and should sleep, and rise night and day, and the seed should spring and grow up *he knoweth not how.*"

But though unappreciated by the many, there were those among her companions at school who understood and loved her, and with some of these she formed life·long friendships.

One little girl of six years old was so devotedly attached
to her that she was miserable if they were separated, and
when Ruth passed on to more advanced schools, the child
gave her indulgent father no rest till she was allowed to
follow her. It is to this friend we owe these particulars
of Ruth's early life. Ruth, being two years the elder, did
not fully reciprocate this affection at first, but as they grew
up their hearts were knit together like sisters. This circumstance shews that Ruth had already begun to exercise that
influence over others, which was felt so remarkably throughout her life, and which death itself has not destroyed. She
has left her impress on those who loved her; the letters she
wrote still feed their souls, and her simplest words are re-
called and dwelt upon as the choicest treasures of their
memory.

Ruth was sent for final instruction to a writing-school for
girls, where she doubtless acquired the clear penmanship of
which she made such liberal use in after life. None can
read the many volumes of manuscript she has left behind
her, without feeling how much the legible handwriting has
added to their value. Her neat dress and her exquisite
needlework shewed the same habit of doing common things
well, so characteristic of well-ordered minds. As a scholar
she was not brilliant, but always took a respectable place.
She was considered very religious by her companions, for
though speaking little on the subject, her influence was
fearlessly used in checking whatever she knew to be wrong.
She one day heard a passage of Scripture quoted irreverently,
and hushed the speaker with instant reproof. Years afterwards the companion whom she had reproved spoke of the
occurrence, saying that the impression it made upon her was

never lost, and that the influence now remains upon her own children.

When Ruth was about fifteen, her father, being advanced in years, and possessing little of this world's goods, became anxious that she should learn something which might be a means of maintaining herself in case of his removal. With this view he apprenticed her to a milliner in Nottingham, with whom she continued for three years. Miss Byrne, the head of this millinery establishment, was a Christian woman, and a member of Mr Bryan's congregation. In these days, when so much is brought to light of the sufferings of milliners' and dressmakers' apprentices, it is refreshing to hear the testimony of those employed by Miss Byrne, that they were as happy in her service as at home. Family worship was held morning and evening, and Miss Byrne seems to have stood in the relation of friend and adviser to her young people. In Ruth's diary, which was commenced when she was seventeen, and continued up to the time of her death, we find the following extracts :—
"I went with Miss Byrne this morning for a walk; enjoyed it very much. She seems to think there is good hope even for me. Surely I have not deceived her. I think I told her all I felt; but hope and encouragement seem almost impossible. I have been informed by one of my companions, that Miss Byrne has with pain observed in me a spirit of censoriousness and sneering. I sneer! the last person in the world who ought to do it, feeling so guilty myself. I am afraid I did not receive the reproof in a proper spirit ; but felt hurt, as it came from those younger than myself. Lord, subdue the abominable spirit of pride which I feel, and

enable me to overcome the censorious looks which are observed in me."

The diary from which this extract is made is altogether a remarkable production. Forcible in language, and often minute in detail, it portrays with equal vividness the course of her outward life, and the joys and sorrows of her inward experience. Most interesting is it to trace, through the long series of closely-written volumes, the growth and development of the divine life in her soul, and as the feeble handwriting of the girl of seventeen gradually forms itself into the clear and decided characters of her later penmanship, so the weak blade of grace, shooting up from the seed of the Lord's planting, is seen to take root downwards and bear fruit upwards, till it ripens into the "full corn in the ear" of mature Christian experience.

As far as concerns outward circumstances, this diary is a tale of sorrow, but a mere glance over the faded pages will shew that occasions for thanksgiving were with Ruth Bryan not few or far between. She was always on the watch for mercies, and every special token of the Lord's kindness is marked in the diary by an "Ebenezer." Sometimes she writes the word in large strong characters, but often in the later volumes she emphatically marks each bright spot in her life-journey by the figure of a stone, rudely sketched in ink, with suitable inscriptions upon and around it. Another feature of interest in these MS. volumes is the record of prayers in times of need, or of hopes founded on some special promise, across which, years afterwards, she has written the answer of the prayer, or the fulfilment of the hope. These memoranda give to the autograph journal a reality such as no printed copy can convey. Her spiritual anxieties were now continually deepening, and few could have guessed the terrible conflict which went on under that calm and reserved exterior. In her diary she thus pours out the anguish of her soul: "Oh, keep me humble, keep me from self-deception! begin the good work, if it is not yet begun! Oh, may I not be a castaway! Break, break this stony heart! How long, Lord, how long? Make me *feel.* Oh, leave me not to this insensibility! What argument can I use? Oh, leave, leave me not! Suffer me not to perish! Mercy, mercy is all my plea; for Christ's sake, have mercy on me! Oh, precious, precious Christ Jesus, be Thou my Saviour, Husband, Friend,—*my* Jesus and my all. Jesus! Jesus! Oh, that Thou wert precious to my soul!"

But while thus crying out, "Who shall deliver me from the body of this death?" she diligently used the means of grace, and was persevering in prayer. Remembering the promise to united prayer, she induced one or two companions to join with her morning and evening, in supplicating the blessings of which each felt her need, and the practice was found to be mutually helpful. Ruth felt great difficulty in praying before others, but she bravely persevered, seeking special help to overcome the shrinking of her sensitive nature. She also took opportunities of speaking to her companions about their souls, though she could not as yet direct them to the Saviour, as one whom she had herself known and found.

When she had been about two years with Miss Byrne, her father's health began to fail, and this trial added fearfully to her mental sufferings. Her grief at the thought of losing him was intense, and when, some months after, the blow actually fell, poor Ruth was almost overwhelmed, feeling oppressed and stupified with sorrow, and pressed down under a weight which she knew not how to endure. This breavement involved a change in her outward circumstances. Mrs Bryan naturally wished that Ruth should return to her, now that she was a widow and alone, and to this Miss Byrne kindly consented, though the term of apprenticeship was not yet expired. Ruth now entered upon a quiet, yet busy home-life with her mother. They were left but insufficiently provided for, and it was necessary to eke out their scanty income by the labours of their own hands. Ruth relinquished her former employment of millinery, (which was distasteful to her, as seeming to minister to the vanities of a world from which she desired to be separate,) preferring to work with a clear conscience at plain sewing. Mrs Bryan, (being always a little too anxious about the things of this life,) suffered her daughter to attend so closely to her work as to injure her health, and seclude her almost entirely from the society of her friends. The press of work may partly account for the interruption in her diary, which was discontinued about this time. When it was resumed cannot exactly be known, as a large portion has evidently been cut away. Those missing leaves contained a painful record which Ruth would gladly have torn out of her memory too.

By way of further adding to their resources, Mrs Bryan resolved to take in lodgers, and thus a temptation was thrown in the way of poor Ruth, under which many of the Lord's children have succumbed for a time, even if they have not, concerning faith, made shipwreck. It seems scarcely consistent with the prudence to be expected from a mother having a young daughter at home, to take in single men as lodgers, but perhaps Mrs Bryan thought Ruth's retiring manners a sufficient safeguard. So shy indeed was she, that her friends have never ceased to wonder how any person could gain the opportunity of paying his addresses to her,—but this opportunity was found by one of the lodgers, a young man engaged in business in Nottingham, whose attentions, no doubt coyly enough received at first, were eventually only too successful in making an impression on her heart.

Unhappily, this young man was in every way unworthy of her. Less partial eyes than hers were at a loss to discover anything, either in his disposition or circumstances, to recommend him to her favour; and, worst of all, he was living without God in the world. But Ruth loved him, and her affections once engaged, the blinding of her judgment followed. Like too many others, she saw not the actual person whom others saw, but was occupied with a creature of her own imagination, whom she had invested with all the attractions her gifted mind could supply. Her lover did his best to foster this delusion. Knowing that he had to deal with one whose heart had long been set in earnest desire on things above, he sought to please her by feigning a deep religious concern himself. Ruth longed to be the means of his conversion, and her efforts to this end no doubt tended further to lull her conscience to sleep. She was encouraged by his apparent interest in her reading the Bible and praying with him, and greatly must she have rejoiced when he became a teacher in a Sunday school. Still Ruth was the only one deceived. Her friends warned her that she was misled by a hyprocritical profession, and her mother expressed strong disapproval of her engagement, but no counsel or remonstrance could open her eyes. Ruth seemed infatuated, and clung only the more persistently to one whom she believed all others wronged by their harsh judgment and mistrust.

But a hand was holding her more firm in its tender grasp than that of mother or friend ; One who loved her better than she loved herself, had hedged up her way with thorns that she could not find her paths. Very painful means were used for her disenchantment, but no gentler ones would have availed. Ruth at last discovered that her lover was not only hypocritical in his profession of godliness, but faithless to herself; that he was actually paying court to another, and such additional evidence of his worthlessness was brought to light as filled her with anguish as well as shame. The mutilated volume of her diary, from which a mass of leaves has been cut away, testifies to the miserable awakening which could not bear even to look upon the records of that dream. Ruth went down to the low depths of sorrow where the spirit must dwell alone, for sympathy itself cannot enter without inflicting another wound. To one who ventured to allude to her trial, her answer was short and decisive : " If you love me, you will never speak on that subject again while I live."

How it fared with Ruth in this "low place," we cannot tell, nor what communings she held with Him who knew her soul in affliction, though as yet perhaps she fully knew not Him. Her mourning was long and deep; but time brought soothing, if not relief, and she braced herself anew to meet the claims of home and friendship. In the first entry suffered to remain in her diary, she describes her feelings as those of a shipwrecked sailor, who finds the shore on which he is cast to be within sight of home, and can scarcely believe his eyes as he recognises each well-known tree and

b

familiar turn of the road, speaking welcome and peace to him, where he had only looked for destruction. Such comfort she found in a submissive return to her former life, where, instead of warning words and looks of displeasure from parent and friends, she met with smiles and cordial approval, responding to the voice in her heart, which told her the right track was regained, where those she loved could walk with her, and where, above all, she could walk with God. Years passed, however, before her dreams were quite over and her expectations from "the creature" at an end. Hope after hope was extinguished, till at last she ceased yearning after outward happiness, and accepted of the home of her childhood as her final home on earth. Thenceforth her life subsided into the narrow silent channel along which it flowed, little varied, save by added trial, throughout the remainder of her days.

But let it not be supposed that Ruth Bryan's future life was a gloomy one. To dispel such an idea we have only to refer to her published journal, the key-note of which is thanksgiving and the voice of melody. Throughout the later years of her life she lived as seeing Him who is invisible, and, in fellowship with her risen Lord, found fulness of joy such as words failed to express,—at times almost beyond what nature could sustain. She could contentedly see broken cisterns dried up, while able to say, "Thou hast kept the good wine until now." She ceased to sigh over withered gourds, while sitting down with great delight under the shadow of the Tree of Life, and drinking of that river, the streams whereof make glad the city of God.

Not that this blessedness was immediately attained. She struggled on through years of darkness and conflict before (to use her own words) she ceased "seeking in self what our Father has given us only in Christ." The strife and agony of soul through which she passed before entering into rest are detailed in her journal with almost painful vividness. Sometimes grief for missed happiness would have its way, and broke all the bounds she had imposed upon it; sometimes she was well-nigh swallowed up in the rising tide of her inward corruption. This portion of her diary taken in connexion with its later pages, is specially valuable as shewing that Ruth was no angel lifted by purity of nature out of the sphere of ordinary experience; we see her here as a sinful, struggling human creature, with strong feelings and a womanly heart, craving after happiness in this world. One day her soul mounts up in heavenly aspirations; she hungers and thirsts after righteousness, beseeching God to make her His own at all costs; and then, again, we find her in the lowest dungeon of Doubting Castle. She has indolently trifled with evil, thus suffering the enemy to approach her, and in the hand-to-hand struggle that ensues she finds herself overmatched. Again and again she is worsted in the conflict, and we see her eating the bitter fruits of sin, heartsick and exhausted, and groaning under that stony, prayerless darkness of soul which is certain to follow any known indulgence in evil. It is true that this warfare went on below the surface, while her outward conduct was serious and consistent; but sin is none the less sin when its workings are confined to the thoughts of the heart. Ruth meant what she said, when she afterwards told a doubting friend that her own guiltiness had been such that if she had found mercy none need despair.

At last came the day of deliverance. On February 25,

1838, she obtained a view of Christ as her Redeemer at once
from the guilt, curse, and power of sin. She was listening to a sermon at the time, with no special interest, when
the Lord Himself seemed to take her aside, and reveal
Christ to her soul as her own precious Saviour; so that she
who (to use her own words) had entered the house of God
with a sentence of condemnation as it were hung around
her neck, signed with her own hand at first, came out with
a free pardon in its place, signed by the infinite Jehovah.
The decorous congregation little knew what was passing in
the heart of her who sat so quiet and serious in her wonted
place. "The kingdom of God cometh not with observa-
tion;" but the same voice which called Lazarus from the
tomb had now said, concerning the long-captive Ruth,
"Loose her, and let her go."

She entered yet more fully into rest during an illness
which attacked her about a year after, and from which she
was not expected to recover; but neither bodily suffering nor
the immediate prospect of death was able to interrupt the
triumph of her soul. She longed, indeed, to be gone, feeling
that the joys of heaven with which she was favoured had
spoiled her for earth; and she touchingly says in her diary,
"Methinks home is the best place for a spoiled child."

This was not yet to be, however. Ruth had many more
toiling, suffering years to live unto the Lord, before the time
came for her to die unto the Lord. She recovered, and the
joy which had sustained her in illness now brightened the
monotonous round of her daily life. A friend meeting her
shortly after her recovery walking in Nottingham Park,
Ruth remarked to her, "This is my first walk in liberty."
She had entered upon a new era of her life; her heart was

enlarged, and she could run in the way of God's commandments.

Not long after this the congregation of which Ruth was a
member were unexpectedly deprived of their pastor. Great
difficulty was found in supplying his place, and for some
time they were left without any regular ministry. Ruth's
course of conduct throughout this time of trouble was characteristic. She gave herself to prayer, and now commenced
her Friday evening prayer-meetings,—seasons of privilege
which will never be effaced from the memory of her friends.
The primary object of these meetings was to ask guidance
of the Lord in their choice of a pastor, but they were continued long after the originating cause of them had passed
away. The last was held in her sick chamber, within a week
of her death. These social gatherings were small and strictly
private. Five or six friends met at Ruth's house on Friday
evenings, to spend the hours from seven to nine or ten o'clock
in prayer. Though few in number they were one in heart,
and one with their Lord, and seldom did they leave that hallowed place of prayer without bringing away a rich blessing in their own souls. They felt that she who pleaded for
and with them enjoyed near access to the throne of grace,—
that she had power with God, and prevailed. But Ruth also
loved to pray alone with her friends. One with whom she
was thus wont to meet on Sunday evenings, says that during
these seasons of communion and pleading with God they
might have used the apostle's words, "Whether in the body
or out of the body, I cannot tell." She remembers Ruth once
saying, " I wish our mothers could come and find us both
flown away," so thin seemed the veil that separated them
from the unseen glory. She was eminently sympathetic, and

in prayer would remember the cases and interests of her friends as though they were her own. So keenly did she feel for and with them, especially in their concern for unconverted children or relatives, that their burdens would press upon her with heavy and painful weight, and she sometimes would say that none knew how much she suffered from sharing the sorrows of others.

The year 1845 closed gloomily for Ruth, for then the fear began to awaken in her breast, that the last tie to earth would ere long be broken, and that she must travel on her way alone. It seems strange to us that the dispositions least fitted for solitude should often be those appointed to endure it, while others, whose buoyant spirits are able to lift them above all depressing circumstances, have their lot cast in the sunshine of social life. Ruth's nature was peculiarly sensitive and clinging. She loved retirement, but shrunk from absolute solitude as some minds recoil from physical pain. Yet this, she now foresaw, was soon to be her portion. Her mother's health had for some time caused her anxiety, and in the December of 1845 it was further affected by an alarming accident. The poor old lady was walking alone in the streets of Nottingham when a horse and cart ran against her, throwing her down and bruising her severely. She was brought home in a coach unconscious, and the sudden sight of her mother in this state was a terrible shock to Ruth. Mrs Bryan soon began to amend, however, and the happy daughter hoped all cause for immediate alarm was over.

But these hopes were soon to be clouded again. Ruth had been well-nigh overwhelmed by her recent trial, but worse was at hand. The precious stone for the Lord's temple was to be shaped to more exquisite proportions by a wearing and grinding process so intensely painful to nature that only the knowledge of a Father's love appointing it, and the sense of her Saviour's presence throughout the time of suffering, could have enabled her to bear it with patience. Mrs. Bryan's health was indeed partially restored, but Ruth saw with dismay that her mental powers were shaken by the shock, and in spite of all her cares, they continued to decline. Then followed one of those periods more exhausting to strength and patience than the sharpest attacks of sudden affliction. Ruth's one business was to endure, as she tended her beloved mother through all the phases of her failing mind. She watched over her night and day, and would delegate this duty to no other, though kind friends offered assistance, and though she herself was almost worn out with harassing care.

" My dear mother," she writes, June 6, 1846, " is more weak and childish in her faculties. I do feel the need of patience to attend to the constant restless and fidgety requests of a mind under the most changeful illusions, to satisfy which is impossible, because the things imagined have no existence, but which she expects me to attend to, till my poor nerves and frame are almost worn down. The Lord has done wonders in renewing and upholding me hitherto ; may He continue the mercy, and make me dutifully obedient in all things. . . .

" *July* 25.—The last week has been one of the deepest in trial that I have ever known. My dearest mother's faculties are far gone. Oh, it has been heart-grieving to see the stamp of miserable feelings in her dear face, and to hear her think us all unkind and neglectful when doing our very

utmost for her.   Often have I felt almost worn out with
weariness and fatigue, and yet the dear one could not allow
me to rest.   Altogether, it has been most bitter, but I have
sweet refreshings from the presence of the Lord, and this
evening feel a firm and peculiar confidence that, though so
rough, all is right, and He is doing all things well." . . .

"*August* 2.—Many mercies are mingled with the bitter.
One is, that my dear mother, amidst her ramblings, keeps
pleading every now and then for mercy. 'Lord help—Lord
have mercy—do, Lord; do, Lord,' with other such words,
break through the gloom as a gleam of light in a dark place.
Another mercy has been the kind attention of friends in the
hour of need.   I was not left alone when three weeks ago a
sudden emergency came, and my dear mother seemed suddenly struck with death.   Then my dear 'sister' Mary and
her husband came with the willingness of love, and were
unremitting night and day while the emergency lasted.
Also other dear friends the Lord provided for the time of
need.   May He richly reward them all; I deeply feel their
kindness, and my Father's too.   He was the moving cause,
and much I wonder at such undeserved favour. . . .

"*August* 5.—Last evening was one of great distress. My
dear mother would not be controlled, but was determined to
go out, for which she was utterly unfit.   She did go into the
garden, and it was only by force I could prevent her going
into the street.   Oh, what did my heart feel at my dear
mother's great anger and these painful circumstances! Till
twelve o'clock she did not rest; she then fell asleep, and till
near two I was favoured with such sweet communion with
my Lord as made amends for all.   I was sure that though
our precious Christ might appear not to answer prayer, or

not to notice my distress, He was overruling all, and every wave obeyed His bidding. Truly I had 'songs in the night,' and to-day I have stood rejoicing in the will of my Father.

"*September* 27.—Great have been the Lord's mercies to me the past month. I have now great exertion in the day, and very broken rest at night with my dear mother, whose infirmities are many and have much increased, increasing greatly my labour also. I often feel very ill and jaded, but cannot resign my post to another, unless quite obliged. I wish to minister to my dear one to the last, though I could not have believed it possible to accomplish what I do night and day. 'Tis not I, but Christ in me doeth the works: praise Him, O my soul! Death appears to be upon my dearest mother, but the Lord has not yet spoken peace, and I seem to hold Him here in faith and prayer that He will hold her body in life till the Vision has spoken which shall soften the pang of parting, and gain our Lord glorious praise. My Christ is my rest and refreshing in all my weariness. As I lean on Him I triumph; when I confer with flesh and blood, and look to creatures, I get shame and loss. The unknown future which I have so dreaded is coming—to stand alone in this dark drear wilderness; but then my Jesus will be all-sufficient."

In this last extract, Ruth touches on the bitterest circumstance of her present trial. Mrs Bryan had long been a Christian, and her friends had no doubt of her safety; but throughout her illness, her soul was overclouded by doubt and depression. It was sharp anguish to Ruth to see her mother without sensible support in her hour of need, and earnestly did she plead for the sinking sufferer, that the Lord would lift up the light of His countenance upon her, and give her peace.   He, however, who renders no account of His dealings with His own children, saw fit to withhold an answer to this prayer.   Mrs Bryan continued to sink, and no ray of light broke through the cloud.   In ever-deepening gloom the hours and days passed on, but Ruth felt the presence of the Lord was with *her*, even while her mother was passing through this valley of the shadow of death.

" *Tuesday, Oct.* 6.—Watching beside the dying-bed of my dearest mother, and I think she can hardly live through the day.   No word of power in her soul, and her mind quite rambling.   I desire to be this day in great stillness from earthly avocations, and to wait much on the Lord in this chamber of death.

" *Wednesday.*—Still my dear mother lives, but sinks evidently.   I am much alone with her, and am mercifully supported.   The Lord has not spoken, and I hope I am coming to feel completely, ' Thy will be done.'   The Lord go with me through this dreaded hour !   I have had nothing special from Him but this word, 'As one whom his mother comforteth, so will I comfort you ;' and this has been re-iterated in my soul again and again."

The next entry is bordered with a thick black line— token of a life-long mourning.

" *Thursday, Oct.* 8.—The dearest of mothers left this sorrowful world at a quarter-past six this morning."

Her one earthly light, after flickering painfully for so long, and then sinking into feeblest glimmer, had gone out at last, and Ruth was alone.

Alone, and yet not alone.   Her very next entry is a song

of praise. " *Oct.* 10.—With wonderful cordials and comforts of love Divine hath the Lord supported my aching heart. Indeed, He is fulfilling His promise—'As one whom his mother comforteth, so will I comfort you.'"

The "Ebenezer stones" which about this time are thickly sprinkled over her pages are bordered with black, in token of her sorrow, but the upper edge is invariably left white, to signify (as explained by the inscription) that the Sun of joy was beaming on her from above, while all was dark below. She felt keenly, so much so, that for a length of time she could not visit her mother's grave with calmness; but every murmur was subdued, and her soul was joyful in all her tribulation.

Having now no engrossing ties at home, a call to work in a very rough part of the Lord's vineyard was joyfully responded to. She was requested by some Christian friends to visit the Nottingham Refuge for Outcast Girls; and though with much fear and trembling, she undertook the office of weekly visitor, which she held till her last illness laid her aside. How trying she often found this duty is shown by such records as the following:—

" *Monday and Tuesday.*—I was with a dear afflicted friend six or seven hours each day, and I felt sharply the fatigue. I sat up with her on Wednesday night, and was very poorly in the morning, but had a request to go to the Refuge. I felt as if the Lord was laying too much upon me, yet dared not draw back, believing it to be His work. I went, had peculiar power in prayer with the poor girls, came away refreshed, and the Lord seemed to say, ' Will you ever say I lay too much upon you again?'"

"*August* 16.—This morning awoke feeling very ill, severe

cold on my chest, and breathing short and oppressed. After breakfast, it was very wet, and looked like settled rain, when a request came that I would go to the Refuge. The flesh felt it, but the spirit was willing, and dared not withhold. After giving myself to the work, the clouds broke away, the rain was over and gone, and I had a dry walk. Also, the Lord was pleased to give me strength of body, and—what was most gracious—did put a very solemn word in my mouth, causing it to flow freely from a feeling heart. Only six girls were present; but there was deep attention, and I saw one eye moisten with tears which had always been dry before. May the Holy Spirit fasten some word as a nail in a sure place! My heart is in that work in longings for their souls."

"*August* 25, *Friday.*—I have been privileged to go to the Refuge again to-day, when all the inmates were present. The Lord gave me utterance to speak solemnly on the wrath of God in devouring fire against breakers of His law, and of a precious Christ enduring that wrath for His people. One girl wept exceedingly. My heart yearned over her, but I dared not appear to notice it, lest it should be fleshly feeling. Oh, when shall I have to record some solid work, some soul brought out of darkness into marvellous light! For this I wait, and long, and pray."

This desire of her heart was not granted, to her knowledge, though at the time much impression was produced among the girls. She had to labour on in faith; and the results will be made manifest in the day when the Lord maketh up His jewels. It is remarkable that Ruth, so earnestly desiring to win souls to Christ, never knew herself to be the means of the conversion of any, and she often

mourned over her unfruitfulness in this respect. Sometimes she was almost tempted to envy those who were
more evidently useful than herself; though, as appears
from the following extract, abundant consolation was
always at hand :—"'Peninnah had children, but Hannah
had no children.' How this word has sounded in my heart
this morning. It is just like my friend and me, spiritually;
she is made useful to souls, and I am a poor barren thing,
not knowing that one has been called through me. It says
that Elkanah gave to Hannah 'a worthy portion,' and this
is spiritually true of me. 'The Lord is my portion, saith
my soul.' I do rejoice in Him, though the least and most
insignificant of all His members."

But here it must not be omitted that it had been her
wont to pray that, if blessed to the conversion of any, she
might not know it, lest she should be exalted above measure.
We may question the wisdom of such a prayer, as implying
a doubt of the power of divine grace. Surely He who gives
success is able also to give strength to the happy labourer
to bear it with humility ; but, at any rate, it seems singular
that, having so prayed, she should not recognise in her
seeming failure the answer to her request. Her special
work, however, seemed to lie in strengthening and comforting the Lord's people; and for this she was peculiarly fitted
by the severity of her own experiences, and the rich consolations she afterwards enjoyed.

After her mother's death Ruth suffered much from strait-
ness of circumstances, of which her friends knew nothing
at the time, or they would joyfully have lifted this burden
from one who had borne so many burdens on her heart for
them. She had a little property in the Funds, and, be

sides this, she owned several small houses; but these last proved a very uncertain source of income, as the rents were irregularly paid, and frequent outlay was needed to keep them in tenantable repair. The house in which Ruth had always lived with her parents was now too large for her, and the rents and other expenses entailed by it were beyond what her income could meet, even with such additions as the labour of her hands procured. She was urged to reduce her expenses by moving to a smaller house, or to increase her means to meet them, by taking inmates to reside with her; but Ruth loved privacy, and clung to the dwelling which was associated with all the dear recollections of her past. She continually sought guidance from the Lord on this point, and believed she was following His will in continuing to reside alone where she was.

Whether she was right or wrong in this belief, it is certain that it entailed upon her much pecuniary distress, and acute mental anguish in consequence. The approach of the rent-day or the tax-gatherer filled her with dismay, and to borrow or to postpone payment was alike repugnant to her upright soul. The first year after her mother's death she was in such distress for the means to pay her rent, that she spent the greater part of two whole days in fasting and prayer to the Lord for help in her extremity, tasting no food each day till evening, and continuing for many hours on her knees. After some delay, a seasonable relief came in a remittance of rent from a tenant in London, enabling her to pay her own. The next year she was in similar distress, and though again she fasted and prayed before the Lord, no outward answer came to her request, and she was forced to borrow the needful money. A third season of similar anguish seemed to point out to her that the Lord's will was other than she had imagined it to be, and that she must not look for extra providential supplies for this yearly-recurring need. She therefore sold out of the Funds sufficient of her little property to pay her rent, and thenceforth continued to do so when necessary. This plan, by lessening her stock, reduced her income also; and though she worked at her needle as much as her health allowed, it was only by the most strenuous economy that she was able to provide herself with the common comforts of life. The following is one of many passages in her journal describing the sharpness of her trial and the blessing she found in it:—

"I have been much harassed on account of my temporal affairs, but in the conflict have been brought to close dealing with the Lord. A large demand for half a year's poor-rate has drawn the providential knot still tighter. . . . Yesterday came tax for highway rate, which, with the other, only left me a few shillings in my purse. I cried to the Lord to have pity, and before noon was sent £1, 2s., which was owing for needlework that I have done. How timely! How merciful! What a ray across my dark path! It is like a gift from the Lord. . . . . 'The Israelites came to the impassable place, and the enemy behind kept them from turning back; they must go forward; but the sea is there, and no bridge; and, when the strange command is given by their leader, the waters shall wonderfully withdraw to either side, and between the liquid walls they shall safely pass over, to the honour of their God.' This seems like me. I have come to the place of hedging up. I have looked all ways for an outlet, and cried to the Lord for it, but in vain. I find deliverance *in* the trial, not *out* of it; and now, while going through the deeps, my sighs are changed for songs."

Yet, though so sorely straitened herself, her liberality to others passed all bounds of wordly prudence, and sometimes perhaps could hardly be justified at all. She had that royal spirit which gives uncalculatingly, not reckoning what she could spare, but what the needs of others required. A friend of hers lost largely in the railway panic of 1848, and was so cast down by the misfortune that her distress seriously affected her health. Ruth visited her constantly, trying to speak comfort, but in vain. One day she appeared as usual with the little black bag on her arm, in which she generally carried her Bible. "I have tried all that words and prayers can do," she said, "aud now I have brought my money." As much of her little fortune as she could lay hands on was in that bag, turned into ready money for the use of her friend. This was offered to her with such eager desire for its acceptance, that the refusal of her gift cut her to the very heart. So keen was her disappointment, that her friend's husband afterwards regretted not having taken the money as a temporary loan, to be speedily returned with interest, so that Ruth might have had the pleasure of rendering service to one she loved.

But it is written, " Give, and it shall be given unto you ; good measure, pressed down, and shaken together, and running over, shall men give into your bosom;" [1] and this truth was strikingly exemplified in the case of Ruth Bryan. The Lord raised up friends for her who had both the means and the will to minister to her comfort, and who held it a privi-

[1] Luke vi. 38.

lege to provide her with change and enjoyments, for her health's sake, far beyond the reach of her own scanty resources. It was during a visit to Ockbrook, which was arranged for her by one of these friends, that the compiler of these letters first became acquainted with her, and the interview was singularly characteristic. Ruth was alone in the sitting-room of the little inn where she was staying, when her visitors entered, bringing her a beautiful bouquet of flowers. Her appearance presented nothing remarkable to a casual observer. She was a slight, spare woman, of about forty, dressed with great neatness in black, which she always wore after her mother's death, just till the time of her own drew near, as will by and by be noted. Her complexion was pale, with light hazel eyes, and her small features were somewhat sharpened by suffering, but the expression of her countenance was animated, and even joyful. She seemed instinctively to draw spiritual instruction from every object around her, and the sight of the flowers at once suggested a train of happy thoughts to her mind. "What lovely flowers!" she exclaimed; "how sweet they are—how very beautiful! That rose, it is delicious, but not so beautiful as the Rose of Sharon. I could never describe His beauties, nor tell you a thousandth part of His glories. As the leaves of this rose unfold one by one, so does Jesus reveal Himself little by little to the soul that is kept waiting upon Him, and looking to Him. He has so attracted my soul, that I can say, 'Whom have I in heaven but thee? and there is none upon earth that I desire beside thee.'"

To another friend, who saw her shortly after the death of her mother, Ruth remarked, that during the last Friday's prayer-meeting she had been at the very gate of heaven. "I have had a very comforting thought lately," she said, "in remembering 'Thy Maker is thine Husband.' It is so sweet to think, Who is to manage the house? Surely the Husband. Who is to pay the debts? The Husband. Who is to order everything? The Husband. And who has a right to remove anything from the house that has taken too much of the Bride's heart away from Himself? Why, surely the Husband. And that is what He has done in removing my dear mother, for since then, He Himself has been more precious to my soul. I see Him in it all, and that stops repinings and murmurings."

Ruth delighted greatly in fine scenery, and her friends knowing this, so arranged her changes from home that she visited some of the loveliest spots in the kingdom. Here her natural mind expatiated in beauty, while her spiritual discernment saw in the glorious objects around her "patterns of things in the heavens." Thus she enjoyed the loveliness of earth while her soul was feeding on Jesus. She saw Him in all, and all in Him. She writes thus from Matlock Bath in the summer of 1850:—

" We have such a view from our lodgings as quite enchants me. I have not the power to describe it; but the romantic beauties of the scenery make me weep with delight, and often afresh exclaim, How beautiful, *how beautiful!* I can hardly look out of the window quietly, it is so grand, so majestic. . . . . Words can never express the wonders of either grace or nature; they have no richness, verdure, or fulness. They seem quite insipid when the heart has felt His love, or the eye beheld the wondrous works of His hands. . . . . I am writing on Temple Terrace, with a wood-crowned hill in front, the river Derwent rolling at its foot, and often little boats gliding about beneath our windows making it look like fairy-land. The Heights of Abraham are at our right, and the clean white houses studded about amongst the green thick foliage, look beautiful indeed. As my eye rests on the wood or plantation, or whatever it is which thickly covers the side of the high hill opposite our window, I constantly think of that passage, ' Let all the trees of the wood clap their hands before the Lord.' Ah! amongst them all our Apple-Tree excels, and for His love let rocks and hills their lasting silence break."

She thus describes another spot near Matlock which she visited with her friends :—

" We went to the Rowter Rocks, Birchover. They are very singular. We saw one large piece some yards long, through the centre of which is a natural opening large enough for us to go through, following each other in a low stooping posture. At the entrance there was upon the rock green moss of the most beautiful lustre, which shone like the richest silk velvet. Other huge pieces of rock were so placed, that they could be made to move quite easily. I could move one of from six to eight tons weight, and the guide moved one of fifty or sixty tons without difficulty just with his hands only, and also seven other pieces together ; the whole quite ponderous. No human power could have placed them thus ; though so easily moved because just suspended upon each other, yet the most of them are too immense to be thus fixed by any creature force. We had an extensive view from the top; it was a treat to me ! To see a rock as the *Lord* has formed it, a fissure *He* has made in it, a detached portion so huge that no mortal force or skill could place it in the position it occupies ;—to see the

beautiful moss covering one part, the various plants and
shrubs spontaneously growing in another, and often springing
out of the chasms between the rocks—all just of the Lord's
own doing,—this is much more enchanting to me than all
the beauties of the far-famed Chatsworth. Most magnificent,
indeed, these are; but oh, what labour and cost to embellish
and beautify the grounds by imitating rocks, fountains, and
waterfalls, and at immense pains cultivating plants of foreign
origin! All has its beauty, but there is something artificial
and unreal about the whole, while amid these rugged rocks
and lovely valleys, in the flow of these winding rivers, and
bursting forth of these mineral springs, nature is at home,
and we see the wonderful works of our God in their own
loveliness. It is here my natural heart revels, and my natural
taste is gratified. It is said these rocks are just as they
were left by the deluge. At anyrate, they lie just as thrown
by an Almighty Hand, whether left thus at the deluge, or
rent asunder when our conquering Saviour came forth from
the rocky sepulchre in which He had been entombed, or
whether they have been split and scattered at some other
trembling of the earth,—all has been under the control of
Him whose mighty power we recognise in these wondrous
masses. And oh! methought what must be the terror of
those souls who shall wish such rocks to fall upon them to
hide them from the awful frown of Him that sits upon the
throne, and from the wrath of the Lamb. I had, too, a
sweeter thought as we sat under the cool shade of one over-
hanging piece. It was of Him who is a shadow from the
heat, as well as a refuge from the storm. We found this
cool rock grateful in the weariness of a hot summer's day,
but how much more welcome the shade of the Living Rock

when the poor pilgrim is ready to faint from the heat of
temptation and trial. Indeed all things in nature are full of
Him, when the dear Testifier takes off the veil. We went
up the Heights of Abraham on donkeys. I thought of the
father of the faithful, and the mountain he had to ascend to
sacrifice the child of promise, and what acute feelings he
must have had. As we rode on, Ann reminded us Who once
rode upon an ass. Ah, indeed, the Highest was meek and
lowly, and entered Jerusalem riding upon an ass's colt; what
majesty in meekness was there! May we not only ride
as He did, but have His lowliness—the mind that was in
Christ. Having ascended, we enjoyed a most commanding
and beautiful view of the surrounding country. As we
came down we went through Rutland Cavern. I was much
delighted to see the wonders in the bowels of the earth ;
we had traversed the side of the mountain, and now saw
its interior, which my poor powers cannot describe. In one
place was a bed of coal, in others lead, a green carbonate
(I think) of copper, spar, petrefaction, &c. There were
several natural arches and openings, and in one place the
immense parts of the rock striking about looked like the
roots of the mountain, just as we see those of large trees,
only so gigantic. Looking up, in some places it seemed to
me as if the interior of the earth resembled a honeycomb,
—such openings, cavities, and juttings about. I could have
stayed for hours examining this kind of anatomy of the
mineral kingdom, for it is really like the veins, arteries, &c.,
being laid open to view. I think there may be much spiritual instruction from these natural developments. We see
there is often a hidden vein for usefulness which requires
an opening to discover it. So in the Word, and so in Pro-

vidence, there is a vein not seen on the surface. We must dig deep for these hid treasures, and there must be openings which we cannot make, but by the Spirit's light do discover while we are searching like the miner for the expected ore. And as we are led on deeper into heavenly things, what ever-new wonders do we find! Not that they then begin to exist, but are developed like the various strata in this wonderful earth."

Thus she drew honey out of the stony rock, and her soul was satisfied therewith.

"We went to Chatsworth, and saw the beautiful house and grounds; the latter were most to my taste, but neither like the wild scenery of these romantic and lovely rocks and dales of Matlock. . . . . The many curiosities in the house made my head and eyes weary, so that most welcome it was to go into the grounds, and inhale the fresh and reviving breezes. Here we saw an artificial tree, which the gardener made suddenly to send forth water from every part like a shower-bath. After this we saw water gush out of a rock, and flow most refreshingly. This reminded me of the Israelites, and their smitten rock and welcome stream, and of the spiritual Rock which followed them through the dreary wilderness, of which Rock the *living* souls drink, and which rock was our precious Christ. . . . . Miss C—— and I having lingered behind, we hastened after Mr and Mrs R——, who were in sight. They had just gone through a narrow pass between huge pieces of rock which had been purposely placed there. In attempting to do the same, we found ourselves enclosed in rock, and did not know what to do. We went a little way back, but could not get out. Mr and Mrs R—— and the gardener stood laughing and telling

us to come through, and we were quite puzzled.   At length
they said, ' Turn that stone ; ' it seemed impossible, ' for it
was very great ; ' but at length we tried, and found it turned
upon a pivot, going back quite easily, like opening a gate.
Thus was this insurmountable difficulty overcome, like many
others in our way through this wilderness.   We see a huge
stone in the way, and think we can never get on, but ere
long an opening is discovered which we never thought of.

" We went on, saw the Conservatory, and many fountains ;
then the kitchen gardens, the beauties of which cannot be
described by me ; also many rare plants in the hothouses,
especially a very wonderful water-lily [1] in a place on purpose for it, where it is beautifully thriving.   The health of
the plant is much promoted by keeping the water in constant
motion ; this is done by a small wheel, placed there on purpose.   I was reminded how the Lord's people often thrive
most when exercised by trials and afflictions ; these are like
the small wheel which keeps the water in motion, and pro-
motes the growth and beauty of the plant.   They, in like
manner, keep the soul in an upward motion by the exercising
of the Holy Ghost, and thus its health and vigour are much
promoted.

" While we were in the grounds at Chatsworth, some deer
were killed.   The shots alarmed the rest, and they bounded
in a large number (perhaps more than a hundred) to the
side of the river, and all plunging in swam across for safety.
The splashing noise of so many in the water at once was
very striking, as well as the sight of them singular, and the
spiritual illustration beautiful,—the hunted hart panting for
the cooling stream, the timid deer venturing into the watery

[1] The *Victoria Regia.*

element to escape the gunshot of the enemy. So the weary soul thirsts for the waters of salvation, and the tempted one is driven contrary to the meaning of the foe to plunge afresh into that River of Life, the streams whereof make glad the city of God."

In the spring of the next year, 1851, a small social party of Christian friends visited Great Malvern, of whom Ruth was enabled to make one. Here she had great enjoyment, not only of natural scenery, but in fellowship with many of the Lord's people, and above all, with the Lord himself. She seems, during excursions from home, to have been specially on her guard lest the change and charm of outward circumstances should dissipate her mind, and interrupt close communion between her soul and her Saviour.

She writes from Malvern :—" We were just going to start from Birmingham, when I found I had lost my bag off my arm. It had in it some papers and my small Bible, which is much valued, from being once my own dear mother's; it has also been my companion at the Refuge, and beside many a sick bed. All search and inquiry was made but in vain; we were told it was not in the carriage we had left, and could not be found. The train set forward, and my heart felt sad, but I looked to the Lord, and begged Him to restore it or bring some good out of it, making what the bag contained as good seed to some other heart. After we had gone some distance, and were stopping at a station, the Guard unexpectedly came to the door with the lost bag, saying it was found in the other carriage. I trust I did return thanks to the Lord, who can notice a falling sparrow, or a lost bag, or things less than that. . . . . The first view of

Malvern Hills was very solemn and striking to my mind, but when I saw the extensive and lovely prospect on the left hand, it quite overcame me, and I was actually obliged to turn away and burst into a flood of tears. I was very weary, and poor, frail humanity could not bear to gaze on so much loveliness, stretching out in miles of verdure and foliage all around. Well! but a short space, and weakness and weariness will be no more ; we shall see as we are seen, and know as we are known. The works of Immanuel's hands delight and overpower us now ; the glories of His person will beam upon us then in bright effulgence ; nor shall we want a veil through which to behold them, but be able to bear and bask in their fullest radiance, reflecting back His glory to His praise."

Sometimes a spiritual thought is rather hinted than expressed, as in the following note of a morning walk :—

" *Thursday.*—Again I had an early walk alone to bid adieu to Malvern Hills and beauties, and to commit my future way to the Lord. I saw more than thirty sheep singly following each other upon a very narrow path from hill to hill a good way up the side. They looked very singular.

" Went to Worcester, and then down to the ' potter's house.' We saw the granite and chalk ground to powder, then put into water, and so made into clay to form the china of. (' Ye are the clay, and I am the Potter, saith the Lord.') In the clay state it does not look as if it could ever be transparent at all. Then we saw vessels formed on the wheel at the pleasure of the potter ; none of them were marred, so we thought our view must betoken the new creation, which is complete in Him, and is never marred. Other clay was put into a mould, the impression of which it exactly took.

"We saw also the kiln, where the vessels are burnt when made into the right shape. The extreme heat and fury of the fire made me think of the seven-times-heated furnace, and those who were thrown therein rather than dishonour their Lord, and yet in passing through the fire they were not burned, neither did the flame kindle upon them, for He was with them there. We saw the china painted, which is all done with the pencil and brush like a landscape. The colours looked very dull, and they told us the vessels must be burnt again, which would bring them out in brightness and beauty. My friend touched my arm, and immediately I saw that so the Lord must do with His vessels; they must have the fire in some way to bring out clearly the works the Holy Ghost has wrought in them,—faith, hope, patience, and the grace of supplication.

"Then we saw some being burnished after they had come out of the fire, (which is the third the vessel goes through,) that is, though the colours are brightened in the fire the gold still continues dim and dull; so it is rubbed with the *blood-stone*, which makes it brilliant and beautiful. Ah, indeed! I think the Lord's gold wants rubbing too, and better to bear hard rubbing than not to reflect His praise?"

This excursion to Malvern refreshed and strengthened her for the time, but on her return home her health soon failed again; and at times she suffered severe pain from a hidden cause, too soon to be developed into terrible disease. Her friends seeing her still ailing, took her with them in the autumn of the same year to Bridlington, for the benefit of sea air. This was her first sight of the ocean, and it filled her with delight and wonder. " I did feel," she says, " as an atom or a speck in the view of that vast expanse of waters, so betokening His greatness who governs them by a word and holds them in the hollow of His hand. . . . . In the evening we all walked again upon the pier to enjoy the moon and the ocean. The sky was cloudless, the moon nearly full, and the flood of light on the calm surface of the sea most beautiful. I thought how lovely grace appears as it shines in the waters of affliction,—it is Heaven's light reflected in earth's sorrows. . . . . We parted beneath the moon's cold rays, but hope to meet in glorious day, when the light and heat of our Sun of Righteousness shall never be withdrawn."

"*Monday, Sept.* 14, 1851.—What new beauties! A clouded sky and dark-looking sea. Its waters reflected the clouds—not heaven's lamps, or the covenant blue—but still they remain the same behind the clouds. The scene teaches me that we are to walk by faith, not sight. Afflictions may be trying and the clouds dark, but the chart says, ' Let him stay himself upon his God.' But just now as I sat at breakfast the sun's rays burst through the edge of a cloud, just skirting the horizon with beauteous light on the face of the waters. This looked like a good hope through grace beaming with immortality entering into that within the veil, and brightening the edge of this life's dark sea. But as I gazed with delight the beams burst through another cloud, enlightening the nearer waters, while they were still dark between that and the shining horizon. This seemed like manifestation, the Lord lifting upon us the light of His countenance, but still teaching us the need of faith, for there will be many dark days between the present enjoyment and that glory which just beams in the distance.

"While I was thus musing a vessel appeared far away, sailing in glorious light, and then another came on the dark waters between the light of manifestation and that of glory, enjoying neither the one nor the other. These vessels looked like two believers, one almost in port, sailing joyfully in light and love, with the storms of life nearly passed away; the other, as safe, but under a clouded sky, with many a storm to come, pressing on towards the same heavenly shore; their course is the same, though just now their appearance is different. Ah! and their end will be the same, for they are both seeking, and shall find, immortality and glory in the presence of the Lord God and the Lamb.

"*Tuesday.*—The sea not quite so calm as it has been, and very dark-looking. I have been thinking of our Black Sea—the sin and corruption of our fallen nature—where go the ships. Ah! many a vessel of mercy has gone down in those deeps and feared overwhelming, but has seen the Lord's wonders of deliverance there. In that Black Sea are creeping things innumerable and hateful; there goes that Leviathan, who stirs up the mire and dirt, and seems to make this deep of corruption boil like a pot of ointment, till the Lord rebukes him, and discovers the Red Sea, into which all the guilt of this corruption is cast, even the blood of Jesus which cleanses His people from all sin.

"Thou beautiful sea! Thou preachest to me of myself and my glorious Lord. As thy waves roll on I see my many changes, and in thy reflecting the azure of heaven I see that He changes not, but is ever the same to me, and in

tribulated waters His fast, firm covenant is most strengthening to behold.

"As I walked on the beach I was looking for nice stones,
but felt my ignorance to discern those which were of any
value. This word came to my mind—'Be ye not unwise,
but understanding what the will of the Lord is,' and I thought
how often the flesh tries to pick up something it likes, and
hopes it is the will of the Lord, when, indeed, it is quite
contrary—a common pebble instead of His precious stone.
Lord, teach me to know Thy will, and conform me to it." . . .

She again writes:—"On reaching Flamborough we saw the
old lighthouse, which looks as if it had stood many a storm,
then went forward to the one in present use. The pieces of
rock around it are very wild, and the sea-view beautiful; it
looked almost as if we were driving into the sea. We alighted
at the door, and going in, ascended a hundred and twenty
winding steps to the room where the lights are. It is a small
round place, windows all round, through which the light is
seen thirty miles out at sea. I am at a loss to describe this
singular piece of machinery. It is something like a large
chandelier hanging from the centre of the roof, only much
more ponderous. It has three sides, on each of which are
seven lamps, each placed in a reflector of a round form, like a
flattish basin, made of copper, and lined with silver, beautifully bright. The copper tacks were all inside, the bright silver
being next the lamps and towards the windows, which makes
the light reflect very brilliantly. Seven of these reflectors
have their surface covered with beautiful crimson glass; thus
the lamp is enclosed, and the light richly red. The rest have
no glass. At the back of each reflector is a tin vessel containing oil for the lamp, and from each lamp ascends a pipe

which conveys away all the smoke through a chimney at the top; thus all is kept clear, that the light may not be at all intercepted. All the lamps are lighted at sunset, and burn till sunrise every night through the year, and the whole while burning is kept revolving all together by machinery like the works of a clock. It turns quite round in seven minutes, so that the red side may be seen in every direction, thus convincing those out at sea that it is a true light from the land, guiding them to a shore, but warning them of a danger.

"We were much delighted with the sight,—it spoke of so many spiritual things to our minds. The light so high,— 'a city set on a hill that cannot be hid,'—the grace of God produces effects which *must* be seen. The light so bright,— 'let your light so shine before men that they may see your good works, and glorify your Father which is in heaven.' The vessel with oil to every lamp,—'the wise took oil in their vessels with their lamps.' Those who are made wise unto salvation have not only the lamp of profession, but grace in the heart, which, by renewing of the Holy Ghost, keeps the outward light burning steadily. It was most beautiful to see the oil-vessel at the back of every reflector supplying the lamp and turning about with it; thus the believer, though turned about in the vicissitudes of this changing world, has still the oil with him,—grace in the heart can never be lost. But, moreover, we saw another room containing thirteen barrels, which held a hundred gallons of oil each, and from this storehouse the vessels are constantly supplied. How this reminded me of that word, 'Of His fulness have all we received, and grace for grace.' This is the secret of the vessels being kept supplied and the lights burning. In Christ for His people is an inexhaustible store of grace and of the Spirit, which He had without measure, that they each in their measure may receive thereof.

"Then those lights with the crimson glass seemed like such souls as Hart,[1] who have much fellowship in the sufferings of their Lord. How chastened and solemn the light they shed, though not the less bright for the crimson hue! They have deeply felt sin, and deeply felt salvation, and have best learned in the scenes of Gethsemane and Calvary how to hate the one and value the other. Sin pierced the Saviour, and His precious blood must flow to save His people from their sins. If this heart might breathe a wish, it is to be one of these crimson lights, knowing only Christ and Him crucified, and glorying only in His cross.

"But we are only 'light in the Lord,' and here I see these lights shew forth Christ, who is the light of His Church wherever she be. He is the only True Light for a poor sinner, because He has a crimson side to meet crimson sins, for 'without shedding of blood there is no remission.' When, condemned by the Law, the poor soul is doing business in the dark waters of corruption, how welcome the red light of the Sun of Righteousness, the crucified Lord of glory beheld by faith! He sees also the glory of His person, (like the other white lamps,) as the brightness of His Father's glory and the express image of His person.

"Truly this is a lighthouse to me, because it has been as a similitude of my Lord and His Church. But, moreover, the whole of every night a person watches in this tower where the lights are, to keep them burning brightly, one man till twelve o'clock, another till sunrise. This reminds one of those solemn injunctions to 'Watch,' in Matt. xxiv.

[1] The author of the Hymns.

42, and Mark xiii. 34-37, and in Luke xxii. 46, 'Why sleep ye? rise and pray, lest ye enter into temptation;' also it suggests watching for the word of the Lord, as in Hab. ii. 1, ' I will stand upon my watch, and set me upon the tower, and will watch to see what He will say unto me, and what I shall answer when I am reproved;' and also waiting for a sense of pardon, as in Psalm cxxx. 6, ' My soul waiteth for the Lord, more than they that watch for the morning; I say, more than they that watch for the morning.' Further, I was much struck on reading in a printed list of regulations hung upon a wall as follows: ' No bed, or sofa, or any other article whereon to recline can be allowed in the room where the lantern is—a constant watch must be kept.' This spoke a powerful word to my soul on the danger of self-indulgence and carnal ease. Beware, my soul, of sinful sloth! No bed, no sofa for these men in the place where they should WATCH. This time-state is thy place of watch, Heb. vi. 12; 1 Pet. v. 8. Surely I shall not soon forget the Flamborough Lighthouse."

Many similar entries in her journal describe the pleasures and occupations of this sea-side sojourn. Among other objects of interest she describes a lifeboat, with all its apparatus for the rescue of the perishing. She collected sea-weeds, and watched the lapidary at his work, giving intelligent attention to all things around her, and drawing from each object and circumstance its appropriate spiritual lesson. In a few weeks she returned to her "Bethel-home" at Nottingham, to take up the cross of her struggling daily life once more.

But, to continue our narrative, a yet sharper thorn in the flesh was to be her portion than any disappointment in the Lord's work, to which we have already referred, or any pressure of mere outward poverty. The great adversary understood the weakness of our nature when he said, "Skin for skin, yea, all that a man hath will he give for his life; but put forth thy hand now, and touch his bone and his flesh, and he will curse thee to thy face." But Satan understood not the power of grace as evidenced in Job, and now made to appear in Ruth. Before her youth was well past, symptoms of cancer manifested themselves, and though the disease lay dormant for many years, it was at length developed in its most terrible form, and, after causing her years of anguish, brought her finally to the grave. But this affliction only gave occasion for a fresh triumph of grace. The enemy thrust sore at her, but his weapon was caught and blunted on the shield of faith. She was more than conqueror through Him that loved her. Bodily suffering seemed rather to intensify than to lessen her joy,—she passed singing through the furnace, leaving to others the evidence of actual example, that those in whom Christ dwells have nothing to fear, even from those visitations which nature recoils from with the greatest trembling and abhorrence. Her fortitude was extraordinary. No one ever heard her complain; suffering was not allowed to hinder her avocations, nor to cloud the cheerfulness of her countenance. A slight start or shudder would sometimes betray that a spasm of agony had taken her by surprise, but otherwise her sedate calmness was unruffled, and her sufferings revealed themselves only in her sharpening features and the gradual wasting of her form. Full as she was of sympathy for others, she desired no commiseration for herself. A friend expressing pity for her received almost a sharp

d

answer. "Don't pity me!" she said; "every one has their own burden, and I have this." She was wont to speak of her affliction as her Lord's messenger of love, her "healed disease."[1] "The form of the fourth"[2] was with her in the furnace, and the raging flames lost all power to do aught save to burn asunder any remaining bonds which might have hindered her from walking in the full liberty of the Lord.

Doubtless, her long course of trial, inward and outward, had strengthened and armed her for the endurance of bodily suffering. Pain came not to her as it comes to those who have settled down amid earthly hopes fulfilled, and with present joys springing up freshly around them. Every tree in which she could have built her nest was cut down; every hope was shipwrecked with which she set sail in life. She was "spoiled for earth," and earth was spoiled for her. The onslaught of the enemy was made on one who had nothing more to lose, whose treasure was in heaven, where no moth or rust, or consuming disease, could touch her hidden store of joy. Her clay tabernacle might be taken down by a slow and painful process, but in heart and mind she had already ascended to her mansion in her Father's house, and dwelt there in communion with her Lord, who had prepared a place for her with Himself.

In the spring of 1852, her kind friends took her to Beaumaris, where the strange dress and language of the Welsh people awakened her liveliest interest, while the mountain scenery was to her a source of never-ceasing delight. "The latter half," she writes, describing her journey, "of the road from Chester to Bangor is truly beautiful. I began to feel

---

[1] Exod. xv. 26.   [2] Dan. iii. 25.

very weary, but was quite revived by the scenery. On one side of us rolled the waters of the Irish Sea, (I suppose,) and on the other were ranges of the Welsh hills, rising one after, and one above another, in such grandeur as I cannot describe. I had heard enough to raise my expectation greatly, and feared a disappointment, but the reality very far exceeded all my conceptions. At Conway we passed through a tubular bridge, where the sound of the carriages was very peculiar. We only just caught sight of the castle. The scenery here was most picturesque and beautiful. We went through several long tunnels, but were mercifully preserved safe in person and calm in feeling. . . . We arrived at Beaumaris between six and seven, finding most comfortable lodgings kindly prepared by our dear friend, who came, after we had taken tea, to bid us welcome. We were glad to retire early to rest after travelling all day, having first set up an Ebenezer to the praise of our faithful God.

"Our new 'lodge in the wilderness' is beautifully situated. In front of our windows roll the Menai Straits; we have a full view of Penrhyn Castle on the other side, and at the back, dark mountains rise majestically one above another. Some of their tops are at times covered with snow, and often they are enveloped in clouds, their appearance varying much with the alternations of cloud and sunshine. The vessels are constantly passing us when the tide is up. The scene is altogether very striking. It is most singular to see the Welsh women in their hats, short-gowns, and woollen petticoats.

" We went to see the church, where are many tombs of persons who were lost when the *Rothesay Castle* packet was wrecked. The sight was mournful, and yet hopeful, through the belief that some there were found in Jesus. One lady was found on a piece of wood. She had torn up her white dress, and hoisted up the pieces for a signal of distress. She was just alive when found, but died very soon. Her husband was found on the Lancashire coast, and is buried in another place. The vessel was wrecked in sight of Beaumaris, and, humanly speaking, through the fault of the captain, who was not sober. How mysterious such events! What wonders of providence may eternity open! What wisdom we shall perhaps discover in those very circumstances which now most puzzle us. The mighty helm of providential movements is not left to chance; it is governed by infinite wisdom; it is managed by One who will do injustice to no one; and who says, 'Be still, and know that I am God.'

"The tide is down, and I have just been much delighted, while sitting at breakfast, to observe the anchors of two vessels which are lying close in front of the window. They are cast deep into the ground, and that word sweetly occurred to mind, ' Which hope we have as an anchor of the soul, both sure and steadfast, and which entereth into that within the veil, whither the Forerunner is for us entered.' While I was musing a sailor went and attempted to pull up the anchor, but did not succeed. As I watched him the thought came, how like the enemy of souls, who tries hard to remove the believer's hope from Christ, and from the faithfulness of God, and from the promises. He does shake it, but cannot take it away, for the God of hope sustains it. . . . . While I write a small boat with sails is passing by. The wind is brisk and contrary, and has just turned it quite about, which seemed to bring them to a stand; then turning again, they go slowly forward. Is it not thus with us when the wind of adversity or tribulation or temptation blows hard against us? We cannot press forward as before; perhaps the first sudden gust seems to turn us quite round with our hearts and thoughts and anxieties all earthward, and we cry, 'Turn Thou me, and I shall be turned, for Thou art the Lord my God.' And when turned, it may be we can only just stand against the contrary wind without making any way; but let us remember *that* wind is both to try and to strengthen our faith, which often groweth exceedingly under such exercises, and soon the Lord does help us a little onward, though sense and feeling say, 'All these things are against me.'

"At two o'clock a dear friend took us to see that masterpiece of science and skill, the Britannia Tubular Bridge. It is indeed most wonderful, far surpassing any conception which can be formed of it. The bridge consists of four immense iron tubes, the ends of which are placed upon lofty and massive stone towers. Upon each corner of the bridge is placed an immense statue of a lion in couchant attitude, said to be each twenty-five feet long and thirty tons in weight. The length of the four tubes is said to be considerably more than a quarter of a mile. They are joined together upon the towers, and thus form a bridge, in which the trains pass over the Menai Straits. They are divided into two parts like arcades, (I find each of these parts is a separate tube,) one for the down, the other for the up train, and in each is a walk upon a wooden causeway beside the rails. I was greatly astonished at the size. The height is inside twenty feet at the centre, and eighteen feet nine inches at the ends. We walked down one tube, and back through the other; it is not quite dark in the very middle, and far from it at the ends. There are two million iron rivets in the bridge, which look like large buttons all about it, and the whole weight of iron in the tubes is nearly ten thousand tons. A train went through as we waited outside; the noise was almost terrific. We went up by steps to the top, which commands a most beautiful prospect. At a short distance is the seat of the Marquis of Anglesea, and very near to the bridge is a small spiral monument, which is erected over eighteen workmen who are interred there, having died from accidents during the erection of the bridge. I was much gratified in seeing this wonderful passage over an arm of the sea, which I can but so poorly describe. As we returned home the word Passover came sweetly to mind. The bridge is a way to pass over the water, and Christ is our way to pass over from curse and wrath and condemnation to eternal glory. 'Christ our Passover was sacrificed for us,' and He is the Father's way to pass over our sins honourably. 'When I see the blood I will pass over you.'

"Sabbath. No service but in Welsh, which we heard in the evening, but without any profit, or at all feeling the power of the Spirit. It was like the 'unknown tongue' in 1 Cor. xiv. 11–17. But yet it was a precious day to my soul, which, by the power of the Spirit, was kept in much melting and brokenness. I had sweet meditation upon the mountains of Judea as I gazed upon those of Wales, and upon Him whose immaculate feet trod them in travail of soul for His Bride—' He went out into a mountain to pray, and continued all night in prayer to God.' 'And every man went unto his own house.' 'Jesus went to the Mount of Olives.' 'He went up into a mountain, and He opened His mouth and taught them.' He suffered His last anguish on the Hill of Calvary, and after His resurrection He met His disciples by appointment on a mountain of Galilee. How He has honoured the mountains, and favoured unworthy me with sweet musings thereupon! I think it was in part fulfilment of a promise He gave me so graciously before we came; it was Matt. xxviii. 7–10. How do I prove that no change of place or circumstance prevents communion when we are living by the faith of the Son of God. . . . . .

"We called upon a cottager known to my friend, but the poor woman understood only a little English, which was a barrier to conversation. She said that Welsh did her the most good, but that Jesus was all the same, though we could not understand each other. . . . . After dinner I had a nice sunny stroll on the beach, then called upon dear Mrs Hughes, and again felt it sweet to converse of Him whom, having not seen, we love. I told her I had been thinking of the disciples going to Emmaus, and how Jesus joined them as they walked and were sad. She replied that she had thought He would often join us if we talked of Him more. She told us they had to-day been burying an aged saint who died very happy, but was very poor; that when a wealthy lady was here last year she gave Mr Hughes some money for the poor, and that then this aged one had scarcely any shoes to her feet, so he gave her a pair, which were the last that she had. Another poor believer, a widow with three children who has a mangle, had been accustomed to have a pair of good stout shoes for winter from some friends who visited Beaumaris, but last year they went to France instead of coming here. The poor widow did not know how to get shoes, and Mr Hughes then gave her a pair out of this lady's money. The poor thing wept for joy, and said

· she should not thank any one but Jesus Christ, for He knew
what she wanted, and it was He who put it into the heart
of one far away to send that she might have shoes. . . . . .
We went to visit this poor woman.   She looked very shy at
first, and knew very little English, but when I mentioned
the dear name of Jesus as the best friend, she was all delight, and by broken words with signs made us know that
He was her Friend and always so, and that like David she
thought of Him night and day.   Our hearts seemed touched,
and tears gave manifestation of those feelings which could
not find utterance in words.   We quoted some Scriptures
which she understood and said, 'What a pity—what a
pity!' (meaning) that she could not talk to us.

"*Sabbath Morning.*—Through divine mercy and free
favour the Lord of the Sabbath and the Spirit of the Sabbath are present, though the outward privilege of the sanctuary is absent.   Be silent all my flesh, for the Lord is in
His holy temple of the new heart.   Jesus is such a Saviour,
so mighty and so merciful, that mountains of the blackest
guilt may be safely trusted with Him—His rich atoning
blood will cleanse from all.   We have so little enjoyment
of its efficacy because, like Naaman the Syrian, we are so
proud, turning away to some creature effort and in actions
saying, 'Are not Abana and Pharpar, rivers of Damascus,
better than all the waters of Israel?   May I not wash in
them and be clean?'

"*Friday Morning.*—We this day went to Bangor, and
were marvellously astonished at the slate quarries belong-
ing to the Hon. E. D. Pennant, who lives at Penrhyn
Castle. . . . They are six miles from Bangor, and consist of
an immense rock of slate which is cut out from the top to

the bottom, laid open as it were in indented form. There
are many shelvings round it, on one of which we walked to
observe the wonderful works going on in getting and shaping the slate. There are more than two thousand men employed. About two hundred tons of slate are daily taken
away to different parts of the kingdom and to America.
The guide told us that £2700 are weekly paid for wages.

"It was a most remarkable sight. The hacked and rugged
sides of the quarry are dotted all about on the shelvings with
little huts for the workmen, where they go in during the
blasts, and the men are seen in all positions upon the slant-
ing sides hewing and boring, with thick ropes round them
to hold them on. It is so large and high that from where
we stood they looked only like tiny pigmies, or little ants
popping in and out of the holes in the rock. I could not at
first believe they were men, they looked so different to those
who were working near us ; but this showed the immense
height of the place. We were there during a blast. At a
set time a man comes and blows a horn at the very top of
the rock, at which signal nearly all the men are most curi-
ously seen running into the huts. Then the gunpowder
which has been put in goes off, and the sound is very grand,
roaring through the interior of the mountain like thunder,
or cannon after cannon, and the smoke is seen issuing out at
various parts up and down the sides. It is the inferior kind
of slate which is blasted ; the best is got with tools.

" After the blasting, we saw the men dividing and shaping
the slates for use. It is very singular to see how easily
large pieces split through when two chisels are driven in at
the end, and one pulled each way. This, the guide told Mrs
—— to do, and thereby she divided a piece of slate perhaps

large enough for a small gravestone. Accidents frequently happen to the men from blasting, and other things; and close at hand is an hospital for them, with two surgeons, one always there. It was altogether a wonderful sight, and I could like to have stayed much longer, but it was time to depart.

" As I stood and gazed upon the rock excavated all round, its different shelvings, great number of workmen, and their varied occupation, I was reminded of the Lord's ministers, and of all those whom He employs in the gospel for the good of poor sinners. Some souls are hewn out of the mountain of old Adam, the quarry of nature, by His word in the mouth of His servants; others are brought out with great terror, like the blasting which makes the earth quake and the mountains tremble at the presence of the Lord.[1] His word is both a fire and a hammer to break the rock in pieces, and bring out His chosen from the original rock, whence they shall all be hewn to be built upon the Rock of Ages. For this they need squaring and forming after they are separated, and in this work we saw many men employed, who seemed to me answerable to those ministers whose work is amongst the saints, for their further instruction in right-eousness and edifying in the faith;[2] they are busied in cutting off those irregular edges, or things of the flesh, which do cleave and plead for indulgence, also in strengthening and encouraging to endure the cutting process.[3] Others are Sons of Thunder, and seem made for setting forth the terrible majesty of the Lord, the evil of sin, and the danger of the sinner.

" When all the men ran into their little places of shelter,

[1] Acts ix. 6, 9, xvi. 26, 30.   [2] Eph. iv. 11, 12.   [3] 1 Thess. iii. 3, 13.

just before the blast, we were reminded of "Enter into the Rock and hide thee in the dust, for fear of the Lord, and for the glory of His majesty;' 'The lofty looks of man shall be humbled.' I cannot tell with how much spiritual interest I looked upon this sight, seeing what various methods and instruments the Lord employs to prepare for the temple of the second Solomon above, where shall be no noise of axe or hammer ever heard,—all this rough work is done below.

"But there were immense heaps of refuse, and men constantly employed to remove it away. This is solemn. 'The wicked is driven away in his wickedness.' 'He that believeth shall be saved; he that believeth not shall be *damned.*' I hardly dare write the word, but so it must be. 'Many are called but few chosen.' See to it, O my soul! that thou rest not in hearing the call; there must be the obeying it,—the obedience of faith,—or thou wilt be but as the refuse slate, 'whose end is destruction;' and the condemnation of the lost will be a just one, for they love and live in those things which God condemns, and for which things the wrath of God comes upon them.

"Last evening, as we were walking home, we saw a woman sweep before her house, gather up some dust in a dust-pan, and throw it into the sea close at hand. I thought nothing then, but now so sweetly feeling the efficacy of Jesus's blood, it just strikes me that thus our Father has done. He has gathered up all the inherent and actual sin of His people, and thrown it into the ocean of redeeming blood, where it sinks like lead in the mighty waters, and never shall rise to condemn them to death. And He will do it for each experimentally. 'Thou wilt cast all our sins into the depths of the sea,' because 'He hath laid upon Him the iniquity of us all.' In due time He enables faith to do the same thing, to keep casting the felt and hated filth of sin into the Red Sea of precious blood, exclaiming, 'I thank God through Jesus Christ our Lord,' so that 'in all these [hated] things we are more than conquerors through Him that loved us.' 'Thanks be unto God who giveth us the victory through Jesus Christ our Lord.'

"It is well that the heart, as well as the house, should often be swept by the searching Spirit,[1] and the rubbish cast out by faith of His operation, the conscience purged by blood. See Heb. ix. 14.

"In our last conversation with dear Mrs Hughes, she quoted Prov. xvi. 3, and feeling rather at a loss for the English of it, said, 'Commit thy *bundle* to the Lord, and thy thoughts shall be established.' I thought there was much sweetness in this rendering; the 'bundle' may comprise so many things which are wearying to carry, and fill the heart with anxious and disturbing thoughts. Therefore let us seek grace daily to commit the bundle to the Lord, that our thoughts may be established in Himself, the Hope of Israel, and the Saviour thereof in the time of trouble.

"Mrs Hughes reads everything in English but the Bible, and that always in Welsh. They all say the Welsh Bible does them most good, and that they can feel it most. Those who know English are much at a loss in quoting Scripture, which they seem to find difficulty in translating."

But to proceed—Ruth's life was varied by several other journeys—two to Filey, and one to Edinburgh. This last was very formidable to her, as she had an especial fear of

[1] Ps. li. 10.

railway travelling, and the thought of going to Scotland by express train made her tremble for days beforehand. This timidity was inherent in her sensitive nature, and though her soul rejoiced in triumphant security, the constitutional peculiarity was never wholly overcome. The appearance of a mortal disease in her frame did not ruffle her peace, while other remote dangers threatening herself or her property awakened the liveliest alarm. She shuddered beforehand at crossing the Menai Bridge, having heard some one speak of its slender appearance; and once at Ockbrook she lost a night's rest through hearing that a window in her empty house had been left unbolted, and this while acute pain and the seeming near approach of death only stimulated her joy in the Lord. The same sensitiveness made her feel reproof as keenly as when a child, and a slightly sharp word from a friend would vex and agitate her for days. Of such weak clay are the vessels of glory moulded!

She writes at Brighton:—"Through the Lord's mercy we arrived here safely. When we reached London we took a fresh train, and the porters very orderly took our luggage and weighed it; they then said, 'Now you have no more to do with it,' putting a ticket upon it. When we had been hurried into our train, I inquired, and found that the luggage was put into another, which was also going to Brighton. They said it would be all right, but it seemed strange to me, and I felt disconcerted for some time. I found even such a little thing enough to try faith, and prove it very weak. My heart did cry to the Lord and commit it to Him, feeling ashamed to be so moved, while my dear compaion in travel was quite easy. However, in about half an hour, the Lord broke in upon my soul, and

spoke His peace, seeming lovingly to reprove my fears, and
renewing the words first given for the journey, 'It is I, be
not afraid.' Then, as we passed through an arch, He
shewed me that, as that arch would not be perfect if one
brick were wanting, so if one trial, great or small, were
wanting in my lot, faith and patience would not have perfect work, 'that ye may be perfect and entire, wanting
nothing.' Thus I was sweetly instructed and refreshed. At
first I prayed that the luggage might stare us in the face
when we got to Brighton; but as the Lord talked to me, He
brought me to be willing to lose it all if He saw good; but
when we got to the station, we inquired, and were directed
a few yards forward, where it all stood waiting for us."

In strange contrast with such records as the above stand
many others like the following :—

"My heart leaping and dancing this day, because the
body again totters and weakens. Jesus, my Saviour, I long
to be perfected! Come, O Beloved, say, Arise, come away!
Earth is not now my country, and even dear Christian
friends do not respond to my ardent breathings after Jesus,
the rightful Sovereign of my heart. I know not what fire
and water await me, but it matters not, for I shall neither
burn nor drown.

"I had a very sweet view of death this morning. I saw
that this mortal flesh is just like a veil upon my spirit, and
I seemed to hear my Beloved say, 'At death, I shall only
come to turn the veil aside, because I want to see thee
face to face.' And if disease should remove the veil of
this flesh with a rough hand, my dear Lord will sustain
me, and one view of Him will swallow up all remembrance
of self-suffering."

Truly Ruth was one of those who "out of weakness are made strong!"

Her first visit to Filey was in 1856, and a friend accompanied her. A Scotch minister who was staying there called one day upon them, but only Ruth's friend talked with him. Ruth herself sat unobserved in a shaded corner of the room during his visit listening to the conversation, which was entirely of the love and glories of Jesus. The minister never saw her till, as he was taking leave of her friend, Ruth emerged from her retreat. "I must thank you," she said, warmly giving him her hand, "for speaking so well of my precious Lord." Indeed, her thoughts were so taken up with Christ, that no other topic of conversation was heartily welcome to her.

Her second visit to the same place was marked by a more striking incident, which gave a new interest to the few remaining years of her life.

It has been already stated that Ruth was the child of Mr Bryan's third wife, and younger by many years than the children of his former marriages. Her half-sister had married a minister, in Lady Huntingdon's connexion, named Lee, and died early, leaving two children, a boy and a girl. Mr Bryan took the boy, and brought him up as his own. When about fourteen, this youth, John Bryan Lee, was sent to London, where he had several uncles, and where it was hoped he would make his own way in business. He did not prosper, however, and was soon surrounded by difficulties, which ended in his leaving England for Australia. For forty years his friends never had tidings of him but once; and Ruth in her diary often mentions him as the subject of her thoughts and prayers. At length a cousin of his, Wil-

liam Bryan, of Derby, emigrated to Australia, and, shortly
after his arrival, took an active part in an election of magis-
trates.   He was appointed teller of the votes, and looking
over the list of names, he recognised that of John Bryan
Lee.   He at once claimed the owner of that name as his
kinsman; and, notwithstanding the changes wrought by
many years, the cousins recognised each other.   John Bryan
Lee had by that time become a wealthy man.   He had commenced life in Australia by keeping a school, and afterwards
set up a store, or shop, which so prospered as to yield him a
large fortune.   At the time William Bryan discovered his name
in the list of voters he was married, and living in a hand-
some house of his own.   The exile of many years inquired
eagerly after his friends at home, and was especially anxious
to hear news of his aunt Ruth, and his sister, Esther Lee.

John Bryan Lee wrote accordingly to Ruth, and the
letter making inquiries for Esther was received by her while
at Filey.   Ruth was perplexed, and carried her perplexity to
the Lord.   She had heard nothing of Esther since the death
of her father, Mr Lee, and possessed no clue whereby to discover her present abode.   "You know," she writes to a
friend, "how earnestly dearest J. B. Lee besought me to
search after his sister Esther, and perhaps I told you that I
wrote to London, and found that they knew nothing of her,
but had heard that she was married.   Well, one night the
week before we came here, a thought came into my mind
which I believe the Lord put there.   It was, to write a few
lines, stating that her brother John was alive, give her my
address, that she might send for more particulars, and then
direct it thus : Esther Lee, daughter of the late George Lee,
formerly minister of the Countess of Huntingdon's Chapel,

Wallingford, Berks. I had many questionings, and reasonings, and shrinkings, it looked so absurd, because her father has been dead above forty years, and if she was married her name would be different. However, at last I did it, and put it into the post myself, committing it to the Lord, and entreating Him to find her, if He willed dear John to be thus indulged. Last Monday, to my surprise and delight, a letter from Esther Lee arrived. Mine had been forwarded from Wallingford to Esther in Worcestershire where she is, not married, but governess in a family. She was, of course, astonished and delighted. We never knew each other. Truly, I felt it was the Lord's doing, and that nothing is too great or too small for Him to manage, to shew Himself the hearer and answerer of prayer."

Esther, at the time she received the letter, was laid up with a broken leg, but she soon recovered, and sailed to join her brother. The little history had a sad end after all, so far as earthly expectations were concerned. On reaching her brother's home in Australia, Esther found him once more in poverty, ruined by the dishonesty of his shopmen. He was unable to maintain her, and she was forced in that distant land again to take a situation as a governess. But Ruth, though saddened at the news, felt none the less that God had guided her in her perplexity, and owned His wisdom, while unable to comprehend His dealing with one whom she joyfully believed to be His child.

This characteristic entry occurs in her diary the March following :—

" To-day received a dear letter from my beloved John Bryan Lee, with a ring of colonial gold, which he begs me to wear for his sake. All outward ornaments I laid aside years

ago, when I found the Pearl of great price, and have no
desire to resume them; but I think I must wear this pledge
of love till death, because it comes from one so long lost, so
wonderfully found, both by the Lord and by me. The Lord
bless him and his with all choicest covenant blessings!"

Ruth had now almost done with earthly journeyings, and
was looking forward with bright expectation to her departure to her final home. Her disease increased fearfully, and
her sufferings were intense. Combined with this affliction
were distressing trials in her private life, her heart being
wrung by the ingratitude of some whom she had impoverished herself to serve, and whose unkindness embittered all
her declining years. But she was one in spirit with her
Lord, and could say while taking each cup from His hand,
" The cup which my Father hath given me, shall I not drink
it ?"

"I have much inward fever," she writes, "making me
restless and uneasy at night, but I have been led to see this
fever my Father's servant, and obeying His will. He says,
'Fever, go to that child, and work in her frame, and disturb
her rest;' and it comes, but all is in covenant love. He has
said also, ' Cancer, go to that child, and wound her flesh,
and sap her strength;' and it has come, and is doing His
work and His will, but all is love."

"The waters of affliction have risen higher this month,
but, safe in my living Ark, I am unhurt. It is sharp to flesh
and blood, but right to faith. I am not always light and
bright in my feelings; but oh! what blessed security and
solidity do I find in my precious Rock. There I am, come
what may. 'The Lord shut (her) in '—in the Ark, and in
the Rock for ever. Happy, *happy* though unworthy R. B.

Angels might envy our mighty joy, for they never knew joy in tribulation and suffering,—in safety, and peace, and joy in the flood and in the flame.   Oh, it is so real, so very real, because so contrary to every grain of the flesh.   Hallelujah!"

Her strength declined rapidly, and she became emaciated to the last degree.   Her friends marvelled, and she wondered herself, at what her frame was able to endure, and yet continue in life.   She was seen on Sabbath days slowly tottering to the house of God, leaning on the arm of her servant, when in such a state of suffering that she could not bear the motion of a vehicle.   Her weakness had obliged her to give up visiting the Refuge, but her weekly prayer-meeting was still a gathering-point for the few friends who were with her, pressing on earnestly to Zion, with their faces thitherward.   Ruth's prayers at these seasons were the outpouring of a heart brimming over with love beyond utterance.   Her mouth was filled with arguments drawn from the Word of God, and she would plead the promises of Jesus, and remind Him of His works on earth, as one speaking with Him face to face.   Her prayers were almost wholly in Bible language, for her mind was so steeped in Scripture that her thoughts clothed themselves naturally in the expressions of Holy Writ.   On one occasion her rapture of devotion was such, that two hours passed, while her praises and pleadings poured forth without check or stay, or any weariness was felt by herself or her companions. The language of her heart seemed to be, "I have found Him whom my soul loveth; I held Him, I would not let Him go."

At last she was confined entirely to the house, and there anxiously yet quietly awaited the summons to "come up higher."   When she at last discovered in her frame the

tokens of nearly approaching death, it was a high day of
festival to her soul. A friend found her removing from her
cap the black ribbons which, as before noticed, she had
worn habitually since her mother's death, and replacing
them with white ones, as for an approaching bridal. " I am
going to my wedding," she said; " the Bridegroom must
not find me in mourning." Her natural timidity had in
former days made her shrink from the thought of her last
hours, but now that she was actually drawing close to the
dark valley, its terrors were all done away, and she saw only
the form of Him who had passed through it before her.

Her last prayer-meeting was held on a Friday, less than
a week before her death. The little group of friends assembled in her room, and knelt around the bed where she lay.
Her face was of a ghastly whiteness, her features and hands
so attenuated as to be almost transparent, and the process of
dissolution so far commenced that the circulation had ceased
in her lower limbs. But the spirit so sustained her frame
that the actually dying woman lifted up her clear voice for
twenty minutes in what was less a prayer than a triumphant
song of praise, commencing, " I will extol thee, O God my
king!" One by one she named her friends, and made
earnest petition for them, committing them to the care of
Him whose face she would so shortly see. But for herself
Ruth had nothing more to ask. Her heaven was begun.

For the last two or three days of her life she was free
from pain, and able to converse with the various friends who
visited her. All clouds were past and gone for ever, sorrow
and care were forgotten, as she lay basking in joy too deep
for outward demonstration. She remarked to one who
visited her on Thursday, (July 26, 1860,) that she had been

thinking her heart was like the sheet beheld in Peter's vision, full of unclean beasts; that it had belonged to God in His own purpose from all eternity; then it was let down to reveal to her what was in it, and again had been drawn up to heaven, there to remain to all eternity. "I have been wondering," she afterwards said, "why such a one as I should wear a crown, but now I have found out the reason. A crown will be given to me that I may cast it at the feet of Jesus." She seemed to think the time of her translation was close at hand. "His chariot wheels tarry long," she said, "but He will come—He will not tarry."

That day was her last on earth.

Her early friend, Mary T——, was with her in the evening, and begged earnestly to be allowed to stay with her through the night, but Ruth refused this, saying, "No, dear sister, no; it would interrupt communion." Her friend still hesitated to leave her. She feared some sudden change might take place, and that the one servant in the house might be unable to summon her in time to see her beloved Ruth again in life. But Ruth's answer was, "Leave it, dear sister, leave it with the Lord, and see how well He will manage it." As Mary left the room in sorrow, Ruth said cheerfully, almost playfully, "Farewell, dearest!"

Throughout the night her voice was raised in prayer so audibly that the servant thought she was calling her, and drew near to the door, when she became aware that the dying one was in close converse with her Lord. She was pleading not for herself, but for others, especially for a mother and her children, whose name the listener could not catch. The servant described her prayer as being just like conversation. Some refreshment was taken to her early in the morning, as she appeared weaker than usual. A char-woman who had been sent for to assist in the house looked into the room shortly after, and then went and told the servant that Miss Bryan had not taken her breakfast. They both hastened to her, and found her just sinking. The presence of the charwoman (which seemed a providential answer to Ruth's faith) enabled the servant to send for Mary T——. This earliest and latest friend hurried breath-less to the house, and found her just gasping her last. Mary bent over her, and said, "Looking unto Jesus." Ruth took no notice. Even that beloved Name could wake no further consciousness. In another moment she had exchanged faith for sight, and the lower court of the Lord's house on earth for the presence-chamber above.

Thus she entered into rest early on the morning of July 27, 1860.

The following was found among her papers after her death :—

"To My Executors.

"Please, dear friends, let my body be kept a week, if it can be without inconvenience to those in the house. I have a foolish fear of being buried alive.

"Please let my funeral be like my dear mother's. Give the friends hatbands tied with white, which will not be improper, as I am unmarried. I should like it, because the white will betoken the joy of the spirit, while the black shews the corruption and dishonour of the flesh. No hearse but the shillibeer.[1] I have been a pilgrim all my life, and let me so be buried. I should have liked a walking funeral, only it is too far. Bearers three." She then gives their

---

[1] A hearse and mourning-coach in one.

names. "A good oak coffin, very plain. To my dear mother's funeral several friends and the minister came to tea. I should like the same to come to mine, and, of course, C. B. and M. A., the bearers, to have tea in the back parlour, and any other friends you like to tea with you. Let the converse be of Jesus only, with reading and prayer after tea.

"I do not like funeral sermons at all, but if any of my dear friends wish it, let it be from my own dear passage, 1 Tim. i. 15. Not studied, but very simple, all about JESUS. Nothing about unworthiest R. B.—only praise Him for saving such a sinner; and do tell poor sinners much about Him, and about the way of faith.

"Hymns—'Why should we mourn departed friends,' (Watt's,) and 'Rock of ages cleft for me,' and 'Hark the voice of love and mercy sounds aloud from Calvary.' Very easy, simple tunes, such as all can sing, that there may be a blessed sound of praise below while I join the ever-new song above, 'Worthy is the Lamb.' Oh do not let there be flourishing tunes, or any flourish connected with unworthy me. O Lord, pour out Thy Spirit, that Thy people may have a blessed time, and be all absorbed in Jesus.

"I should prefer no funeral sermon, but if it would disappoint my dear friends not to have one, I leave it with them.

"Perhaps there will be room on the grave-stone for the following; if not, shorten it, but put nothing about me :—

'Christ in me the hope of glory.'
'Here also rest the remains of Ruth Bryan, daughter of the above,
Who slept in Jesus. Aged .'
'My flesh also shall rest in hope.'

"Dear friends, 'To depart and be with Christ, is far better;" wherefore rejoice in my joy all who are left behind, and be not slothful, but followers of them who, through faith and patience, are inheriting the promises.— The Lord pardon the slothfulness of yours, gratefully and affectionately, "RUTH BRYAN.

"Please give my maid, Ann Croft, mourning, because she wishes to wear it. I would have none mourn for me while I shall be so glad. She has been faithful and kind to me, and has stayed with me at pecuniary sacrifice, and I wish her to be rewarded. Please let her have some one in the house with her while she stays; I mean to help her. Also, I wish her to have such of my clothes as I have not left to any one else.

"I should like my plate divided between my dear nephews, John Bryan Lee and Charles Bryan, and my nieces M. A. H. and G. L.

"The gold ring I wear to go to Australia for John's daughter, Esther Ruth, also my silver mug marked R. B."

1.

"Jesus! the sinner's friend,
　　We hide ourselves in Thee;
God looks upon Thy sprinkled blood,
　　It is our only plea.

2.

"He hears Thy precious name,
　　We claim it as our own;
The Father must accept and bless
　　His well-beloved Son.

3.

"He sees Thy spotless robe;
　　Thy blood has cancell'd sin;
The golden gates have welcomed Thee,
　　And we may enter in.

4.

" Thou hast fulfill'd the law,
    And we are justified ;
  Ours is the blessing, Thine the curse :
    We live, for Thou hast died !

5.

" Jesus ! the sinner's friend,
    We cannot speak Thy praise !
  No mortal voice can sing the song
    That ransom'd hearts would raise !

6.

" But when before the throne,
    Upon the glassy sea,
  Clothed in our blood-bought robes of white,
    We stand complete in Thee !

7.

" Jesus ! we'll give Thee, then,
    Such praises as are meet,
  And cast ten thousand golden crowns,
    Adoring at Thy feet !"

CONTENTS.

TO E. M.

lxxvi CONTENTS.

TO MRS H.

LETTERS OF RUTH BRYAN.

––––––––

THE following letters were addressed by Ruth Bryan to one who was then almost a stranger to her, but whom she had once met under circumstances which drew out all the tender sympathies of her heart. E—— M—— and her sister had then recently been in deep affliction through the loss of a mother; and Ruth, having known the bitterness of such a trial herself, could well enter into their feelings. But her chief desire was, that the chastisement by which the sorrowing sisters were then exercised might afterward yield to them the peaceable fruit of righteousness, and this led her to write to one of them. The correspondence thus begun was continued up to the time of her death; and it is hoped, that the counsels which proved so profitable to one, may be the means of blessing to many. Throughout her letters, it will be seen that her grand aim was to set forth Christ in His fulness, and to turn the spiritual eye from self and every other object to Him, as the one way to pardon, peace, and holiness.

I.

*All spiritual blessings are in Christ Jesus, and to be
dispensed to the poor and needy.*

TO E. M.

High Pavement, Nottingham, *Nov.* 1848.

Dear Miss ——, There is in my heart a strange and
unaccountable drawing towards you and your dear sister, a
full tide of feeling which will break through all opposing
timidity, and find its way to you, in the shape of earnest
longings after you " in the bowels of Jesus Christ," that He
may be formed in you "the hope of glory." I should not
mention this, but in the hope that it may be from the Lord,
and for His glory, which He can accomplish by the most
weak and insignificant means. With this encouragement,
then, I venture to write to you in that Name, through
faith in which the lame do "leap as an hart," "and the
tongue of the dumb" is made to "sing,"—that Name which
is to the believing soul " as ointment poured forth "—the
Name of Jesus, who was so called because He should
" save His people from their sins." This well suits a sin-
sick soul. His name is also Emmanuel, which is "God,
with us ; " "God manifest in the flesh ;" God taking our
nature—becoming our brother, born for our adversity—to
bear our griefs and carry our sorrows, to be tempted as we
are tempted, that He might for us conquer the tempter, and
deliver His tempted brethren. He can pity, for He has felt ;[1]
He can relieve, for He has broken the power ; He "was in all

[1] Heb. ii. 18.

points tempted like as we are, yet without sin." Satan tried every arrow in his quiver; but our glorious God-man repelled them all. Satan foiled the first Adam with one temptation, and all his seed in him; he came against the same nature in the second Adam, "the Lord from heaven," in whom again a seed was included to stand or fall with Him. And here our nature came off victorious in union with our glorious Head. Truly it makes my heart glow to see Him as our champion on the battle-field, vanquishing our foes—Satan, sin, the world, our old man, and death itself. They have all been so overcome by our spiritual David, that they shall never be the destruction of the least lamb in His flock. The lion and the bear may come out together against them, and seem just ready to devour; but He will arise, smite the beasts of prey, deliver His trembling one, and none shall pluck it out of His hand.

This is precious consolation to such as feel they have no might at all, and feel, too, the world drawing, Satan prompting, sin striving, and the flesh lusting. Oh, what should we do at such times if we had not One to fight for us, and fight in us too! We should certainly be "swallowed up quick," but the Lord has laid help upon "One that is mighty;" and this mighty One that is for us is more than all that can be against us. What makes it so beautiful is, that Himself is our very strength and victory; so that our weakness and inability are no hindrance at all. Of this one of old was so well convinced, that he exclaimed, "When I am weak, then am I strong." What a paradox to carnal reason! and how long we are learning this lesson perfectly, by reason of the working of our carnality and self-love!

Our Father has determined that Christ shall be all, and

we nothing. To accomplish this experimentally, He undoes our work. When we have been washing with nitre and soap, He plunges us in the ditch; when we seem to be getting on a little better than usual, He turns us upside down. This is hard work, and while the process is going on, we think it must be for destruction, for we appear to grow worse and worse. But in truth it is for salvation—to show ourselves to ourselves, to bring us to forsake ourselves,[1] and to give us Christ, instead of ourselves.[2] Oh, what a blessed exchange ! It is worth being spoilt in all the labour of our hands, and marred in our very best things, to possess such a treasure. There can be no drinking of the living waters while we have a price in our hand, be it much or little ; no buying the gospel wine and milk while we have any money ; no triumphing in "the Lord our righteousness, " while we are hunting about for shreds of our own, and sewing them together. All this is Christ-rejecting and God-dishonouring.

Therefore be not cast down at the Lord's ways towards you, for if we are anything, or have anything, Jesus cannot be everything ; and if He be not everything, He is nothing. He must be all, for holiness and happiness, for justification and sanctification,[3] for acceptable appearing before God and suitable walking before men, for holy living and happy dying. Do we want good works ? we are " created " unto them in Him.[4] Do we desire "the fruits of righteousness ?" we are filled with them by union with Him.[5] In short, our Father has "blessed us with all spiritual blessings" in Him ;[6] and the reason we do not enjoy them more is

---

[1] Luke ix. 23.   [3] 1 Cor. i. 30.   [5] Phil. i. 11.
[2] Gal. ii. 20.   [4] Eph. ii. 10.   [6] Eph. i. 3.

because we seek them in ourselves. Oh to have the single
eye which looks at Jesus only! Then would our whole body
be "full of light." But thus to venture right away from
self is a venture indeed, and can only be done by the power
of the Holy Ghost. It is He effects that blessed closure of
the soul in Christ, which is like the weary dove getting into
the ark; and you know she was pulled in after vainly seeking rest elsewhere. May you have such a precious pull of
Divine power, that you may enter into rest by believing;[1]
which faith is "not of" ourselves, it is the gift of God.[2]

When once admitted to the loving heart and loving arms
of Jesus, you will find that which would superabundantly
compensate for more than a thousand years waiting: such a
complete and blessed salvation,—such a precious and glorious Saviour,—such fulness in His work, blood, righteousness,
love, and person, as to eternity will never be fully developed,
—and such blessed entrance thereinto by faith now, that,
though I dare not trust myself to speak of it, I sincerely
wish you its happy and speedy enjoyment. May the sweet
love of Jesus constrain us more and more to speak well of
His name, and may its savour perfume our souls, lips, and
lives, that men may take knowledge of us, as being much
with Him, and much like Him! May you have full experience of those words, "Wherefore also we pray always
for you, that our God would count you worthy of this calling,
and fulfil all the good pleasure of his goodness, and the
work of faith with power; that the name of our Lord
Jesus Christ may be glorified in you, and ye in him, according to the grace of our God and the Lord Jesus Christ."[3]—
Yours, affectionately,   R. BRYAN.

[1] Heb. iv. 3.   [2] Eph. ii. 8.   [3] 2 Thess. i. 11, 12.

II.

*Christ proved to be all-sufficient in near views of eternity,
and recommended to seeking souls.*

TO E. M.

OCKBROOK, *April* 1849.

MY DEAR MISS ——, It was not my intention that your
kind notes should be so long unanswered; but true, indeed,
is Jer. x. 23, and my heavenly Father had prepared for me a
journey I then knew not of; I mean down into the valley of
affliction, having been much prostrated in health since I had
the pleasure of hearing from you. The descent was gradual,
and quite safe, for I was enabled to lean upon my Beloved,
who kindly granted me, that as the outer man was weak-
ened, the inner man was renewed by the Spirit day by day.
From the beamings of celestial glory which sparkled through
the crevices of a decaying body, I joyfully hoped soon to
put off mortality and enter the presence-chamber of my Lord,
to behold Him, not "through a glass, darkly," but "face to
face;" to see that countenance, once "marred more than any
man's" for my sake, but now in resurrection glory, shining
above the brightness of the sun in his meridian splendour.

Such was my anticipation, but apparently not my Lord's
intention at this time, as He is now gradually strengthening
this poor tabernacle, and sending me back a second time
from the very gates of the Celestial City. May He condescend to be glorified in my return to the discipline of the
wilderness, and pardon my unwillingness. Perhaps He is

saying to me as before, "Now the man out of whom the devils were departed besought him that he might be with him: but Jesus sent him away, saying, Return to thine own house, and shew how great things God hath done unto thee."[1] And my heart says, "We cannot but speak the things which we have seen and heard;"[2] and, "Come and hear, all ye that fear God, and I will declare what he hath done for my soul."[3] I must come to you again in the sweet name of Jesus; and if ever one poor sinner more than others had cause to extol that precious name, it is she who now addresses you; in whose soul it is "as ointment poured forth;" in whose ear it is more melodious than music; and in whose hand it is a staff either to pass over Jordan, or journey forward in the pilgrim road. Feeling the most vile, worthless, and unlikely of all creatures to have sat down so blissfully at the banquet of Love, this poor heart must praise the Founder of the feast, who is also the substance of it, and who, by His own irresistible power, sweetly brought me in, and then said, "Eat, O friends, drink, yea, drink abundantly, O beloved;" "For my flesh is meat indeed, and my blood is drink indeed." Having thus partaken of life, I am constrained to testify in my feeble way that this is the bread of God, which nourisheth the soul; this is the wine of the kingdom, which cheereth the heart, and, with the oil of the Spirit, doth make the face to shine.

Moreover, having just come from very near views of eternity, I must solemnly testify that Christ only is the Rock upon which the soul can be safe and triumphant, when the waves of death seem going over the body. At such a time the world stands afar off; friends can only look on, or look

[1] Luke viii. 38, 39.   [2] Acts iv. 20.   [3] Ps. lxvi. 16.

up; and all that is to come appears a vast *for ever*, either in the fiery wrath, or the blissful presence of the Lord God and the Lamb. Nothing can be solid but "Christ in you, the hope of glory." To realise this at such a moment is worth a thousand such worlds as this; and, indeed, whatever you may be called to give up, is not worth a name in comparison of a precious Christ. My heart glows with a desire to speak well of His dear name, His finished work, His glorious person, and, if it might be His will, to set other souls on fire of love or longing after Him. For what do I away from my glory-home, but to be a savour of Christ, telling poor dead sinners, that whatever be their profession, they are "feeding on ashes;" that "a deceived heart hath turned them aside" from the only way of salvation? I would also seek to encourage poor, trembling souls, who are already brought into judgment, and feel the sentence of death in themselves, to put their case, bad as it is, into the hands of the "Wonderful Counsellor,"[1] prevailing Intercessor,[2] and "Advocate with the Father," who is "Jesus Christ the righteous."[3] I think, beloved, He is just what you both seemed to need when you wrote to me, for the sentence of death appeared to be working deeper, that you might not trust in yourselves;[4] and the goodliness of your flesh seemed to be fading, I hope, by the blowing of the Spirit Jehovah thereupon,[5] to make way for the beauty of Jesus. By your words, your comeliness seemed turning into corruption,[6] and the Lord, with inward rebukes correcting you for iniquity, was making your beauty to consume away like a moth.[7] Though

---

[1] Isa. ix. 6.
[2] Rom. viii. 34.
[3] 1 John ii. 1.
[4] 2 Cor. i. 9, 10.
[5] Isa. xl. 6, 7.
[6] Dan. x. 8.
[7] Ps. xxxix. 11.

to your feelings these dark discoveries make against you, they are in truth for you, for it is the *light* that maketh manifest; and better that the leprosy should be disclosed, than have it working death unheeded. The things over which you lament were within when they troubled you not; and now they are disclosed, the great enemy would suggest, You are too filthy for the fountain, too cold for the fire, too much diseased to appear in the presence of the great Physician. He does this in a wily way, bringing to mind, when you would approach the mercy-seat, some shortcoming or misdoing, in order to turn your eye away from that sprinkled blood which is the sinner's all-prevailing plea. May the Comforter reveal Christ, as He convinces of sin, and take of His precious things, and set them against your vile ones, giving you heavenly skill and understanding to plead His precious blood against your sin, His perfect obedience against your constant disobedience, His power to heal against your desperate disease.

You know those before the throne overcame Satan "by the blood of the Lamb;" and our victories must come in the same way. Yet this way we are so slow to learn, because it is completely out of and against that self which it is so hard to leave. However, the Holy Spirit will not forsake His own work; the least beginning shall have a sure ending, for He will perfect that which concerneth us. David tells us how *he* became such a skilful warrior: "It is God that girdeth me with strength." "He teacheth my hands to war." "By thee I have run through a troop; by my God have I leaped over a wall." There is a very encouraging word in Heb. xi. 34, "out of weakness were made strong"—strong through faith; which faith leaves the creature and creature-

working behind, and fastens upon a precious Christ, determined to go through all, trusting in Him, and saying heartily,
" God forbid that I should glory save in the cross of our
Lord Jesus Christ, by whom the world is crucified unto me
and I unto the world."[1] My soul earnestly desires that you
may obtain " like precious faith " to venture wholly upon
Jesus; and though that faith should seem small " like a grain
of mustard seed," it will not prove a delusion; for "He
knoweth them that put their trust in Him," although sometimes they know not to whom they really belong.   May it
please our gracious Lord soon to reveal Himself, as you
desire, and grant you that sealing of the Spirit[2] for which
you long.   May the Lord bless you indeed, enlarge you out
of self into Christ, and keep you from evil, that it may not
grieve you.   So prays, yours affectionately,   R. BRYAN.

1 Peter v. 10; Eph. iii. 14-19; 1 John v. 21; Jer. xxix.
11-13.

III.

The matchless love of Christ as the Bridegroom.

TO E M.

(To be received, " if the Lord will," on her wedding-day.)

Oct. 31, 1849.

And why does dear Miss —— wish for a line from the
humble, unworthy Gleaner, when so many tender sensations
will be thrilling round her heart ?   Is it that she thereby

[1] Gal. vi. 14.   [2] Eph. i. 13.

desires to forsake all, (even when her net is drawn to shore right full of mercies,[1]) and follow Jesus only? Is it that she longs, on the very day she receives her earthly bridegroom, to give him back to the Lord, and, embracing her heavenly One, to become so absorbed in Him that He shall ever be between her soul and her heart's best earthly love? If thus it be with her, the Gleaner's heart warmly says, Amen! and may the Lord say so too.

Dear Miss ——, as you have requested me to send you a line at this season, it would be unseemly in me to withhold it, but I humbly confess that it is not in me to write what you desire. Wherefore, let us look up to the dear Testifier of Jesus, that under His Divine anointing our meditation of Him may be sweet. It is as the heavenly Lover and Bridegroom of His Church we just now love to think of Him. Oh, what a contrast to the very best earthly husband! They love and choose because of something congenial and pleasing, and in hope of a faithful return of affection. But He, our wondrous Ishi, loved, chose, and determined to betroth and espouse unto Himself, in the certain fore-view of debt, disgrace, and sin; ah, and of unchaste wanderings too, for He says, " I knew that thou wouldest deal very treacherously and wast called a transgressor from the womb." Yet, through all He loved, and from all He has redeemed with His own precious blood. When His spouse "hath played the harlot with many lovers," His marvellous language is, "Return, for I am married unto you," thereby overcoming His faithless one with the very love which she has slighted—a love, indeed, beyond compare. May its fires afresh be kindled in your soul, that you may now count all things but loss, yea

[1] Luke v. 6-11.

even as dung, for the sake of such a Beloved. Did Jacob
serve seven years for his Rachel, by day in the heat, and by
night in the frost, and did they seem but as a day unto him
for the love he had to her? Our spiritual Jacob has far
exceeded him. He left the throne of His glory for His poor
Rachel, and took her humble flesh in the form of a servant,
and for her sake served thirty-three years under the Law.
He bore the heat of temptation, weariness, and thirst, as well
as the cold of reproach and scorn, with the contradiction of
sinners against Himself. This He thought not too much;
for when He had finished the work on her behalf, for her He
cheerfully entered upon the most bitter part of His sufferings, which made even His mighty heart to thrill with
agony, while His dear lips prayed, "O my Father, if it be
possible, [with the rescue of my Bride] let this cup pass
from me; nevertheless, [ah! who can tell what was in *that*
word, nevertheless] not as I will, but as thou wilt." Behold
the depth of his unflinching love! The cup of curse must
be drunk, or the captive Bride must perish. And now He
takes it, nor turns away till every dreg is gone; and the
same sacred lips which emptied it could say in triumph, "It
is finished!" For the joy that was set before Him (of possessing His betrothed) He endured the cross, despising the
shame, "and is now set down at the right hand of God," till
the blissful consummation before assembled worlds, when
it will be joyfully proclaimed, "The marriage of the Lamb
is come, and His wife hath made herself ready." Then
shall the spiritual Jacob and Rachel meet and embrace,
and part no more for ever; she awaking up after His likeness shall be satisfied, and He seeing her in glory, (the
very travail of His soul,) shall be satisfied likewise.

" Haste, blissful dawn of endless day,
　　When sin shall cease, and death shall die,
And Christ His glory shall display,
　　And beam upon our longing eye.

" Then, wrapped in everlasting bliss,
　　'Midst heaven's innumerable throng,
His love shall all our powers employ,
　　And be the theme of every song."

" Wonder, O heavens ! and be astonished, O earth !" that this most glorious Immanuel, the Prince of Peace, whom angels worship, and before whom the seraphim bow, should from all eternity engage to come and seek His Bride from this poor world, and claim her for His own. Yet so it is. But she is filthy and polluted ![1] Then His own precious veins shall pour forth the rich crimson flood to cleanse her,[2] and His Spirit shall open the fountain to her for her sin and uncleanness.[3] But she is naked and bare.[4] Then He will cast His skirt over her,[5] and will for her weave in the loom of the Law[6] fine linen— clean and white—a robe in which she shall be meet to appear at His court. Moreover the Spirit shall bring near His righteousness,[7] clothing her with " the garments of salvation," and covering her with the " robe of righteousness," "as a bridegroom decketh himself with orna-ments, and as a bride adorneth herself with her jewels." But she is diseased[8]—she is a leper,[9] yet will He bring her health and cure, for He says, " I am the Lord that healeth thee ;" and He is actually made to be sin for (her),[10] that (she) might be made " the righteousness of God in Him." But she has no personal charms—she is ugly. Then He will put His

[1] Ezek. xvi. 6 ; Job xv. 14-16 ; Isa. lxiv. 6.
[2] Rev. i. 5.
[3] Zech. xiii. 1.
[4] Ezek. xvi. 22.
[5] Ezek. xvi. 8.
[6] Rom. v. 19.
[7] Isa. xlvi. 13.
[8] Isa. i. 5, 6.
[9] Ps. li. 5.
[10] 2 Cor. v. 21.

comeliness upon her, and through it her beauty shall be perfect. But she is poor, so He bestows Himself and His fulness upon her, and thus endows her with a good dowry. But she is unwilling, and has no heart to the match, for she obeys a hostile prince;[1] her delights, too, are in the world and the flesh. A new heart will He give her, and a right spirit will He put within her; the Spirit shall make her willing in the day of His power, "and take away the name of Baalim out of her mouth," so that, prostrate at His feet, she shall say, "Other Lords beside Thee have had dominion over [me], but by Thee only will [I] make mention of Thy name." And now that the Spirit has touched her heart, she feels she is diseased, and discovers her filthiness[2] and nakedness, knows she is ugly and poor, and cannot think the Bridegroom's heart is towards her, or that she can find favour in His eyes, and therefore she cries out, "I am black," "behold, I am vile," my comeliness is turned in me into corruption; but He overwhelms her by responding, "Thou art all fair, my love, there is no spot in thee." Then she exclaims, "Set me as a seal upon Thy heart, as a seal upon Thy arm, for love is strong as death." He replies, "Fear not, for I have redeemed thee; I have called thee by thy name, [Hephzibah,] thou art mine." Now she ventures, with a captivated heart, to declare, "My Beloved is mine, and I am His. He is the chiefest among ten thousand; He is altogether lovely."

Thus do the matters of this marvellous betrothment and union go on, "which things the angels desire to look into," and devils desire to defeat. The first desire shall be blessedly gratified;[3] but the other shall be disappointed, for none shall be able to pluck His loved one out of His

---

[1] Eph. ii. 2, 3.　　　　[2] Rom. vii. 8, 9, 18.　　　　[3] Eph. iii. 10.

hands; and against her the gates of hell shall never pre-vail. Praise Him for ever for such love as this!

Well may it be asked, Who is this wondrous Beloved that would go to such depths for His spouse, and on whom the weak fair one is leaning as she comes up out of the wilderness? Ah! He is the same who, from all eternity, was the great "I Am," the mighty God, by whom all things were created, who is before all things, and by whom all things consist. It is He who, in the fulness of time, scorned not the lowly Virgin's womb, but became a babe, and was found in fashion as a man. The same glorious Person who was seen coming from Edom, with dyed garments from Bozrah, glorious in His apparel, travelling in the greatness of His strength, who did tread the winepress of Almighty wrath alone, and of the people there was none with Him. It is He whose countenance is as the sun shining in his strength, yet whose "visage was marred more than any man's, and His form more than the sons of men." He is a holy One of the holy ones, and yet "a man of sorrows and acquainted with grief; holy, harmless, undefiled, and separate from sinners," and yet "numbered with the transgressors." Under the weight of sin and its punishment, Jesus agonised in the sacred garden of Gethsemane, and sweat as it were great drops of blood falling down to the ground. Oh, those rich, rich drops from His precious veins, of more value than all the gold and gems His hands have made!

This is the matchless Bridegroom of whom we speak. His love has saved, and it does kindle the soul now trying to tell of His worth, who, on Calvary, was stretched on the accursed tree, and there finished the love-scene of His mystic sufferings. Come, sit with me a moment beneath the shadow of

His cross. It will not mar, but heighten the joys of your nuptial day. Look up, and remember it is as a Husband He hangs bleeding there. It is the Bridegroom, in love for the Bride, enduring those unknown pangs. See how His holy flesh is bruised with scourging, and His precious hands and feet pierced with rugged nails. How is His heavenly brow torn with pricking thorns, and His dear side with the cruel spear; each gaping wound proclaiming, Man is guilty—God is love. But God is justice too! Oh, see His precious blood trickling down. It flowed forth for sinners like me—like thee! Look and wonder; look and be comforted; look and adore.

> " Here look till love dissolve your heart,
>   And bid each slavish fear depart."

Say, does not your very soul move towards this glorious Well-Beloved! and will it not join mine in saying—

> " Bruised Bridegroom, take us wholly,
>   Take and make us what Thou wilt."

O glorious Lord, we worship Thee! Thou art fairer than the children of men! Grace is poured into Thy lips—

> " Thy beauties we can never trace
>   Till we behold Thee face to face."

We love to meditate on Thy sufferings, but rejoice that they are over. Thou hast suffered, and thou diest no more! Thou art gone to *our* Father and to *Thy* Father; and we are expecting thee to "come again" and receive us unto Thyself, to be with Thee, and behold Thy glory, when, in nobler and sweeter strains "we'll sing Thy dying [and yet never-dying] love, and tell Thy power to save," while with open face and ravished heart, we gaze upon Thy matchless beauty. . . . . Please, excuse my many words. It is to me a thrilling subject, full of blessedness; and the very writing it has been a lattice through which my precious Beloved has shewn Himself. Oh, may He shine on you; and when you give your hand and heart to ——, may the Holy Ghost rouse you in powerful enablings to give yourself more fully to Jesus than ever before. I come not to you with worldly compliments; they beseem not our holy religion, and the peculiar people. But I come with an honest heart, desiring for you both every choice covenant blessing, with the sweetest mercies of the new estate upon which you are entering, and that these may be to you but as the shadows of a substance, you, in and through them, coming by the Spirit's power to fuller enjoyment of union and communion with our all-lovely Immanuel, and with the Father in Him. May your union be of the Lord, in the Lord, and for the Lord. May His name be glorified, and Jesus doubly precious to your souls. The theme wants more than an angel's power to tell all its fulness.—Ever yours in Jesus.   RUTH.

Hosea ii. 19, 20.

IV.

The long patience of the Husbandman.

TO E. M.

HIGH PAVEMENT, NOTTINGHAM, *May* 10, 1850.

MY DEAR MRS ——, All health and peace to you in our glorious Covenant-Head. My soul desires that yours may prosper, and greets you affectionately in that dear name which, when breathed into the soul by the Holy Ghost, is

B

truly precious.[1]   Precious indeed He is, but not to the carnal mind; to such He has no form nor comeliness, no beauty,
that they should desire Him.   There must be spiritual life,
spiritual sight, and spiritual appetite, before a glorious
Christ can be appreciated in His preciousness and suitability.

These gifts, my beloved friend, I believe you have received
through rich sovereign grace ; and it can be truly said, "You
hath He quickened, who were dead in trespasses and sins.'
This one mercy of quickening, this first communication of
grace, is a sure pledge of glory, according to Phil. i. 6.
Eternal life is the same in kind, though not in development,
in "the blade," "the ear," and "the full corn in the ear."
The great Husbandman is watching over all, giving sun
and rain as well as storms and frosts in due season. We like
the showers and sunshine, but would rather go on without
the cold and stormy weather, which is likewise needful, and
often very conducive to our spiritual growth.   I have often
said before the Lord, "Search me, O God, and know my
heart : try me, and know my thoughts : and see if there be
any wicked way in me, and lead me in the way everlasting."[2]   But when a cutting north wind has come, I have
complained, little thinking that it was just an answer to
my prayer. Perhaps you may pass through some such experience, and in these wintry seasons you may think that
growth is stopped, and life will soon be gone ; but no, it is
"incorruptible seed" of which you are born, which liveth
and abideth for ever.[3] Amidst our many changes, how
encouraging is this thought ; and also the knowledge that
the great Husbandman has more interest in the seed than
it has in itself.   "Ye are not your own," but His who

---

[1] 1 Pet. ii. 7.   [2] Ps. cxxxix. 23, 24.   [3] 1 Pet. i. 23.

bought you with His blood. You are His portion, His inheritance, in whom He will be glorified.

Truly the gospel of the blessed God, while it is most
strengthening as shewing all the work to be His, is most
humbling, as shewing all weakness and sin to be ours. Had
it not been so, such mighty cost and pains would not have
been needful for our redemption. I pray that the oil and
wine of gospel grace may flow into your soul, for this makes
us nothing, and Jesus all. I hope you are well, and that
the Lord is making your holiday a holy day unto Himself
by His own presence and power. The Lord be with your
spirit, and strengthen your faith, and make all needed
grace abound towards you, dear Mrs ———.—So desires, with
much love, your very affectionate, but very unworthy,

Ruth.

V.

*Earthly things bedimmed by clear views of the glory of
Christ.*

TO E. M.

Bethel Cottage, *Aug.* 27, 1850.

Very dear Mrs. ———, In the precious Name which is
above every name, I come to inquire, Is it well with thee?
Does the vine flourish, and the tender grape appear?[1]
and do you find the savour of the Beloved's ointments
give a very good smell? Is Jesus increasingly precious,
more than ever desirable? Is He, in your esteem, better

[1] Song vi. 11.

than rubies, and all the things that may lawfully be desired not to be compared to Him? Is the Holy Ghost sharpening your appetite for this Bread of Life, so that with more ardent longings you are saying, "None but Jesus?" When He is in the right place, other things will be so; it is His rising in the soul that makes them sink to their proper level; and oh! He is so worthy, so suitable, so altogether lovely, we cannot prize Him too much, or hold Him too fast, or lean on Him too heavily. All I can say of Him is nothing, so mean is it, so far below His worth; but through rich grace, I, a vile sinner, have tasted and handled of this precious Word of life, and found such blessed benefit, such soul-invigoration, that I want to set others longing for these royal dainties.

Perhaps I might think that the Lord will do His own work, and I am only meddling in vain, if I did not read in His Holy Word about "exhorting one another," and "stirring up pure minds by way of remembrance." But, as these things are there, I venture; and if by many poor attempts I may be used to stir up but one warm loving remembrance of Him, I shall be thankful. Satan is ever striving to divert the mind from this object. He will allure or alarm, he will use what is pleasing or painful, anything to keep the soul from closing with Christ, from looking unto Jesus, and believing in Him for life and salvation. Nevertheless, all those who are ordained unto eternal life shall believe in spite of his efforts, and all those in eternal union with Christ shall close with Him by living faith. Cords of love shall entwine, the bands of a man shall draw, till the poor soul is brought into conscious union with the Beloved, and can say, "Who loved *me*, and gave Himself for *me*."

Oh, the blessed provisions and securities of the ever-lasting covenant, which is ordered in all things, and sure! Not only are all things made ready, but the soul is made willing to receive them; the appetite given, and the required garment put on.[1] The precious Saviour is a free gift, and the faith which receives Him is a free gift also; the blood which cleanseth is Heaven's royal bounty, for freely did it flow from the veins of heaven's King, and the application of it is Heaven's sole prerogative. By mercy, not by merit, do all the blessings come. This salvation is for the poor, and the poor only, and they must be stripped even of their rags. It is not enough to confess that their rags are filthy and worthless, they must be parted with, and this necessity touches very closely the heart of the old Adam. But all must go, that Christ may wear the crown,—that he that glorieth may glory in the Lord our righteousness.

How is it with you, my beloved? Are you stripped of your own righteousness, emptied, and bankrupt? If so, I hail you blessed, for "the poor have the gospel preached to them;" and it is written, "When they had nothing to pay, he frankly forgave them both." Nothing to pay! how our proud flesh does murmur and complain, and only wish that it had something to bring! But why? "He hath magnified the law and made it honourable." He hath endured every stripe that justice required, paying every farthing the creditor demanded, and that in Heaven's own coin, for "without shedding of blood is no remission." His pure blood was freely shed that sin might be honourably remitted. "The soul that sinneth it shall die." He dies, "the just for the unjust, to bring us to God;" and when at the close of His

[1] Isa. lxi. 10.

work He cried aloud, "It is finished," there was not a voice heard in heaven, earth, or hell to contradict him. Take courage, then, my beloved; we can afford to be poor with such "unsearchable riches in Christ," and all He is and has is ours, for "my Beloved is mine, and I am His." "All things are yours, for ye are Christ's, and Christ's is God's." He is "Head over all things to His body the Church."

"Ah! but," say you, "I want to know more clearly that He is mine. I want personal application and appropriation." Well, this is not unlawful coveting; go on longing, for this very same Jesus "satisfieth the longing soul, and filleth the hungry soul with goodness." You want to know your sonship? "We are children of God by faith in Christ Jesus;" faith is the manifestation of sonship, and by it we come to the enjoyment of family privileges. Living faith is the gift of God, and "faith cometh by hearing, and hearing by the Word of God." While Rebekah was listening to Abraham's servant, I trow there was a moving of her heart towards his master's son, for when asked if she would so quickly leave all for him, she said, "I will go." So, perhaps, while you are hearing of the "things which are Jesus Christ's," the Holy Ghost will be kindling love and longing in your soul, bringing it to believe and venture. May the blessed Comforter speedily make you as willing as Rebekah, and work in you the same obedience of faith. She went forth, and her faith was not in vain; she found her husband more than she forsook for him. So shall you; for eternity will never unfold all the love, loveliness, and glories of our wonderful Emmanuel. Oh, I do want to know more of them here, and thus have all the things of earth bedimmed!

Sweet Testifier of Jesus! Thou Wind Divine! "awake,"

and " come," and blow away the dust of earth, and clouds
of flesh and sense, which seem to come between us and
our souls' Beloved, revealing Him in warmer love, more
manifested union, and more endeared communion. Oh,
make us walk in Him!

> " Closer and closer may we cleave
>   To His beloved embrace,
>   Expect His fulness to receive,
>   And grace to answer grace."

If for Jesus you pine, come join to beseech Him for more
of His love. Come, O Thou Beloved! into the garden of
our souls; breathe upon the graces of Thy own Spirit there,
that the spices may flow forth for Thy regaling. Eat, O
Beloved! Thine own pleasant fruits, and give us, Thine unworthy ones, to find Thy fruits sweet to our taste—the
fruits of Thy love, of Thy doing, of Thy suffering; give us
to feast on Thy rich fruits,—to eat, by faith, Thy flesh and
blood, and thus live by Thee.[1] Say to us, "Eat, O friends!
drink, yea, drink abundantly, O beloved!" for Thy " bid-
dings are enablings." Amen. (Eph. iii. 20, 21.)

Now if there should be one drop of living water for your
refreshment in this little vessel, give God the praise. To
Him I commend you in love.—Your very affectionate, but
in myself, very unworthy,   Ruth.

I send you Phil. iii.

[1] John vi. 57.

VI.

Bearing one another's burdens.

TO E. M.

HIGH PAVEMENT, *Sept.* 25, 1850.

VERY DEAR MRS ——, Lady L. S. wished me to write to you again. Wherefore, "send, Lord, by whom Thou wilt send," only let these absent ones be fed with food convenient for them, and Thy name be glorified. Breathe, Holy Comforter, on our souls that they may be quickened; breathe in providences, that we may be edified by them; breathe in the written Word that we may be instructed; breathe on the Rose of Sharon, the Incarnate Word, that by the fragrance thereof our souls may be revived and refreshed; breathe upon these hearts, that we may commune sweetly in and of, the Beloved, for the Divine glory, and our soul-strengthening. Amen, amen.

Jesus is the never-tiring theme. It is He who is the precious stone, which prospereth whithersoever it turneth.[1] On the mount of high communion He is precious; in the valley of humiliation He is precious; also, unto you that believe, He is precious. Faith is the "Christ-receiving grace;" by faith we apprehend Him, by faith know more and more of His preciousness, by faith have the felt benefit of His blood and righteousness,[2] and by faith cast anchor on this Rock, when to sense and feeling all is dark and stormy.

[1] Prov. xvii. 8. [2] Rom. iii. 22, 25.

Ah! indeed there are seasons in experience when we can neither see nor hear nor feel Him whom our souls love and long for; and all within seems barren and powerless: then is the trial of faith, and the time for its exercise. If we are walking by sense, our confidence will be shaken, and we shall draw wrong conclusions;[1] but if faith prevail, we shall not be greatly moved. The soul does not voluntarily choose to be "a spring shut up, a fountain sealed," neither, if under self-direction, would it prefer to travel "three days in the wilderness and find no water." We would rather linger always at Elim, beside the wells and the palm-trees. Thus sense would grow mightily, and faith become weak for want of exercise; but He who ordains all our encampments, and who is to us "instead of eyes," knows best where to lead us; having determined that "faith, though the smallest, shall surely be tried."

Wherefore, my beloved and longed-for, "think it not strange concerning the trial which is to try you, as though some strange thing happened unto you." Whether that trial be inward exercise from indwelling sin, or the fiery darts of the wicked one, or outward affliction, or something in prospect which makes the heart tremble; for all these, and every other, we have the promise, "My grace is sufficient for thee, my strength is made perfect in weakness." What can be weaker than a worm? Yet the Lord says, "Fear not, thou worm Jacob, I will help thee, saith the Lord, and thy Redeemer, the Holy One of Israel." "I will hold thy right hand, saying unto thee, Fear not." "When thou passest through the waters I will be with thee, and through the rivers they shall not overflow thee: when thou walkest

---

[1] Isa. xlix. 14.

through the fire thou shalt not be burned, neither shall the flame kindle upon thee." These are sweet cordials for a time of weakness and trial. The Lord fulfil them in your experience, and grant that your faith fail not. May you be kept instant in prayer, "watching thereunto with all perseverance" to learn the mind of the Lord respecting you. Times of trial are inquiring times.—See Gen. xxv. 22, 23; 1 Sam. xxiii. 2, 4, 11; 1 Sam. xxx. 8; 2 Chron. xviii. 4; Job x. 2. There are those now living who can testify to the Lord's glory, that they have found a great blessing, in the close dealing with God to which they have been brought by afflictive dispensations under the Divine exercising[1] of the Holy Ghost. It is spoken of ancient Israel that "the more they were afflicted the more they multiplied and grew." Often, indeed, is it thus with the spiritual seed of Abraham, being "chastened of the Lord" there is growth out of self into Christ. Blessed is it when we turn our face to the wall; that is, away from every creature expectation, and pour out our hearts before Him. One who did so, in the bitterness of his soul, had afterwards thankfully to say, "O Lord, by these things men live, and in all these is the life of my spirit; so wilt Thou recover me, and make me to live." The Lord grant you like experience, that with me you may have to say, "It is good for me that I have been afflicted."

My heart earnestly desires for you that the present dispensation, and what may be approaching, may be very much sanctified, that the Lord's name may be glorified, and you come forth as gold, saying, "I know, O Lord, that thy judgments are right, and that thou in faithfulness hast afflicted me;"[2] and heartily choosing, as Moses did, "to suffer afflic-

[1] Heb. xii. 11.   [2] Ps. cxix. 75.

tion with the people of God, rather than to enjoy the pleasures of sin for a season." [1]

> " For though our cup seems mix'd with gall,
>   There's something secret sweetens all."

Is it not so ? Have you not found some drops of Divine
love in this bitter cup? May the Beloved further shew
Himself through this lattice, and walk with you in this furnace, causing some bands to be burned off that you may
walk at large in the way of His commandments. It is better
to walk with Jesus in the fire, than to walk after the flesh
in the slippery places of worldly indulgence and carnal security. I hope He has a special favour towards you, and
means to have you walk very closely with Himself. Would
that I could speak more worthily of our precious Well-
Beloved, who may safely be trusted in the flood and in the
flame. Praise Him, O our souls. Adieu, much-beloved.—
Your very affectionate   RUTH.

1 Thess. iii. 3.

You have many petitions to present to the King just
now. Psalm xx.—From   R. B.

VII.

Christ is all.

TO E. M.

Dec. 1850.

VERY DEAR MRS ——, I cannot but again inquire, Is it
still well with you ? Has Israel's God proved faithful in
your time of need ? Have you had strength as your day ?
and can you now say, " It is good for me that I have been

[1] Heb. xi. 25.

afflicted ? "   The cloud of affliction or trial often looks very
dark at first. " Men see not the bright light which is in the
cloud, but the wind passeth and cleanseth them."[1]   The
Holy Spirit by His Divine exercising comes with the affliction, and then is discovered some light of instruction, and
the dark cloud is found to be full of mercy, and " breaks
with blessings on our head."   Earnestly do I hope this is
the case with yourself and your husband.   I desire mercies
of the God of heaven for you my beloved, that when you
come to the tribulated waters they may either divide, that
you may go over dryshod, or, if they overflow, that their
depths may only prove to you the deeps of God's mercy,
faithfulness, and love.   May you feel the Rock firm beneath
while the billows roll over your head ; and may you be
brought up again with a new song of praise, even " salvation
is of the Lord."

Our God is a refuge for us.   Our Rock will stand the
storm.   Our Guide may be safely trusted, though we see
neither sun nor stars for many days.   He sees us when we
can see nothing but gloom, and cannot see Him at all—
when we have not one glimpse of the King in His beauty.
He hears us when we cannot hear Him, for He seems to
answers us never a word ; but many an answer of peace is
prepared, while the poor petitioner is suffered long to go on
pleading in sackcloth and ashes.[2]   Our God is wonderful
in His way of working ; and, for myself, I must confess
that He generally deals very contrary to my expectations ;
but " He doeth all things well."   It is

> " Sweet to lie passive in His hands,
> And know no will but His."

---

[1] Job xxxvii. 21.   [2] Dan. ix. 3, 23.

I have proved my own strength to be perfect weakness, my own wisdom consummate folly, and my own righteousness filthy rags. What a mercy, then, to be stripped of all, and have Christ for wisdom, Christ for righteousness, Christ for strength, Christ for purity, Christ for power, Christ for beauty, Christ for holiness, Christ for acceptance above, Christ for our daily walk, Christ for our daily work, Christ for rest, Christ for food, Christ for medicine ; yea, to know nothing among men or before God, but Jesus crucified and glorified.

But, say you, I cannot make so free with Christ, I dare not claim Him for everything. Perhaps not, and we read that Ruth felt no claim upon the mighty man of wealth when she fell at His feet to thank Him for a few handfuls of corn,[1] and a morsel at meal-time. But there was the secret of relationship behind, and she afterwards found a claim and made it, nor did she do so in vain ; for she obtained not only her hands full and her veil full, but also the Lord of the Harvest Himself. I trust ere long you will be thus led on by the Spirit from gleaning ears of mercy and pardon, to say, " Spread thy skirt over me, for thou art a near kinsman." He will then acknowledge relationship, and give you that freedom of love which may now appear almost presumptuous, though indeed it is not so. Where Christ is thus revealed in the soul in His fulness, He is to be to us instead of ourselves, and all besides; as Rutherford says, "Not myself but Christ, not my ease but Christ, not my honour but Christ." Oh ! blessed are they that can deny themselves, and put Christ in the room of themselves. Ah, indeed! this is the true starvation of the flesh, and the true strengthening of that inner man, the life of which is Christ.

[1] Ruth ii. 10.

Well-beloved friend, if you have not yet full possession, I hope you are Christ-hungry and Christ-thirsty ; then I am sure you will not die for want, for such are blessed and shall be filled.   Take encouragement.   May the Lord give it, and make your soul as a watered garden, for He shall come down as the rain, as showers that water the earth.

All this is from one who has had an exchange of hearts with Jesus, and therefore he is the never-tiring theme.   That He should be the constant subject needs no apology, but only that He is not more worthily spoken of.   Ah, indeed ! of all words and similes, we may say—

> " All are too mean to speak His worth,
>   To set Immanuel's glories forth."

To His loving heart and powerful arm I again commend you for all you need, and may you both receive of His fulness, and grace for grace.—Yours affectionately,

RUTH.

Col. ii.

VIII.

The deceivableness of the form without the power of godliness.

HIGH PAVEMENT, *June* 11, 1851.

MY DEAR MRS ——, ... This is a day of much lip-profession without real heart work, and the "kingdom of God is not in word, but in power;" " it is within you."   This is what Satan seems in this day to be most fighting against.   He does not oppose a general profession of religion, which is now

deemed respectable; nor does he mind great strictness in outward form, as that is often a means of lulling the conscience
into false peace. He will not even disturb a sound creed, and
much zeal in contending for the truth of the Bible, so long
as they rest only in the natural judgment, whereby they induce vain confidence and terrible self-deceiving. The great
enemy of souls will endeavour to keep all in peace who have
a name to live, but are dead; and if one of his subjects pass
over either from gross sins or from the more refined pleasures
of this perishing world to an outward profession, he will not
be alarmed ; for he cares not whether souls perish under the
title of worldling or of Christian, so that he may get them
into his own fearful condemnation. Nay, I believe if he see
one become restless under some sense of sin, and that he
cannot urge that poor soul on further in the old way, he will
transform himself into an angel of light, and recommend
reformation and outward duties, such as reading and hearing
the Word, taking care to substitute form for power.

Oh! the dreadful danger of such souls, soothed into carnal
security ; but only blinded to their danger, not delivered
from it. Better were it to endure years of anguish in weeping, and seeking for mercy by Jesus Christ, than to be turned
to such " a refuge of lies," and to walk in such " sparks of
their own kindling." Better to walk in sorrow all one's life
than to lie down in sorrow at death to end in eternal woe.
May the Lord deliver souls thus deceived from this snare of
the great fowler, so that they may thankfully say, " The
snare is broken, and we are escaped " by Divine power into
that kingdom of God which is not meat and drink, (or outward things,) but righteousness, peace, and joy in the Holy
Ghost. Ah ! my loved friend, it is this stronghold which

Satan fights against, and fallen flesh is in league with him. Outward form and bodily exercise may be tolerated, but inward power is represented as contemptible, unreasonable, and is called fanaticism and enthusiasm, yet the world of glory is full of this, swelling broader and deeper the anthem of praise to the holy Lord God and the Lamb. Without this divine life within, no soul of man can be saved, as the great day shall declare. It is, indeed, fearful to think what that terrible day will reveal; and of all characters, I think those seem in the most fearful condition who have had Christ on the lip, but not in the heart, as in Matt. vii. 21-23. My heart often says : "Search me, O God, and know my heart; try me, and know my thoughts; and see if *there be any* wicked way in me, and lead me in the way everlasting."[1] True it is our vigilant foe does not mind a new creed, but he hates a new heart. He does not object to outward reformation, but hates inward regeneration, and also the regenerated. He does not fear good words of prayer on the lip, but he well knows he shall suffer loss when it is said of a soul, " Behold, he prayeth;" for—

> " Satan trembles when he sees
> The weakest saint upon his knees."

O ye trembling souls, let not the subtle serpent drive you from this stronghold; your God will hear and help you. He has taught you to pray ; He will answer your prayers. If He long delay, He is worth waiting for. If He shut His door against you, it is only to make you knock the louder. It is better to wait on God for His salvation in sackcloth and ashes, than to wait on the world and the flesh clothed in scarlet; "for the end of these things is death."

[1] Ps. cxxxix. 23, 24.

It matters not who may deride or scoff, or how your own evil heart may shrink from the contempt of the cross. "How long halt ye between two opinions ? if the Lord be God, follow him; but if Baal, then follow him." You cannot serve them both. Oh, be wise. If the world and Satan and the flesh seem too strong for you, as they surely will, go into your closet, and pour out your heart before the Lord ; He will be a refuge for you. "He giveth power to the faint ; and to them that have no might He increaseth strength." The sighs and groans of a broken heart are heard in the high court above, and the tears of a contrite spirit are audible there ; for before the throne is Jesus, the Brother of the broken-hearted, the propitiation for sin, the Advocate for sinners, who loathe themselves for their iniquity.[1] That blessed Saviour understands all the broken utterances ; He knows what each would say if he could, and "He ever liveth to make intercession for them."[2] It may be the law condemns thee, O trembling one; conscience condemns thee ; thoughts, words, actions, all condemn thee. Be it so, and may it be thy mercy, and the beginning of thy salvation, for this is like the power with which the Holy Spirit begins in the soul, thereby translating it out of the kingdom of darkness "into the kingdom of God's dear Son."[3] The religion of Jesus is a religion of power ;[4] and if, through the power of the Holy Spirit, there is a discovery of sin and condemnation, may Jesus say, "Thy sins,"(oh, the sweetness of personality !) "*thy* sins, which are many, are all forgiven thee ;" then the burden is lawfully lost, and the soul has solid peace. Thus shall it be with every one quickened by

---

[1] 1 Kings viii. 38, 39.
[2] Heb. vii. 25.
[3] Col. i. 13.
[4] 1 Cor. i. 18, 23, 24.

C

the Spirit. Satan may strive to drown and stifle the conviction, but it will return with double misery, and the burden
grow heavier and heavier, until the poor soul finds there is
no way of escape but through the blood of the cross. May
the Spirit enable you to come just as you are! Dear Mrs
——, I know you are seeking for Jesus, may He soon be
found of you.—From your affectionate but unworthy

RUTH—a sinner saved.

IX.

Signs of spiritual life.

TO E. M.

"Look unto Me, and be ye saved."

HIGH PAVEMENT, *Sept.* 15, 1851.

BELOVED MRS ——, I thought much of you last evening, while hearing a sermon from Phil. i. 6. "The day
of Jesus Christ" was spoken of, as the day when He
comes to receive the soul unto himself; and the glorious
day when He will raise the body in His own likeness. It
was said, how surely the Lord will carry on His work in the
soul, through all the doubts, fears, temptations, sins, and
corruptions which assail it, and are bitterly felt before Jesus
is revealed. Though they threaten to swallow up and destroy, the Lord is above them, and will secretly maintain the
precious life He has given. Perhaps, however, the great
point with some is, whether they have this life. They are

thoroughly established in the comfortable doctrine we speak of,—the final perseverance of the saints,—but fear they are not one of them. How is it with you? Do you hunger and thirst for Christ? Do you plead, pant, groan, strive against sin and for salvation? Then you are alive, and it is eternal life, which cannot die; incorruptible seed which cannot decay; and grace which was given to you in Christ before the foundation of the world;[1] nor can anything which occurs in time take it away. I well know the night is long and dreary to the quickened soul, while the Lord delays His coming. It is no longer "alive without the law," but the Spirit has brought the commandment home; it bears upon the conscience heavily; and in the pure light of that holy law is discovered evil, only evil, and that continually; fresh sin at every turn; new stumbling at every step. It is night with the soul, and "he that walketh in the night stumbleth." Though the law is light,[2] it is only to make manifest evil,[3] not to guide in the way of peace. The Holy Spirit must do that. The light of the law upon the black soul only makes its night more horrible before it has found the Law-fulfiller; the sun has not arisen, and corruptions creep forth to its great dismay. But He that shall come will come in the set time, and will not tarry. He knows them who love His appearing, and will not let them long for it in vain. As in His law they have seen their own darkness and deformity, so in this light they see light, even the light of life when He comes; and then they learn that all those sharp reproofs of instruction were the way of life, though, indeed, they felt like death and destruction.

I am not writing to you merely from the map, but mark-

[1] 2 Tim. i. 9.   [2] Prov. vi. 23.   [3] Eph. v. 13.

ing down a few of my own steppings, that you may thereby trace whether you are in the footsteps of the flock; and though this cannot satisfy you, because the way is not the end, yet it may comfort and stimulate you afresh to press on towards the mark, looking for and hastening to the coming of the day of Christ in your own soul. There are times when the hands hang down and the knees are feeble, and the soul says, " Our hope is lost, we are cut off for our parts."[1] Then a word from the Lord, through a fellow-traveller, does good, like a medicine ; the Word of the Lord is precious in those days when there is no open vision. I mean when the soul has never been able to say, " I have found Him whom my soul loveth," and cannot make the personal appeal, " Thou knowest that I love Thee," but does long to know, it is loved of Him. Then it sometimes gets a sweet melting season in hearing that others have trodden the same in and out path ; and a feeling of comfortable hope that " being in the way," the Lord will ere long meet with it, and lead it into the House of the Master's brethren.[2] Be it mine to welcome you there in the appointed season, and to try to encourage you while you occupy the waiting-place. It is at least a safe one : " Blessed are all they that wait for Him." But through unbelief we are too apt to think we shall wait in vain, and He never will come to us; although He has said, "They shall not be ashamed that wait for Me." This passage was very sweet to me in days gone by, when tasting the wormwood and gall ; and it is so still. My soul hath the bitterness still in remembrance, and is humbled in me,[3] for instead of tasting only, I deserve to be drinking to all eternity ; but He hath taken the cup of trembling out of my hand, and

[1] Ezek. xxxvii. 11.　　　[2] Gen. xxiv. 27.　　　[3] Lam. iii. 19, 20.

hath given me the cup of salvation and blessing. He hath brought my soul out of prison; and dealt bountifully with me, and now I like to point other poor prisoners to the way of escape.

I know the heart of a "captive exile," as well as of a stranger, and would not impose heavy burdens; but you know how happy I should be to hear from you. How blessed when the captive exile, described in Isaiah li. 14, experiences the deliverance spoken of in Zech. ix. 11, 12. Affectionate remembrance to you all in the Beloved. May the blessing of the Lord flow freely in your family circle. 2 Thess. iii. 16 and 18.—Yours ever, RUTH.

X.

Encouragement to a burdened soul.

TO E. M.

HIGH PAVEMENT, *Nov.* 14, 1851.

VERY DEAR MRS ——, Grace, mercy, and peace be with you, from God our Father and the Lord Jesus Christ, by the anointing and teaching of the Holy Comforter. "For," said our Lord, "He shall teach you all things, and bring all things to your remembrance, whatsoever I have said unto you." "He will guide you into all truth:" "He shall glorify me, for He shall receive of mine, and shall shew it unto you." The Holy Spirit is the living guide to Jesus. It is He who says, with power, "Behold the Lamb of God, which taketh away the sin of the world." It is He who convinces of sin, who wounds, and probes the wound, and lays open the evil of our nature, causing us to know that we are corrupt within and without. But He not only thus discovers the malady, He also applies the remedy. He just abases the sinner to exalt the Saviour; and gives the deep sense of sin that the great salvation may be more appreciated and enjoyed. We are as bad as we can be, and it is needful to know it; but our knowledge of it will not save us. It is, "Look unto ME, and be ye saved, all the ends of the earth." Some seem to glory in their deep discoveries of depravity; but nay, rather "let him that glorieth, glory in the Lord."

The end of a thing is better than the beginning: the beginning of the Lord's teaching is to know ourselves; the end to know Him, whom to know is life eternal, and happy is it for those who tarry not in all the plain, but amidst all the sense of sin and the loathing of self, are kept pressing on, crying, "That I may know Him;" "that I may find Him;" that I may be found in Him;" "I press towards the mark;" "I long for the prize."

We read, Luke vi. 19, "And the whole multitude sought to touch Him: for there went virtue out of Him, and healed them all." Their miseries pressed them on to seek His mercies; and so the poor woman with the issue of blood; it seemed incurable; it made her unclean. How dare she approach the Holy Jesus? How dare she presume to touch His unspotted garment? Ah, but she believed that He had virtue, and that *that* virtue was to be received by faith; and thus she obtained the cure. "Jesus said, Somebody hath touched me; for I perceive that virtue is gone out of me." She had believed with the heart, and thus He drew her on to confess with the mouth, and then He openly gave her the full reward of her faith,—"Daughter, be of good comfort : thy

faith had made thee whole ; go in peace."[1]   Ah, many are
now thronging and pressing Jesus by noisy profession, but
only a few are getting the healing virtue, and those are
unclean diseased ones who think themselves most unlikely
of all.   But of Him they hear; and "faith cometh by hearing."   To Him they are brought, for "all that the Father
giveth me shall come to me;" and they do not come in
vain, for "him that cometh to me I will in nowise cast out."
"All power is given unto me in heaven and in earth."   Yea,
power to forgive sins also.   Yes, my precious Saviour, with
hand and heart do I subscribe thus ; Thou hast power to
save those whom none else could or would; for "Thou
hast clothed such a vile sinner as I am" with the garments of salvation.   Thou hast covered me with the robe
of righteousness.   Therefore my soul doth greatly rejoice
in the Lord, and is joyful in my God.   Oh, those words,
"My God," when lawfully and feelingly uttered, have in
them a world of blessedness !

Well, you see how it is with me.   I am still delighting in
the love of the altogether lovely Jesus; but not half enough.
What think *you* of Christ?   Surely my heart's desire is, that
He may be enthroned in your affections, for "He is worthy,"
and the more unworthy you feel, the better He will suit you.
In your flesh "dwelleth no good thing."   While you dwell in
that tent you will find evil, only evil.   Like the father of the
faithful, you will have to go forth into the land[2] which the
Lord will shew you; but He must order all your journeying, as He says, "I will guide thee with mine eye, I will instruct thee and teach thee in the way which thou shalt go."

It seems, however, that at present you are under the

[1] Luke viii. 43-48.   [2] Deut. viii. 7-9.

ministry of condemnation, because you are resting in your own righteousness, which you will never establish, as it is contrary to the law of faith.[1] The contrast is, "There is therefore now no condemnation to them who are *in* Christ Jesus, who walk not aiter the flesh, but after the Spirit." This is the ministry of righteousness which follows the other and exceeds in glory; for the work of righteousness is peace, "and the effect of righteousness quietness and assurance for ever." Here is that which establishes us. "Thou hast set my feet upon a rock, and established my goings." "Believe in the Lord your God, so shall ye be established."[2] " In righteousness shalt thou be established."[3] "He that stablisheth us in Christ and hath anointed us is God,[4] who also sealeth us with that Holy Spirit of promise, which is the earnest of our inheritance."[5] All the operations of that Spirit in the soul are either to make known or make way for Christ; the latter seems at present His work in your heart. He is discovering your evil, and shaking your movable things.[6] Like John, He goes before the Lord to prepare His way. Be of good cheer, this Divine Messenger betokens that the Lord is at hand. He would not have shewed you all these things if He meant to destroy you. "I commend you to God, and to the word of His grace, which is able to build you up, and to give you an inheritance among all them that are sanctified" "through faith which is in Christ Jesus."

The Lord bless you, and grant you the instructions of wisdom for the training of your dear child, and all else you are called to.

And now, farewell! May you be brought home at the

[1] Rom. x. 3.
[2] 2 Chron. xx. 20.
[3] Isa. liv. 14.
[4] 2 Cor. i. 21.
[5] Eph. i. 13, 14.
[6] Heb. xii. 27.

appointed season in safety, and with dew resting upon your branch. As Mr ——— is a lover of husbandry, he perhaps will not be offended with the Christian love and greeting of a gleaner, who can feelingly say, "The Lord bless thee,"[1] and make thee a blessing.[2] This is the true wish of my heart for you both.—Your very affectionate

RUTH.

XI.

The blessings of affliction.

TO E. M.

"Behold, I will bring it health and cure, and I will cure them, and will reveal unto them the abundance of peace and truth."

HIGH PAVEMENT, *Sept.* 22, 1852.

MUCH BELOVED AND OFTEN-REMEMBERED FRIEND, The tidings received from you this morning made me sorry, and yet I must say, "It is well," for I do believe it, knowing that "He doeth all things well." May this trial be as a lattice, through which Jesus will shew himself to your souls. Trial is one, which He often looks through, with much tenderness,[3] upon His redeemed ones. He looked through the pillar of fire and cloud, to trouble His enemies, and hinder their flight;[4] but He was in the fire and cloud to preserve and guide His people safely through the deep, so that not even a little one was left behind. It might be that "little faith" looked at the walls of water, and feared they

[1] Ruth ii. 4.   [2] Mic. v. 7.   [3] Isa. lxiii. 9.   [4] Exod. xiv. 24.

would give way; but those fears did not make the promise of none effect, though they might rob the soul of comfort. Was it not wonderful that the same cloud, which was light to Israel, was darkness to the foe; and the same water, which was as walls of salvation to one, was death and destruction to the other?[1] So it is with bodily afflictions and providential trials; to the worldling they are destroyers of his best enjoyments; to the child of God they are often the very high road to them. To the worldling they are only bitter; to the other it is a mingled portion, for

> " Though their cup seems mix'd with gall,
> There's something secret sweetens all."

"I will sing of mercy and judgment; unto Thee, O Lord, will I sing." And it is as of old: "howbeit our God turned the curse into a blessing."

Last evening, the love of God,[2] its gift, its effects, and its consummation,[3] were simply and sweetly spoken of. Oh, indeed! the love of God is a precious theme with those who feel it and who can say, "We love Him because He first loved us. What an amazing love to bestow such a gift! My soul does muse and marvel. Bring it home to yourself. Think of giving one of your sweet babes to poverty, hardship, toil, disgrace, and a torturing death. You could not do it even for your loved husband; and they are not as lovely as that precious, spotless Lamb, and they are not as much beloved as He. Yet His Father gave Him, and bruised Him, and "put Him to grief" for the ungodly,[4] for enemies,[5] for the unjust.[6] Truly, herein is unparalleled love.

---

[1] Exod. xiv. 28, 29.
[2] John iii. 16.
[3] Rev. vii. 9.
[4] Rom. v. 6.
[5] Col. i. 20, 21.
[6] 1 Pet. iii. 18.

May the Holy Spirit apply it, shed it abroad in our hearts, and encourage us to come unto the Father by Him.

The Lord hath prepared of His goodness for the poor; so if you are learning your poverty, it is to prepare you for the feast prepared for you.—Your affectionate　　RUTH.

XII.

Difficulties met.

TO E. M.

HIGH PAVEMENT, *March* 7, 1853.

DEARLY-BELOVED AND LONGED-FOR IN CHRIST JESUS, "Grace, mercy, and peace be multiplied to you by the revelation of Jesus Christ." "Blessed are all they that wait for Him." "Wherefore gird up the loins of your mind, be sober, and hope to the end for the grace which is to be brought unto you at the revelation of Jesus Christ." Fashion not yourself according to the former lusts in your ignorance; "be not conformed to this world, but be ye transformed by the renewing of your mind, that ye may prove what is that good and acceptable and perfect will of God." "Not by might nor by power, but by my Spirit, saith the Lord of hosts." When we last conversed together, you mentioned having received encouragement from Romans x. 13, and having lost it again by the first clause of verse 14, and some remarks upon it, and you seemed to confine the words, "Have not believed," to the faith of appropriation. Now, I must still say the passage does not convey this meaning to me; and I will mention one or two passages of Scripture which seem to me conclusive, that the faith of appropriation is not essential to a right calling upon God, though certainly where that faith is enjoyed, there will be stronger assurance of an answer.[1] "He that cometh to God must believe that He is, and that He is a rewarder of them that diligently seek Him,"[2] shews the need of faith in coming to God, which is the same as calling upon Him. It is a faith in what He is, and what He does, and seeking Him on *that* ground, to have respect to what is in Him, not what is in ourselves, as in Ps. lxxxvi. 4, 5. Again, in Matt. ix. 28, the poor men had been calling upon the Lord. He questions them as to whether they believed in Him, not as to whether He *would*, (for He does not try them in that way,) but as to whether He *could* do this, and then He gives them, according to their faith, the thing they asked of Him. In Mark i. 40 is a short confession of faith—"If thou wilt thou canst make me clean." The poor leper had heard of Jesus, believed in His ability, and therefore called upon Him; not because he had obtained the benefit, but that he might receive it, for he felt himself in a diseased condition. It does not seem faith of appropriation, but faith of expectation; inducing the cry of need to one who has power to help, like, "Lord save, or I perish." The sense of need, the faith that He can, and the hope that He will, supply that need, induce the cry for help, the Holy Spirit working in all this to bring the poor sinner and the precious Saviour together, that the remedy may be proved, as well as believed, to be just suited to the malady. You know we value a thing when we believe that it is exactly what we need; we value it then enough to seek it; but it becomes still more precious to us when we enjoy great bene-

[1] 1 John v. 15.　　　　　[2] Heb. vi. 7.

fit from it. So it is with Jesus. Faith of appropriation can talk much more in praise of His blessings and benefits, while faith of expectation is all on the alert to be a partaker of them. Have you not such faith as the latter ? Do you not so believe on Him as to call upon Him for salvation ? I do not wish to make you rest in what you have, but yet I would not have you give place to Satan, who is trying to stop the breath of prayer by saying that you cannot call upon the Lord aright because you have not faith. The way to get more faith is to look to Jesus, its Author and Finisher. May the Holy Spirit help you so to do.

You mentioned being cast down by Psalm xli. 11, " By this I know that thou favourest me, because mine enemy doth not triumph over me," because your inward enemies seem to triumph over you. Did you not forget that word, " Gad, a troop shall overcome him, but he shall overcome at the last," and I believe, indeed, that most of the Lord's soldiers experience this before they can say, " By thee I have run through a troop ;" and " By my God I have leaped over a wall." Our own strength must be exhausted, that out of weakness we may be made strong; and our own efforts in creature will and power be proved of no avail, that we may feel and know that the battle is the Lord's, and cry to Him for help, whilst giving Him all the glory. I was much struck the other day in observing, that though Joshua bid the captains set their feet on the necks of the five kings, he himself slew them. So it is with our spiritual Joshua ; He alone could finish transgression and make an end of sin. He has done it, and in the set time does, in the experience of each of His children, take away the dominion of their corruptions, though their lives are prolonged for a season like those beasts mentioned in Dan. vii. 12. If you, beloved, have not yet had that sensible overcoming given which you desire, be not cast down, but cry unto the Lord, and you shall ere long find it, as in 1 Chron. v. 20, 22. Many have realised this who have felt like the Psalmist, in Ps. vi., with regard to these inward foes. The Lord pardon what I have wrongly expressed, and clear up to your mind how He has answered that call which rested only in His power, without being sure of His will. "If thou wilt, thou canst make me clean;" and He said, "I will, be thou clean." Perhaps your heart will join me once more in saying, " Lord, increase our faith."

I sincerely wish you every blessing and covenant-favour. My love be with you all in Christ Jesus.—Yours,

RUTH—less than the least.

XIII.

Counsels how to meet daily cares.

TO E. M.

Saturday Morning.

MUCH-BELOVED FRIEND, My heart has just been much drawn out towards you in Isaiah xxviii. 26, "For his God doth instruct him to discretion, and doth teach him," desiring that you may have the experience of it in those domestic and secular cares which must necessarily devolve upon you; that you may not set them as a "wall between" your soul and your God. May each anxiety and perplexity, which seems to have more of Martha than of Mary, be to you just an errand to Him who is Head over all things, to His body the Church, that you may commune with Him in them and by

them, and thus walk with God while you walk in the duties
of your family and station. How beautiful to read from the
23d verse of the same chapter, and to see that the Lord so
minutely instructs the labourer how to prepare the ground
and sow the seed, as also how to prepare the corn for food.
Also in Exodus xxxi. 3–6, xxxv. 25, 26, and xxxvi. 2, how
encouraging to read of the Lord putting wisdom into the
hearts of men and women to guide their hands, though their
work was for the Tabernacle, and ours for the circumstances
in which He has placed us, saying, "Occupy till I come."
He will as really instruct us as He did them.

How touching also to read of David going to inquire of
the Lord about everything with such sweet simplicity, asking
whether he should go against his enemies,[1] and pursue those
who had robbed him,[2] even telling the Lord of a report he
had heard about Saul, and asking if that were true.[3] Satan
and the carnal mind would say, "It is not right to approach
the Lord in such inward confusion ; wait till the mind is
more calm and spiritual." But David came in the midst of
all, bringing his doubts and uncertainties with him, and in
all the Lord answered him, so that it was with him as with
Jotham—"He became mighty because he prospered his
ways before the Lord his God."[4] I cannot tell you how
precious these thoughts have been to me, or how often I
have resorted to them to encourage my heart to trust in the
Lord in secular things, and to expect His teaching in daily
cares great and small. Though I have mentioned it before,
I just stir up your mind by way of remembrance, because
you seem to be laid upon my heart in this thing. I know

[1] 2 Sam. v. 19.
[2] 1 Sam. xxx. 8.
[3] 1 Sam. xxiii. 10, 11.
[4] 2 Chron. xxvii. 6.

the enemy will fight hard to keep you out of this privilege, trying to make it appear that in different circumstances you could walk more closely with the Lord. This is one of his "devices" to separate us from our God. Oh, for the Spirit's light to discover his snares of darkness! We are each in the best place to glorify the Lord; and present events, whether pleasing or painful, are those in which to be seeking Him. In this sense we may safely say, "Whoso is wise, and will observe these things, even they shall understand the loving-kindness of the Lord."[1] That the Lord may give you this heavenly wisdom in earthly things is the affectionate wish of   R. B.

XIV.

The world seen in the light of eternity.

TO E. M.

High Pavement, *Friday.*

Beloved Mrs ——, How frail are we! . . . . . . How often reminded that these tabernacles have their foundation in the dust! "Dust thou art, and unto dust shalt thou return;" and thus end all the pride and pomp of vain mortals. A few short days they flutter in the sunbeams of pleasure and earthly prosperity, and then lie down in their lowly bed of dust, until aroused by the voice of the archangel, and the trump of God. But in what likeness shall they come forth? Ah! there will be no mistake in that great harvest-day; it will be "to every seed his own body." The seed of the serpent and the seed of Christ will doubtless each have

[1] Ps. cvii. 43.

their own likeness. According to the sowing will be the reaping,[1] which the Day will declare.

O my dear friend, I do more and more like to see things in the light of eternity, the light of the Spirit, which shews things as they really are, and as the Word declares them. I desire this not for the sake of judging others, but that I may judge myself daily and hourly,[2] and not be beguiled by this deceitful and desperately wicked heart, which always pleads on the side of the old Adam, urging in time of temptation, "This is not very wrong, and that can be of no consequence." But ah! away with it all! "There is death in the pot." What saith the Scripture? "To be carnally minded is death. "If ye live after the flesh ye shall die."[3] "He that soweth to his flesh shall of the flesh reap corruption; but he that soweth to the Spirit, shall of the Spirit reap life everlasting."[4] I think that these verses do not refer only to the utter death of the unrenewed state, but also to such a deadness in the believer's experience as "sowing to the flesh" must bring. The truth of this I have sorrowfully proved since quickened into spiritual life, yea, since I have felt Jesus to be precious; and I have had to take to myself the words of Jer ii. 17—"Hast thou not procured this unto thyself, in that thou hast forsaken the Lord thy God, when he led thee by the way?"—and know the experience described in a great part of that chapter and the following one. Oh! what a picture they give of this wandering heart! But the return spoken of in chapter iii., verses 12-14, 22, is wonderful! "Who is a God like unto Thee," pardoning "iniquity, transgression, and sin?" for He not only calls us to, but insures our return.[5]

[1] Matt. xiii. 37–39. [3] Rom. viii. 6, 13. [5] Hosea xiv. 7.
[2] 1 Cor. xi. 31. [4] Gal. vi. 8.

D

They "shall return," snd they "shall revive." This is one of the new-covenant blessings, and a pledge that iniquity shall never be our ruin.

Can this lead to presumption or light thoughts of sin ? Nay, verily : " How shall we that are dead to sin live any longer therein ?" " Sin shall not have dominion over you ;" and though the believer fall, " he shall not be utterly cast down, for the Lord upholdeth him with His hand." He " knoweth how to deliver the godly out of temptations ; " He " will not suffer you to be tempted above that ye are able, but will, with the temptation, also make a way to escape." These are sweet promises to a trembling soul that feels it cannot stand a moment alone, and yet longs to walk in the Lord's way without stumbling; yea, to " run the way of His commandments " with an enlarged heart. Such may be overtaken in a fault, but they will not trifle with sin. They feel it an evil and bitter thing; and if sure that they are delivered from its final consequences, they want deliverance also from its present power. This is the breathing and panting of a regenerated heart ; the new creature, or new man, is " created in righteousness and true holiness," though it dwells in a leprous house. Still its aspirations are after its own element, that of holiness and love; and never will it be satisfied until it awakens with His likeness. No dead soul has these desires : they are signs of life ; He has been there who says, " I am come that they might have life, and that they might have it more abundantly." Precious words to a soul that wants life " more abundantly !"

How thankful I am that you are more spoiled for the world, and that the Holy Spirit is making your conscience tender. I wish every act of conformity to the world may sting like an adder, and bite like a serpent. How cruel! but it is what I wish for myself. I would be as separate in appearance and conversation as in heart; and as separate in heart as I shall wish to be altogether when "He shall set the sheep on His right hand, and the goats on His left." Oh, we would not then have one goat's hair about us, and yet we often tolerate them now. Truly, we owe hearty thanks to the convincing Spirit for all His sharp rebukes. He is that faithful friend who will not suffer us to sin without a reproof; but smiting is welcome from this righteous One; for it is better to sit in sackcloth and ashes under His discipline than be a careless daughter " at ease in Zion." It is true, as you say, we have contending nations within, great and mighty; but the Shulamite is a company of two armies, and the spiritual Joshua says, " As captain of the Lord's host am I now come." With the Lord on our side, we shall put the foot of faith upon the necks of our enemies, and He will subdue them. Fear not! the battle is the Lord's; and though you may often feel foiled, it is to teach you where your strength and victory lie; not in any conquests of your own, but in the achievements of your Captain upon Mount Calvary. There see Him bruise the head of Satan, the captain of the Canaanites; there see your sin pierce Him; there see His Father bruise Him, and put Him to grief for your iniquities, and in your stead. Would you know what sin is, what justice is, what pardon is, what love is, what victory is? You must learn *all* at Calvary and in Gethsemane. I know the Holy Spirit keeps the key of those sacred places; but it is well to wait prayerfully at the gate till it shall be said, in experience, "Unto you it is given to know the mysteries of the kingdom of heaven."

As to the time you have been waiting, it is nothing in comparison with the value of what you are waiting for. The first sight of your name upon the heart of the crucified One, the first beam from His precious eye, will overpay an age of painful waiting. To see others stepping in before you, may sometimes cast you down; and the enemy may suggest: "Jesus has no favour for you." Answer him not a word; cry to his Conqueror, "Let my sentence come forth from THY presence." Do not be ready to believe hard things of that Friend of sinners, whose heart is made of tenderness. "His bowels melt with love." When did He cast out a coming sinner? When did He leave a helpless lamb to the wolf? When did He refuse to deliver a distressed soul, crying, " Lord, help me?"

My hope of you is steadfast, that as He has begun, so He will finish in you the good work, that together we may witness for the dear Redeemer, that He still "receiveth sinners, and eateth with them." You long to love Him more, and well indeed you may, for He is worthy. But do not forget —"We love Him, because He first loved us."[1] When you can by faith know and believe the love God hath to you, your love will flow back again to Him. But now you are doubting and questioning it, which shews your feelings are more under the influence of fear than love. Those whom you see so warm in their love to Him have known and believed His love to them. In fact, the one is the effect of the other. " The love of God is shed abroad in the heart by the Holy Ghost," and then it rises up again to its source. You long to look away from self; but you are like the poor woman who was bowed together, and could in nowise lift

[1] 1 John iv. 19.

up herself. But Jesus will come and break your bands, and make you go upright and look upward. Oh, cry for faith; and may the Lord open to you. I commend you, my precious one, to the infallible Teacher, whose word is with power. In Him I may take a warm adieu.—Yours, &c.

RUTH.

XV.

Encouragements to venture on Christ.

TO E. M.

HIGH PAVEMENT, *May* 1854.

VERY DEAR MRS ——, I have wished to write a line of inquiry, but having been far from well, had not energy enough to do so. When the people of Israel came to Marah, the waters were bitter, so that they could not drink of them, but the Lord shewed Moses a tree, which when he had cast into the waters they were made sweet. There, too, He made for them " an ordinance," and there He "proved them." Thus have I found it many a time. Christ in the trial has taken away the bitterness, and it has been as an "ordinance" to my soul, which has fed upon Him and been strengthened to endure. He has also proved me by these things. Praise, O my soul, Thy ever-loving Lord, who changeth not. "Jesus Christ, the same yesterday, and to-day, and for ever."

I desire to speak to you in love of our glorious Christ, who "hath been mindful of us, and will bless us." He will be with us through life in six troubles, and in death, the seventh, He will not forsake us. He is very pitiful and of tender mercy to every one who knoweth and feeleth the plague of plagues—that of his own heart. "Go, shew thyself to the priest," however bad it be, for "Him hath God exalted to be a Prince and a Saviour, for to give repentance to Israel, and forgiveness of sins." He sweetly invites all that labour and are heavy laden to come to Him, and says, "I *will* give you rest." Are you weary of self, and heavy laden with your sins, and are you coming to Jesus? "Come just as you are," come to Jesus, who says, "Him that cometh to me I will in no wise cast out." Not for hardness, coldness, darkness, wandering, past sin, present sin, the guilt which presses at this very moment, nor for any other, will Jesus cast out a coming sinner. The Spirit convinces of sin, the Father draws the sinner, and the Son "receiveth sinners." So the holy Three in One are engaged in this great work of bringing souls to Jesus; and who or what shall prevent their coming? Shall the world or Satan without, or sin within? Nay, verily, "All that the Father giveth me shall come to me."

But, say you, am *I* given by the Father? Coming to Jesus is a proof of it; desiring after Jesus is a proof of it; hungering and thirsting for Jesus is a proof of it. Listen not to unbelief and Satan, who would keep you away from the only place of victory. Fall down at His dear feet and tell Him all the truth—the very worst of it; and it may be your heart will melt and your spirit soften into contrition in the doing of it; and it may be He will hold out the sceptre and say, "Return unto me, O backsliding daughter; for I am married unto you." But if not so just now, it is better to wait at His threshold than wander; it is better to follow a frowning Jesus than to parley with a smiling world; and however roughly He may answer, or however long keep silence, He will not cast you out.

But why write I thus? It may be you are walking in the light of His countenance, and finding Him near, though in a far off country and a barren land. If so, my heart shall rejoice, and you will forgive any remark that seems out of place. I wish you to draw nearer and nearer to the dear Friend of sinners, and to drink still larger draughts of the river of the water of life, which makes glad the city of God.

The Lord bless you, and be not silent to you, and keep you from idols. May your children be kept in their proper place, blessed of the Lord, held in the Lord, and consecrated to the Lord. You will not wish to gain for them the admiration of the world, because you would shudder that they should hereafter be embraced by it, and embosomed in it. A mother in this vicinity lately lost a precious daughter of sixteen. As she stood over the coffin, she said, "There lies my beautiful girl. Oh, I have been proud of her!" and, turning to a minister who stood beside, "Do you think, sir, the Lord has taken her away on my account, because I was proud of her? I have been too proud of her." I do not know the minister's reply, but that which we are to learn from the mother's deep anguish is very plain—" Flee from idolatry." The Lord make all grace abound towards you. —Your ever affectionate, unworthy

RUTH.

Isaiah xlix. 14, 16.
How striking, Isaiah xliii. 22-26.

XVI.

Christ the Burden-bearer.

" Cast thy burden upon the Lord, and He shall sustain thee."

TO E. M.

Sabbath Morning.

MUCH-BELOVED FRIEND, The above words came to my mind when thinking of your weak health and present anxieties, in both of which I feel tender sympathy. Oh may the Spirit enable you to make use by faith of your heavenly Husband, who is ever present, who is afflicted in all your afflictions, "who hath delivered, who doth deliver, in whom we trust that He will yet deliver."   May you not be carrying your burdens when you have such a precious Burden-bearer, so able, so willing, who says, " Call upon me in the day of trouble: I will deliver thee, and thou shalt glorify me." Pour out your heart before Him.   God is a Refuge for us. Roll your burdens upon Him as fast as they roll back upon you.   This is a very profitable exercise of faith in the time of tribulation; it is one which He much approves, and which often is the means of bringing the soul into an endearing familiarity with Him, unknown before.   Of this, I am a living witness; for it was by means of many weights, and many trials, that I was pressed to try how much I might put upon Him, and brought to know the blessed life of faith in the every-day occurrences and many perplexities of the wilderness way.   I can truly praise Him now for those heavy storms, and "sharp-pointed things," which made every creature help too little, and made me to live in the sympathy of such a heart, and the home of such a love as His. May you, dear friend, have like benefit, and now, even now, find rest in the midst of trouble by realising that infinite love, power, and wisdom are working all things together for your good, and His glory. May the felt utterance of your heart be "Father, glorify Thy name."

May the droppings of the sanctuary this day be refreshing to our souls.—With tender and sympathising love, your grateful and affectionate   RUTH.

P.S.—Mark iv. 37-40. If Jesus seem to be asleep in the storm, it is only for the trial of faith; He is watching all the time, and waiting to be gracious.

––––––––––

The following letter was received under peculiar circumstances. The friend to whom it was addressed had been asked to attend some Highland games, and complied, notwithstanding many doubts whether by so doing she should dishonour her Lord and bring a cloud upon her own soul. On her return home she found this letter lying on her table, written by Ruth without any knowledge of the circumstances, but which truly came as a seasonable word of reproof. It was like an arrow from the bow of the King, drawn at a venture, but directed by the Spirit himself.

XVII.

A word of warning against worldly conformity.

"Adam, where art thou?" "What doest thou here, Elijah?"

TO E. M.

HIGH PAVEMENT, NOTTINGHAM, *August* 5, 1854.

MY BELOVED FRIEND, The above questions came to my mind for my beloved friend, I know not why. This evening I have heard a sermon from the last of these passages, and I must send you the substance of a few remarks, though not in the exact words. "What doest thou here, Elijah?" It may be said to some believers, " What doest thou here, inactive and indolent in thy Lord's cause? Thou wast very lively in the service of Satan and the world; why so inert in the service of Him who bought thee with His blood, and knew what it was to be weary in working for thee?"[1] Again, it may be said to some, " What doest thou here in a place, or in society, where thy Lord is not loved, honoured, or known?" Thy soul will suffer, thy spirituality will be withered, for it is a very tender plant; and it is easily injured. If the believer will be in worldly society, uncalled by Providence, his spirituality is sure to suffer blight. Ah! what doest thou here, Elijah? "What doest thou here?" it may be said again, when the believer is in the midst of mist and gloom, which hide the Saviour from his view. What doest thou here?—thou whom I have ransomed;—thou to whom I have

[1] John iv. 6.

manifested myself;—thou whom the Spirit has sealed;—whom I have loved with an everlasing love;—what doest thou here with darkened evidences? Is it not because you are looking into your own heart instead of looking unto Me, and coming unto Me, who am made unto you wisdom, righteousness, sanctification, and redemption? The Spirit may discover to us what is in our hearts to abase us and lay us low; but if we look into them to find comfort or encouragement, then our evidences will be darkened, the clouds will gather quickly around us, and our dreariness will grow yet more dreary. What doest thou here, Elijah? We must look away from self, and learn that we are not to live upon past experience, however real, or upon past manifestations, however bright; but we must be seeking for fresh incomings of grace. It is a great lesson which we are very slow in learning, not to live upon grace received. . . . .

XVIII.

Victory over self by abiding in Christ.

TO E. M.

August 14, 1854.

My dear Friend, You have been rambling amongst the wonders of nature, but you find, as I have always done, that the works of our Lord's hands, however lovely, will not do without the love of His heart. If that spring be not open to us, it is all as a dry and thirsty land; but when we have freedom there, then every place is cheerful, and "December as pleasant as May."

I see, more and more, that we live very far below our privileges in Christ. Some say that they want to hear more of duty and precept; but truly I find duty and precept very dry, and all condemnation without privilege in Christ. That is oil to the wheels; and if we are living by faith in a fulfilled law, and in the Law-fulfiller, the fruits of righteousness will as surely flow out as effect follows cause, for those fruits are only by Christ Jesus.[1] Precious things are put forth by the moon, (the Church,) as she receives by faith the precious things brought forth by the sun, (Christ,) and in no other way. Hence we often weary ourselves in vain, because we are looking more after the fruit than the abiding in Him from whom alone it can come. "From me is thy fruit found."

It has been well said, that "in a mere legal way many believers have toiled all their time for power over some corruptions, who, like Peter and the rest, have caught little or nothing, because Jesus Christ was not in the company." That, you know, is self-effort; and if any fruit were to spring from thence, it would only be to self-pleasing and self-praise —all "wild gourds," which bring "death in the pot." If we want good fruit, it must spring from the good vine; if we want plenty of fish, it must be by casting on the right side of the ship. If we desire close walking, holy living, much victory, communion, enjoyment, it must come by abiding in Jesus. Hear what Himself says, "He that abideth in me, and I in him, the same bringeth forth much fruit : for without me ye can do nothing."[2]

O precious Christ-exalting, self-abasing grace of faith, be it ours in lively exercise by the blessed Spirit's operation,

[1] Phil. i. 11.　　　　　[2] John xv. 5.

and may Christ be "all in all." It seems to me that we know nothing of His "unsearchable riches;" and yet how we often turn to toys and trifles of time. He is such a precious full Christ : there is enough in Him to occupy and satisfy all our powers in time and eternity. Oh! send out Thy light and Thy truth into our hearts ; let them lead us and guide us to this Thy holy hill; and when our heart is overwhelmed, lead us to this Rock, which is higher than self.

Now, farewell! Every covenant blessing be with you and yours. "They shall be mine, saith the Lord of hosts, in that day when I make up my jewels." We tread a thorny desert, but

> " Judah's Lion guards the way,
>   And guides His pilgrims home."

There we shall meet, from clog and fetter free, to behold our Beloved without a cloud between. Having sipped of the rivers of His pleasure below, we shall drink full draughts above; and in His love and glory be absorbed for ever and ever.—Ever most affectionately yours, RUTH.

XIX.

The simplicity of faith.

TO E. M.

PAVEMENT, *Thursday*, 1854.

VERY DEAR MRS ——, I trust you will not forget the "near way to the City" of which Mr S—— told us. "Believe on the Lord Jesus Christ, and thou shalt be saved." I have been thinking much lately how the apostles gave this direction to every inquiring soul ; but are we not often like Eccles. x. 15 : "The labour of the foolish wearieth every one of them, because he knoweth not how to go to the city." Then how sweetly come in the words of our dear Lord, " Come unto me all ye that labour and are heavy laden, and I will give you rest." If we toil for twenty years, we must come to this at last : "believe and be saved." May the Holy Spirit bring you there and keep you there, "that ye may know that ye have eternal life, and that ye may believe on the name of the Son of God." May He take away the dominion of that giant sin, unbelief, though its life is to be prolonged for a season. Goliath, the uncircumcised Philistine, came forth only to be cut down; may it be so in your soul with the unbelief which seems increasingly to trouble you. The Lord give you faith to put this foe into His hands.—Your very affectionate   RUTH.

XX.

A seeking soul encouraged to come to the Lord's Table.

" Fear not ye. I know that ye seek Jesus which was crucified."

TO E. M.

MUCH-LOVED MRS ——, You are, indeed, on my heart as regards the coming solemnity of the Lord's Supper. I feel that it is a matter between the Lord and the soul, and dare not press your attendance lest I bring you further into bonds; but I may venture to say it is a feast for the poor, the maimed, the halt, and the blind ; also for such as feel they are outside, wandering in the highways and hedges. It was for such the true Paschal Lamb was slain ; surely then such are welcome to the emblems of His death and suffer-ings, of His body broken and His blood shed. If a sense of sin and unworthiness is not to keep us from Jesus the sub-stance of the feast, should it prevail to hold us back from the shadow and type thereof ? Would any self-improvement or self-complacency be a suitable preparation for this ordi-nance ? Are we not rather to come with the sentence of death in ourselves, that we should not trust in ourselves, and so to embrace the Rock for want of a shelter ? Are we not thus to come, feeling that we deserve death, and shew-ing forth that we have no hope of escape but by the obedi-ence, blood-shedding, and death of the worthy Lamb ?

The woman who was a sinner came to weep at the feet of Jesus before she had sense of forgiveness ; and though she presumed to wash those holy feet with her polluted tears, He did not rebuke her, but sent pardon sweetly home to her heart, and she went away with all her sins forgiven.[1] True, it is sweet to come to the table under a sense of pardoning love, but I believe it is safe to come hungering and thirsting for this assurance. " He filleth the hungry with good things, and the rich He hath sent empty away." It is sweet to come with the sacrifice of praise, singing, " Unto Him that loved us, and washed us from our sins in His own blood ; " but it is safe to come with the sacrifice of a broken spirit, for such the Lord will not despise.[2] Surely those who come with the blessing, and those who come for the blessing, are each bidden guests, for who could make a soul hungry and thirsty but the master of the feast ? Christ is the only pass-

[1] Luke vii. 48.   [2] Ps. li. 17.

over from sin to salvation, from condemnation to justification;
therefore to be knocking at this door, in every appointed
means, seems a suitable exercise for those who are feeling
their sin and condemnation. To take the bread and wine
clinging and crying to a crucified Saviour, does not look
like receiving unworthily, since He has said, "Do this in
remembrance of me;" and what better response than

" Dear Lord, remember me."

May the Divine Spirit guide you in this matter; and if,
like Esther, you are led to venture without a positive call
from the King, I shall desire to pray as he of old, "The
good Lord pardon every one that prepareth his heart to seek
God the Lord God of his fathers, though he be not cleansed
according to the purification of the sanctuary," (has not free
exercise of that faith which purifies the heart, or sweet application of that blood which cleanses from all sin.) "And
the Lord hearkened to Hezekiah, and healed the people." [1]
"What, think ye that He will not come to the feast?" Let
us invite Him, and ask Him to make our new heart manifestly His guest-chamber, where the passover shall be truly
eaten in His presence. Who can tell but we may have to
say that He was known of us in breaking of bread.

But if not, be it ever with us as Hab. ii. 1-3, and the
Lord (the Spirit) " direct your hearts into the love of God,
and into the patient waiting for Christ."[2] He is worth waiting for, and says, " They shall not be ashamed that wait
for me." May that be your privilege, whether you come
to the feast, or whether you be absent.[3]—Excuse all this in
true affection, from your unworthy   RUTH.

[1] 2 Chron. xxx. 18-20.   [2] 2 Thess. iii. 5.   [3] Rev. xxii. 17 ; John vii. 37.

XXI.

Christ the only Physician for a sin-sick soul.

TO E. M.

Saturday Night, 1854.

DEARLY-BELOVED FRIEND, These rich words still follow me, He hath " appeared to put away sin by the sacrifice of Himself." That word " sin " feels weighty to a sensible sinner; but oh! that word "Himself!" seems a million times more weighty. "Himself!" the mighty God, the precious Man Christ Jesus; "Himself!" by whom all things were created, and for whom they consist; "Himself!" whose smile is heaven, whose frown is hell; whom all angels worship, and all devils obey; "Himself!" the sacrifice. Such another could not be found; sins deep as hell and high as heaven cannot overmatch it, for it is infinite; sins of scarlet and crimson dye cannot resist its power, for it makes them whiter than snow. See as much as you can of the vileness of self, and the demerit of sin; "Himself," a bleeding sacrifice, exceeds it all. Here is the sweet-smelling savour, or savour of rest, both to the Lawgiver and the lawbreaker. The Lawgiver is honoured, the lawbreaker is saved.

See how He stands most lovingly, as with open arms, saying to every labouring, weary, heavy-laden sinner, " Come." " Come unto Me, and I will give you rest." "I still receive sinners, to the uttermost I save them, and never am weary of healing their backslidings, forgiving all their iniquities, and multiplying pardons as they multiply transgressions against

E

Me; I blot all out with blood, and love them freely and for ever." "Sinner, will not this suffice?" It will if the Spirit apply it, and open in a little measure Himself and His sacrifice in contrast to thyself and thy sins. It will take eternity to know it fully; but that thy heart may find rest and refreshening in it now, is the affectionate prayer of His gleaner, RUTH.

About this time a change may be observed in the tone of Ruth's letters to E—— M——, who, after having sought the Lord sorrowing for many years, was now enabled to see her interest in the finished work of Jesus for the pardon of sin, and her eternal acceptance in Him.

XXII.

A foretaste of glory.

TO E. M.

HIGH PAVEMENT, *August* 15, 1855.

EVER-DEAR FRIEND, Although we have met so seldom lately, I am glad to find our hearts still beat in unison, When I read of your pleasant Highland tour, and its grand scenery, it made my heart bound, for I love the beauties of Nature. But my spirit quickly turned to its own anticipations; for, you know, dearest friend, I expect ere long fully to enjoy High-land scenery too. I am looking forward to the being unclothed, and delivered from the chilling damps of flesh and blood; to the being raised above the vapours of these lowlands, blissfully to range the mountains of myrrh and hills of frankincense in unclouded day; and, more steadily than the eagle, to gaze all the while upon the Sun. O my glorious Christ, what will it be to see Thee, face to face, in Thine own light! to see "the King in His beauty," and be absorbed in His love! This is the climax of love's anticipations; these are the mountains of myrrh and hills of frankincense; even His perfections, His glory, and His transporting charms. Oh! methinks how riveted shall I be; eternal ages will roll on, but still my eyes and heart will have room for no other object but for Him, who was dead for my sake, but is alive again,—my Lord, my life, my all! Those love-prints in His hands, and feet, and side; that precious body broken for you and for me; we shall behold, we shall gaze upon them; and from the scars of those once bleeding wounds, unutterable radiations of glory will beam forth for ever. There we shall eternally see that He was crucified for us—"the Lamb as it had been slain." Truly, I feel that mortality could not bear it; such "new wine" would burst the "old bottle;" but mortality shall be swallowed up of life, and then shall I be satisfied when I awake with Thy likeness.

Modern believers rebuke my deep longings to be "away in the land of praises;" yet in the works of the dear old fathers I find warm-hearted companions, who step on far beyond me in foretasting the glory which is to be revealed. I am not afraid of walking in such company, because it is God, the Eternal Spirit, who enlarges my heart with desire for this land of Beulah, and gives me a sip of the ocean of love,

which none can have without longing for the full draught,
—yea, to launch out into the ocean itself, and be ever
filled.

I am very fond of 1 Cor. ii. 9, 10,—"But God hath
revealed them to us by His Spirit;" and verse 12: "we have
received . . . . the Spirit which is of God, that we might
know the things that are freely given to us of God,"—not
only possess them, which every believer does, but know
them—have them opened and set out before our spiritual
mind; and then out of the abundance of the heart the
mouth will speak of heavenly treasures.

I shall desire to be looking up to the Lord for you, that
you may banquet with the King at the coming communion;
and forget self with its poverty and misery, while He says,
"Fear not, I have redeemed thee: thou art mine." Luke
xxiv. 29 has been very delightful to me; that word, "constrained," how wonderful! This constraining Jesus to
abide is still done by faith in the Spirit's operation. The
King sweetly suffers Himself to be held in the galleries of
the new heart: "The kingdom of heaven suffereth violence;
and the violent take it by force." But how unbelief
weakens; it is like, "The Philistines be upon thee, Sam-
son;" and when his secret of faith is shorn away he is
weak indeed. Those words, "They that dwell under His
shadow shall return," have also been very precious to me.
That "*shall return*" is in some seasons worth more than
words can express.

Adieu! duty calls me away; but the heart would sit
still at His dear feet, receiving the gracious words which
fall from His lips.—Yours, &c.,

RUTH.

XXIII.

A Christmas feast on Christmas-day.

" My soul followeth hard after Thee, Thy right hand upholdeth me."

TO E. M.

Saturday Morning, Dec. 23.

DEAREST FRIEND, Is your heart with my heart this morning ? If so, you will join me in following hard after Him who is our glory and joy, and who is the substance of every type. In finding Him we do indeed inherit substance, whatever be the changes in our frames and feelings. My soul is longing after Him as my Christmas portion and my Christmas cheer; for the Lamb's flesh is heavenly food, and to be feeding upon Him by faith is an antepast of heaven, where the Lamb Himself shall feed us and lead us to living fountains of water, and God shall wipe away all tears from our eyes. Now, therefore, in the wilderness let us be seeking HIM, not seeking merely pleasant sensations of His manifested love and presence, but Himself, for they who so seek shall not be ashamed. Have you thought of Acts x. 11, 12, 16, and xi. 5, 10, on our subject of return. All those ceremonially unclean creatures were let down from heaven and drawn up into heaven again, no doubt primarily referring to the Gentiles; but surely that sheet also typified the covenant in which the whole redeemed family were let down to earth, and all shall be drawn up again into heaven. It seems to be the same with the younger children as with the Elder Brother; He came from God and went to God.

Christmas-day.—I now must finish this in His name which is above every name, and which is truly at this time as ointment poured forth in my soul. I seem to be drinking living water from the well of Bethlehem, and would pour it out again unto the Lord by sending it to some of my loved ones for whom I intensely long, that they may have a Christmas blessing, being filled with the Holy Ghost.

I am all alone in the house, and have had a royal feast in the blessed company of the King, who drew near so lovingly that my soul melted, my tears flowed, and with a glad heart, though unmusical voice, I did sing right heartily, "Crown Him Lord of all." I thought much of that celestial concert in these lower regions, when a multitude of the heavenly host sang His worthy praise. I once scarcely thought to have been here another Christmas, but He who wills it is making it all up me, for surely this is the land of Beulah. He hath brought me into His banqueting-house, and His banner over me is love. Love brought Him from the bosom of the Father. Love made Him take our nature into His own, and thus come under the law as our Husband, by circumcision acknowledging Himself a debtor to do it all, not for Himself but for us. We are dead to the law by the body of Christ, in which body He fulfilled its every jot and tittle, and endured all its penalty. Since, therefore, we are now married to Him, whatever the law has to say about us must be said to Him. He has "redeemed us from the curse of the law, being made a curse for us." It was for this He took the prepared body; it was for the suffering of death He was made a little while lower than the angels. His "goings forth" towards this were from everlasting, and since time began, promise and prophecy, type and shadow, symbol and ceremony, have all been full of Him. There is a covering on all these holy things which none but the Spirit can remove, but when He does so, the soul in which He has been revealed, leaps for joy, as David did before the Ark. In His birth, too, there was a covering of lowliness, so that none but the Spirit-taught mind could discern the Saviour-King or know the Lord of glory. But oh! the amazing privilege of those to whom this blessed Spirit has been as the star in the East, so that from the very ends of the earth they are brought, saying, "We are come to worship Him." That privilege is ours. We have felt the need of Him, have seen His suitability, and are brought to partake of the saving benefit. What can we render? We can only sink deeper in the debt of love by joyfully receiving more, as I, a most unworthy worm, do this happy Christmas-eve.

The mystery of iniquity is great, but the mystery of godliness, God manifest in the flesh, is greater, and swallows the other up in the ocean of redeeming blood, so that when the iniquity of Jacob is sought for it shall not be found, and of Israel there shall be none. O precious Babe of Bethlehem, how wondrous was Thine errand to this land of curse. Though so little and lowly, Thou didst travel down to earth in the greatness of Thy strength mighty to save. Sweetly has my heart been feeling of Thee, "This same shall comfort us."[1] Fare thee well! With much warm love, your ever affectionate RUTH.

[1] Gen. v. 29.

XXIV.

To the Dove in the cleft of the Rock.[1]

EBENEZER.
"Behold the man."
The man that stood in the gap.

" A man there is, a real man,
     With wounds still gaping wide,
   From which rich streams of blood once ran,
     In hands, and feet, and side."

TO E. M.

December 31, 1855.

MY DEARLY-BELOVED, In His fragrant name I must greet
you at this time in remembrance of His mercy, whereby He
visited you with His salvation, and took off your garments
of heaviness, and covered you with the robes of righteousness
and praise ; when the " banner of love " was over you, the
arms of love were embracing you, the object of love was
filling your heart, and you only wanted the wings of love to
flee away and rest for ever in the dear delights of His un-
veiled presence, who was then revealed as your "Ishi"—your
heavenly husband. Oh, it was mercy to you, and to me also.
We cannot forget it, and would sing His worthy praise, who
from all eternity had thoughts of peace to thee.[2] Ah!
dearest friend, you felt as I did when I found him—as in
Luke viii. 38. But He sent us back to learn the excellent
life of *faith*, and do as verse 39. Oh! for ever fresh anoint-

---

[1] This was Ruth's own address to her note.   [2] Ps. ciii.

ings with fresh oil to do it more and more feeling. I do
think this is a safe and sure way to be separated from the
world and those who have a form of godliness only. Such
strains of love and felt salvation are too warm for them.
But having felt the cure, we must speak well of our Divine
Healer. I wish you a fresh baptism into Him[1] by the power
of the Spirit, that it may be your very element to tell "to
sinners round, what a dear Saviour you have found ;" or
to be silent for His sake where you cannot speak to His
honour, saying of all worldly and flesh-feeding converse, "So
did not I, because of the fear of God"—the fear of love·
And for all these things your Lord says, "My grace is
sufficient for thee." In all our journey through this fallen
flesh-and-blood condition, our Divine Judah is with us; He
has stood surety to our Father to bring us safely back, and
set us before Him with joy ; and on Him it devolves to
guide, provide, and speak for us, when guilt is evidently
charged home, as in Gen. xliv. 12-18. Judah was the advocate.[2] We do not hear that the accused Benjamin spoke a
word. In like manner He, our Judah, will also speak through
us when we long to honour Him, but feel unable to say a
word in His name. He is our strength for everything, and
we need not fear to use Him or trouble Him too much. We
are too shy this way, through conferring with flesh and blood.
I have been enjoying Him through Ezek. xxii. 30, 31. A man
was sought for to stand in the gap ; but none being found,
the indignation and wrath came upon the guilty party. It
must fall somewhere—God's judgment must be executed.
But mark the contrast. For us a Man is found. He comes
forth from the invisibility of Jehovah, and in the likeness of

[1] Rom. vi. 3-6.   [2] 1 John ii. 1.

men undertakes our cause, which he had espoused with our persons in eternity, when the council of peace was between them both. He saw there was no man, wherefore He said, " Here am I, send me." And in the fulness of time He came and stood in the gap, and filled up the breach in the law; and on His holy head fell our storm of wrath and punishment. Thus He became our covert and hiding-place ; and because the Holy Jesus was taken and executed, the guilty Barabbas is set free; for there must needs be one released at that feast of the Passover, because it commemorated the release of Israel from Egypt, which typified the release of the spiritual Israel, by the blood of the true paschal Lamb. How has my soul melted in viewing Him thus—as my door of hope and way of escape. All our deliverances come by the blood of the everlasting covenant; and every new view of it brings forth a new song to His praise. May you have the renewings of the Holy Ghost in recounting the benefits of the past year, and may a precious Jesus be the Alpha and Omega of the one just approaching.

You are going to have walks through the Tabernacle ;[1] may the blessed Spirit take off the coverings, that, from the door to the mercy-seat, every whit of it may set forth His glory.

Sweetly remembering what a summer Sun you had last winter, and wishing you frequent renewals of His healing beams, I rest in Him with much tender love.—Your own affectionate, unworthy   RUTH.

Gal. v. 1; Rom. viii. 15 ; 1 Thess. iii. 8, 9, and v. 23, 24.

[1] This refers to some proposed lectures on the Typical Character of the Tabernacle.

The two following letters were written at the request of E. M. for the express benefit of an aged pilgrim, who had complained much of the absence of that peace and joy in believing, of which she had so often read and heard, and which, it is believed, she had in earlier days herself experienced. It was feared that the secret cause of the mischief lay in the variety and multitude of her labours of love, which were permitted to become a snare to her, by drawing her away from that close walking with God, in which alone the light of the King's countenance can be seen. As in these days of religious activity there may be many similarly situated, the letters are now printed in hope that the blessing they are calculated to convey may be largely shared by others, now that writer and reader have been gathered to their rest, and, absent from the body, are present with the Lord, " with no cloud between !"—

XXV.

Spiritual Declension.

PART I.

TO E. M.

HIGH PAVEMENT, *Feb.* 1856.

MUCH-BELOVED IN JESUS, In His ever-fragrant name I desire again to commune with you in Him and of Him; that in so doing He may be exalted, and our hearts caused anew to burn with His love, which is the source of ours ;—His being the cause, ours the effect. It is self-evident that the more we have to do with the cause, the more freely effects will flow. Hence our dear Lord says, "Continue ye in my love;"[1] not thereby implying that His love can be turned away from its objects, but exhorting us to a continued real-isation or apprehending of His love by the lively acting of a Spirit-wrought faith. Thus will our little spark be increas-ing into a flame by constant communication with the fire from whence it springs. Of this communication *faith* seems to be the medium; and if this precious grace be not kept in healthy exercise upon the person and work, the sufferings and death, the blood and righteousness of our dear Redeemer, the soul will be sure to become languid and drooping in its spiritual condition. Prayer, praise, love, joy, peace, and all other graces, will be at a low water-mark; and whatever external appearances or profession there may be, the heart will be conscious of distance and shyness with its Lord.

You know I am speaking of one who has been quickened by the Spirit, and is a living soul, for we may be alive but not lively; we may be active in our Lord's cause, but not spiritual in our own souls; we may be earnest for the salva-tion of others, but not be living in the joys of salvation ourselves; we may be instrumentally distributing the bread and water of life, but not be enjoying daily refreshment therefrom in our own experience. I do sorrowfully think that this is too much the case in the present day; according to that Scripture, "They made me the keeper of the vine-yards, but mine own vineyard have I not kept." May we not say, as our Lord did upon another subject, "These ought ye to have done, and not to leave the other undone?"

The reason why I thus judge is from finding persons so lively in conversing upon what they are doing for the Lord,

[1] John xv. 9.

yet so slow to speak of what He is doing for them. They seem delighted to tell of the great things which are doing all around, but immediately shrink back if any heart-subject is brought home to them. In fact, if one speaks of personal enjoyment of the love, blood, and salvation of Jesus, there is no response from some, but they put it down to the score of egotism; while others refer to years gone by when they did feel Him to be precious, but they confess that they know little of it now. They are so occupied in what they call working for Him, that they hear little from Him, say little to Him, enjoy little of Him, and may truly say, "While I was busy here and there He was gone." It is most lamentable for any living soul to be in constant religious engagements for the good of others, while following Jesus "afar off." Very many such I fear there are, as well as hundreds who only know Him in the judgment, and yet are continually reading, teaching, and conversing in His blessed name. This is a day of great profession, but yet real vital godliness is at a low ebb, and close walking with God in sweet communion is too little sought after. Solemn, indeed, are these facts; we may well say, with David, "Search me, O God, and know my heart; try me and know my thoughts; and see if there be any wicked way in me: and lead me in the way everlasting."

You will not much wonder that I have been led into this train of tought, because we have, more than once, touched upon the subject in conversation; and indeed, dearest friend, I feel more and more the deep importance of being kept in a freshness of experience by the anointings of the Spirit; so that whatever engagements we may have for the good of others, and however abundantly we may be labouring for their salvation, there should still be a constant communication kept up with our dear Lord, and our souls should never rest satisfied without freedom at Court. To be constantly employed in errands for the King, and never to see His face, hear His voice, or receive a token from Him; oh! how chilling to one who has enjoyed His love, has sat under His shadow with great delight, and has found His fruit sweet to the taste. How unsatisfying to one truly longing to taste that the Lord is gracious. The former may well say, "Restore unto me the joy of thy salvation," and the latter, "Remember me, O Lord, with the favour that thou bearest unto thy people! Oh visit me with thy salvation!" When we are enjoying personal intercourse with the King, and by faith walking in Him and living on Him, then will His messages be most warmly delivered, being fresh from Himself. Then will there be evidently a sweet savour of Him, as well as a good word for Him.

I cannot tell you how sad it is to my heart when I find this savour wanting in some who have been long in the Lord's ways, and active in serving Him too. They are cumbered with many things, and too little alone with Jesus, without which we shall become like salt which has lost its savour. It makes me mourn for them, and tremble for myself, thinking of some passages which have often brought me to great searchings of heart, and wrestlings with the Lord; Matt. v. 13; Hosea x. 2, "Their heart is divided, now shall they be found faulty;" and much of Jer. ii., and also Rev. ii. 4, "I have somewhat against thee, because thou hast left thy first love." It matters not what great works there be if the spice of love be wanting. Oh may our gracious Lord bring us closer and closer to Himself, and cause us to dwell in love, and "to comprehend with all saints what is the breadth and length, and depth and height, and to know the love of Christ which passeth knowledge." May He fill us with the Spirit, that by His power we may so testify of what we taste and hear and see, that other hearts may be kindled with desire to enjoy the same blessed fellowship, even as the beloved apostle said, " That which we have seen and heard declare we unto you, that ye also may have fellowship with us; and truly our fellowship is with the Father, and with His Son Jesus Christ. These things write we unto you, that your joy may be full." He desired that they might have joy in the Lord; and the kingdom of God is not in word but in power ; it is righteousness, and peace, and joy in the Holy Ghost. These are things with which the stranger to God intermeddleth not, for such have only to do with the outworks, but " the kingdom of God is within you ; " " and we receiving a kingdom, which cannot be moved, let us have grace, whereby we may serve God acceptably with reverence and godly fear, for our God is a consuming fire."

Oh what an unspeakable mercy, that by the spirit of adoption we can say, " our God," and " our Father ; " and though He be a consuming fire to those on whom sin is found, yet hath He made for us a " way of escape " by the blood of our Elder Brother ; having laid upon Him all our iniquities. These briars and thorns were set against Him in battle, and on His sacred person did the fire of divine justice burn them up altogether. Oh let us turn aside from creature things and see this great sight, for it is heart-warming and Christ-endearing, to see the bush of humanity in that devouring fire, and yet unconsumed ; to behold our precious Surety enduring all the bitter anguish till every sin of His chosen was expiated, and He could triumphantly say, " It is finished." That was indeed "the conqueror's song," and with joy it is re-echoed again and again from the believing heart by the power of the blessed Spirit. "It is finished, and finished for me." The personality of it is the sweetness; here is food for faith, here is a feast for love. In such believing views of a crucified Saviour we get raised above the things of a dying world; and, in realising by faith our union with Him, we can say, "I am crucified with Christ;" then He becomes our life, that we which live should henceforth live only for Him. [1] This is a heart-warming subject, but I must cease. May we have more and more experience of it in the heart, and never be left to rest in the mere "talk of the lips," which "tendeth only to penury" of soul. There is a talking of Christ which is impoverishing, that is, when the lips outrun the heart; but when He is dwelling there by faith, and causing His Naphtali to give goodly words of Him,[2] in such scattering there is increasing; He is honoured, and the soul refreshed.

Oh may He pour out His Spirit upon His people to quicken the dead, and arouse the living who may be in a sleepy state of soul, who need their lamps trimming and their loins girding afresh. May there be great searchings of heart, causing the inquiry, Why, being a King's child, should there be leanness from day to day? Is there not a cause? Is there not bread enough in the Father's house? or, rather, has there not been a turning away from His spiritual provision to some beggarly elements of the creature or the world. May the Lord in mercy restore all such to their first love, and also lead them on to those more blessed revelations of Himself which are to be enjoyed even in the house of our

[1] 2 Cor. v. 14, 15.   [2] Gen. xlix. 21.

pilgrimage. I will yet be inquired of by the house of Israel, saith the Lord of Hosts, to do it for them. The Lord ever bless you with sweet and close communion with Himself.— A warm adieu, with tender love, from your ever affectionate

RUTH.

XXVI.

Spiritual Declension.

PART II.

TO E. M.

HIGH PAVEMENT, *March* 1856.

MUCH-BELOVED IN JESUS, I must send you another thought or two on our last subject. You know it was Spiritual Declension, and consequent want of savour and unction in living souls. We were especially considering the cases of those who have been kept accurate in all outward observances, active in works of charity, and even been zealous promoters of the salvation of others. Sad, indeed, is a case like this; but I am forcibly arrested with the possibility of such being convicted of the state, but not converted from it. An acknowledgment of wandering is not return ; a consciousness of a dry, barren state is not restoration. Perhaps you can hardly conceive a living soul, convinced of being in the wrong and lingering there, without earnestly and diligently seeking after the right—but I can; for this bad, bad heart has experienced what drowsiness and listlessness sometimes follow sleep, when

F

there is no heart to arise and call upon the Lord for deliverance. Seeing the case to be bad, we just shrink from knowing it fully, and fear rather to be thoroughly aroused to reap painfully what has been sown to the flesh, than desire at any cost to be brought back to close communion with our God.

Look at Jonah: he knew he was a wanderer, but there seemed no anxiety to return; he would rather forget it in sleep. The storm was the Lord's messenger to oblige the man to awake him, and the fish His servant to swallow him up; so that from his senseless sleep he must go down to "the belly of hell," to make him heartily call upon his God; and from that low place the sweet song was to be put into his mouth, "Salvation is of the Lord." Not only salvation from hell is of the Lord, but also the many experimental salvations which we need on our pilgrim journey. And oh! it is a blessed salvation to be brought nigh when there has been a following of "Jesus afar off;" and by His precious blood to be purged and cleansed from our own doings, works, and inventions, when they have come to be like a crowd between the soul and Him. It is blessed to have any secret thing taken away which maketh the consolations of God small with us. But here is the trying point,— whatever is between God and the soul must be taken away to restore nearness; and this is a sacrifice at which most of us tremble, finding it easier to condemn the wrong in others, and even to acknowledge it in ourselves, than to ask the Lord honestly and heartily to take it away.

As I said before, there are many in this busy but cold-hearted day, many of the Lord's people who are most active and energetic in His service, but the cream of their communion is gone, and the fire of love has languished. There are sounds of Jesus and salvation on the lips, but none of His sweet savour flowing from their hearts, nor any of His fresh tokens to tell to those who fear His name.[1] Some are in a measure aroused to a sense of their state, but are not delivered from it; they know that it is not with them as in years gone past, but they are too busy to give close attention to personal facts, and to be really diligent to know the state of their own flocks and herds.[2] They desire a change in their experience, but have not time to seek it, and in this sense are like the slothful who "desireth and hath nothing."[3] All their energies go out another way, and they are too closely occupied with their religious engagements to follow their Lord, who withdrew from the multitude into the wilderness and prayed, and who another time "went up into a mountain to pray," and on another occasion "continued all night in prayer to God." O my beloved, did the immaculate Lamb of God so much use retirement and prayer, as we find by many portions of Scripture He did? How much more do we need it who have sin dwelling in us, and often working under the most specious forms! The truth is, we cannot thrive without it.

Where the experience has indeed become as a wilderness, what double need there is to withdraw from the cases of others, and cry mightily unto God to make that "wilderness rejoice and blossom as the rose." Where there has been much talking about gospel day, but long, long night within, what cause is there to withdraw from all, and wrestle with Him, who "turneth the shadow of death into morning."[4] In so doing the feeling of the wilderness state will

---

[1] Ps. lxvi. 16.
[2] Prov. xxvii. 23.
[3] Prov. xiii. 4.
[4] Amos v. 8.

probably deepen before the rejoicing returns, and the night will seem to grow darker before the bright shining of the Sun of Righteousness rises again upon the soul. Still, the blessed Spirit can enable us to endure; and though He keeps the soul waiting for the Sun and watching for Him, "more than they that watch for the morning," yet such experience shall not be in vain, for "blessed are they that wait for Him," and "they that wait on the Lord shall renew their strength." However weak they have become, the Lord does renew His people's youth like the eagles, and causes them to sing as in the day when He brought them up out of Egypt.

It may seem presumptuous in me thus to speak of the state of useful active Christians; but if some are watching while others are working, they should give the result of their observations for the general good; and especially if they dis-cover danger, should give an alarm. Now this is just what I feel. I am fast nearing eternity, and am proving the deep importance of having matters clear between God and the soul. Moreover, He has been pleased to give me much close retirement with Himself, and a little power of observing what is going on in the Church. Finding, therefore, many active members of the royal family shy at court, and having very little personal intercourse with the King, my heart yearns towards them, and the love of Christ constrains me to say, "My brethren, these things ought not so to be;" "shall not God search this out? for He knoweth the secrets of the heart," and if the searching out should be on the deathbed, and the wood, hay, and stubble have to be burned up then, how bitter would it be. Oh, I would cry mightily unto God for myself, and the whole living family, that by His Spirit He would search our hearts as with a candle, and discover to us wherein they are in any measure departing from Himself; also that He would not let us shrink from the light when we feel some convictions of an evil, but cause us to desire and seek to know it fully, and to be brought to the light to have our deeds reproved, and our souls delivered as a bird from the snare of the fowler.

I earnestly desire to know the real state of my case, and to have my soul laid open to the "sword of the Spirit, which is the word of God;" for whom He loveth He woundeth, and whom He woundeth He will heal. Faithful are the wounds of this Friend, though painful; and I would rather covet them than hear Him say, Let her alone; she hath loved idols, after idols let her go. Oh no, my precious Jesus; I could not bear *that,* even for a little while; I want to be continually with Thee in my own experience, to know much of Thy mind, enjoy much of Thy love, and daily to walk with Thee in endearing communion. I want this also for the whole living family, and would especially plead for those zealous workers who are promoting every means to bring others to Thee, yet themselves rarely see Thy face or hear Thy voice, and yet are not in mourning about it. Oh, grant them a revival, a re-quickening, a return, and a daily partaking of those fruits they are commending to others. Put in Thy pierced hand by the hole of the door of their heart, and cause their bowels to be moved for Thee,[1] that with earnest longings they may say, "I will rise now," and go forth and "seek Him whom my soul loveth."[2] O precious Saviour, we would seek Thee for them, and seek Thee with them, for our soul can never be satisfied with dwelling at Jerusalem without seeing the King's face. Shine on us, shine

---

[1] Song v. 4. Song iii. 2.

in us, shine through us; and in such light there will be living warmth. Bring us to sit at Thy dear feet, and lean upon Thy bosom, and through much communion with Thee to be fragrant with Thy perfumes, and thus to be refreshing to each other. Thus shall the Three-cne Jehovah have glory, to whom Thy poor handmaid giveth heartfelt, though feeble praise: "Blessed be the Lord God of Israel, from everlasting to everlasting. Amen, and amen."

One word more, dearest friend. The thought arose in my mind, What is the best means to be used for one conscious of decay, and longing to be restored to freshness of experience? Of course a fresh view of Jesus by faith—"Look unto me, and be ye saved." "They looked unto Him and were lightened, and their faces were not ashamed;" and the place to get this view is the Throne of grace,—"Pour out your heart before Him." When the Lord was promising a gracious return to Israel He said—"With weeping and with supplication will I lead them." While thinking thus, I opened the blessed Book, and was forcibly arrested with these words about the transfiguration of our blessed Lord, " And as he prayed, the fashion of his countenance was altered." Oh, it did tell upon my heart, which went forth in earnest longings that such souls as have descended, in whom the fine gold has become dim, might, in an experimental sense, have it fulfilled in them; being by the Spirit brought into fervent prayer, and as they pray, the fashion of their spiritual countenance might be altered from dimness to brightness, by the glory of their Lord arising afresh upon them, as in Isaiah lx. 1, and 2 Cor. iii. 18. May we also constantly experience the same, for I feel how much we need these Divine renewings. I do like to have some personal applications of what

I write or say, without which we are apt to fall into a mere intellectual way of speaking or writing, which is not wholesome for the soul, and helps to bring about the dearth we have been lamenting.

And now may He, to whom all power belongs, bless what is His, pardon what is mine, and give you that profit in reading which, to His praise I confess, He has granted me in writing—He knows how to speak a word in season. Oh, what joy will it be to get home and see our Saviour face to face.

In Him I remain, with much warm love, your ever affectionate

RUTH—less than the least.

XXVII.

The blessedness of separation from the world.

TO E. M.

" No man can serve two masters: for either he will hate the one, and love the other ; or else he will hold to the one, and despise the other. Ye cannot serve God and mammon."

"The friendship of the world is enmity with God. Whosoever therefore will be a friend of the world is the enemy of God."

HIGH PAVEMENT, *May* 5, 1856.

MUCH-BELOVED FRIEND, How welcome was your letter, and how does my heart feel for you in the stand which you are called to make at this time for the Lord. May you be filled with the Spirit to testify plainly that such things come of the flesh, in which no good thing dwelleth, and that they lead to evil, even to walking after the flesh, which bringeth death into the experience, according to Romans viii. 13. Mark how strong is the expression—"Mortify the deeds of the body." The carnal mind would like to mix with the world, and to compromise a little, desiring not to seem singular, but to let religion appear pleasant and agreeable to all, enjoying innocent amusements and recreations, serving God in this way as well as by other means, and letting both the old man and the new have their part.

How very many are now deluding themselves with such a profession as this, which is a mere *ignis fatuus* leading them on to the pit of perdition. But we "have not so learned Christ." We know experimentally, that if the old man feeds the new man starves, and that they cannot both fatten and strengthen at the same time. Moreover, we solemnly fear that those who can willingly mix with the world, and find no painful effects from it, have not the true life which feels where death is, or the true light which discovers darkness and evil deeds. They may "chew the cud," [1] in a lower sense by talking of the things of God; but they do not "divide the hoof" by separating from the enemies of God, for friendship with the world is enmity with God." What strong language! We are taught that none are clean in God's account but such as spiritually "chew the cud" and "divide the hoof" also. His word is a separating word, His Spirit is a separating spirit, His command is to "Come out and be separate," and the love of Christ constraineth those who are spiritually alive to live not "unto themselves but unto Him which died for them and rose again." "The Lord

[1] Lev. xi. 3–8.

hath set apart him that is godly for Himself ; " and in whatever measure or manner such do " mingle themselves with
the seed of men " [1] they must suffer experimental hindrance
and loss, for they will find it like being clogged with " miry
clay," and who then can be healthily " running the race,"
" fighting the good fight," or using the dove's wings.[2] This
will never answer, my beloved friend ; and whoever would
persuade you to such things, less or more, it must be said,
" This persuasion cometh not of Him that calleth you," for
He persuades Japheth to " dwell in the tents of Shem," not
with the children of Ham. Your love will bear with me in
saying this, though you know these things, and are fully
persuaded of this present truth—and likely it is that you
will be called more and more to carry it out in a practical
way as you go on. Perhaps the Lord may even require of
you to separate more from those who oppose your separation from the world, for He has said, " Evil communications
corrupt good manners ; " and if these persons profess not to
be of the world, yet they do not "hate the garments spotted
with the flesh," which He has told us to do.

Do not be alarmed, my dear friend ; it is most blessed to
forsake all for Christ ; and when He calls you to any new
forsaking, He will command your strength for it ; yea, the
more He circumcises your heart to love Him and your lips
to witness of and for Him, the more will you find mere professors to forsake you. They do not like such warm-hearted
company, and if they cannot win you over to their cold-water
system, they will get tired of the effects of your spiced wine,
which causes the lips of them that were asleep to speak of
Him whom the soul loveth. Nor should I think you an

[1] Dan. ii. 43. [2] Ps. lxviii. 13.

object of pity, but rather of congratulation, if, from the above cause, these compromising ones should go out, one by one, and leave you alone with Jesus and His despised remnant. The more we lose for him the more we find in Him, and to get rid of anything that is between us and Him is a gainful loss. Fear not. " His reward is with Him," and a rich one it is, even the unfolding and enjoyment of Himself. Hear Him say, " Hearken, O daughter, and consider; forget also thine own people and thy father's house; so shall the king greatly desire thy beauty: for he is thy Lord, and worship thou him." It seems as if cleaving to the first Adam family is like a cloud or veil over the beauty of the spouse—forsake them, so shall the king desire, yea greatly desire, thy beauty, which they cannot see or appreciate. How encouraging are these things for you, though many may rise up against you.

How I have run on! Love oils the wheels and moves the pen,—love to Jesus, and love to you, and earnest longing that you may never be drawn into the " doubtful territory," or listen to those who " only consult to cast you down from your excellency." You may remember that true saying, " They who will needlessly mix with the world and worldly professors shall only enjoy a partial Christ." Oh, may you never rest without enjoying a whole Christ and the fulness of Christ, and ever fresh revealings of Him.

I am proving this a place of tribulation, but am joyful in Him, and desire to live by the moment within that small safe enclosure, " Thy will be done." Self is, indeed, a loathsome object, and all its words and deeds have a very ill savour; but He is our place of refuge from it all. The fountain of His blood, the robe of His righteousness, the arm of His power, and the bosom of His love just suit us as we travel through this dreary, dusty desert, encumbered with " the body of this death ; " and so while one makes us groan, the other makes us sing, "Thanks be unto God, through Jesus Christ our Lord." Farewell, my dear friend : soon will the shadows of time flee away, and we shall see our Beloved face to face.—With much warm love in Him, I remain, your ever affectionate but unworthy RUTH.

I wish you the experience of Num. xiv. 24.

XXVIII.

The fulness of Christ.

TO E. M.

" Bless the Lord, O my soul : and all that is within me, bless his holy name. Bless the Lord, O my soul, and forget not all his benefits." " I will sing of mercy and judgment : unto thee, O Lord, will I sing."

HIGH PAVEMENT, *May* 1856.

MY TENDERLY LOVED FRIEND, I cannot tell you with what mingled feelings I read your last note. It is a solace in this desert land, " when spirit can with spirit blend," in Him and His precious love; but I have reason to believe that Sovereignty shines even in this. May we not safely conclude that our gracious Lord keeps the " fellowship of hearts " under His own control, for His own glory as much as anything else ? I am fond of that saying : " True friendship is one soul in two bodies." This explains being understood without effort, and in spiritual things is both helpful and delightful ; for in trying to make others understand we sometimes get into confusion ourselves, and almost mystify to our own minds what before was simple and plain.

How sweet was that portion of Scripture which was applied to you—how precious that covenant word "yet," which bears down all creature unworthiness. Oh! what free love, free grace, free mercy flows to poor sinners through the bleeding heart of a crucified Saviour, all without money and without price! It is wine and milk indeed. Whatever crooks and twists I find in self, creatures, or circumstances, Jesus is always my only remedy, and in Him I ere long discover something just to fit my case. Yet how it seems hidden from us for a season, to keep us sensible that power belongeth unto God; and when the revealing comes, how plain it is that all we need is treasured up in Jesus! We think we never can so lose sight of this again, when we have such riches in Him; but ah! we truly need hourly renewings of the Holy Ghost to keep us in "the simplicity which is in Christ." Oh! most blessed Spirit, keep us from grieving Thee, keep us from slighting Thy still small voice in our souls, which yet is full of majesty. Oh! testify of Jesus, tell us of Him, and take of those things which are His, and so shew them unto us that we may forget our own. Awake, thou divine north wind, and come thou south; blow upon our souls continually to keep them from a dangerous calm. Oh! cause the spices of our Beloved to flow in, and then flow out, that He and we may be both regaled with His *own*, for we have no entertainment for so royal a guest. Precious Beloved, we would have our poor heart Thy guest-chamber, daily and nightly too; we would constrain Thee to abide with us, and beg Thee to turn all out that is an offence. Nothing on earth can compensate Thine absence, for Thou art to us the chiefest among ten thousand, aud the only altogether lovely. Thou wilt not forsake us because it hath pleased Thee to make us Thy Bride, and thou hatest to put away.

How sweet is the free grace promise: " This people have I formed for myself, they shall shew forth my praise." We can say from our hearts, " He is worthy to be praised, from the rising of the sun to the going down thereof." It is well to be looking at these riches of our Surety when our debts are in view, and we shall find there is no default of payment, but such abundance, such ample satisfaction, that " our souls can make their boast in the Lord," and say, "in the Lord have I righteousness and strength." "Who of God is made unto us wisdom and righteousness, sanctification and redemption." Oh! may He be more and more revealed to us by the blessed Spirit.—I remain, with very tender love and sympathy, your ever affectionate

RUTH.

XXIX.

The Believer's power.

TO E. M.

Tuesday Morning.

MUCH-BELOVED AND LONGED-AFTER IN THE BOWELS OF JESUS CHRIST, I fear lest when with you I did not give you a clear idea of what I meant about the believer having spiritual power. I have no idea that we possess in the least an independent power. Apart from Christ we have a power to do evil, but none to do good; yet after union with Him by the Spirit, and after He has been revealed in the soul through faith, it is our privilege to live by faith on His power, which works against our own evils,[1] and brings forth His good fruit in us.[2] It is the privilege of faith to take hold of Him by the power of the Spirit for the continued exercise of faith and every other grace, that there may be strength and vigour in the soul.

But then it is asked, "Have we power thus to live in His strength? and have we power thus to take hold of Him?" Yes, we have, through the Spirit, and by reason of our union with Him. He himself says, "Come unto me." He says, "Labour for that meat which endureth unto everlasting life." He says further, "Abide in me;" and that in so doing there shall be "much fruit." He does not say these things to mock us. His servant says, "Lay hold on eternal life," "fight the good fight of faith," "put ye on the Lord Jesus Christ," "walk in Him," &c., &c. He does not say these things for naught, or only to make us feel we have no power, but to stir us up to prove wherein our strength lies. I would much rather be hourly seeking to have these blessed exhortations fulfilled in me than be defining them to a hair's-breadth, and turning back from these messages of the Lord, saying, I have no power. That is a wrong use of creature inability. It has robbed many a soul of the secret of strength, which is to live in another. In so doing it does not become stronger in self, but more independent of self, and more happily dependent upon Him who never was a barren wilderness to them who trust in Him, and who says, "From me is thy fruit found."

I do not know whether I have made clear to your mind what I wish, namely, that I have no conception of a creature

[1] Luke x. 19.   [2] John xv. 5 ; Phil. i. 11.

power or self-acting power in the believer; but I believe in
the privilege of faith, to go out upon Jesus and find in Him
all we need, to rejoice in Him alone, and *that* even in times
of most sensible poverty and barrenness, as Hab. iii. 17, 18.
Hart's hymn, 88, sets forth the activity of faith very sweetly,
and hymn 79, verse 3, shews the very climax, where it is
truly, "Not I, but Christ liveth in me." So if I were
questioned—Have you any spiritual power? the most conclusive answer would be, "Christ is my power," and by
faith I have the privilege and benefit thereof. I am all
powerlessness, but He is power in me and for me, wherefore
I rather "glory in my infirmity, that His power may rest
upon me." "I can do all things through Christ which
strengtheneth me." May the Lord bring us more into
union-privilege and union-power, which is blessed indeed.
—From your own most loving but unworthy   RUTH.

XXX.

E. M. received this letter at a time when she had been
much harassed by temptation, the enemy of souls suggest-
ing that her past happiness had been all a delusion.

*" Looking unto Jesus" the way to resist the devil and his
temptations.*

TO E. M.

April 1856.

EVER DEAR MRS ——, I am sorry that you are on the

sinking sands of unbelief, but there is Rock at the bottom, and you will sensibly feel it again ere long. "He is my Sun, although He forbear to shine."

> " Though for a moment He depart,
> I dwell for ever on His heart ;
> For ever He on mine."

"Wherefore cast not away your confidence, which hath great recompense of reward," for "the just shall live by faith," but we die by unbelief. Oh! give Him the glory due unto His name, and "give uot place to the devil," but "resist him and he will flee from you." Resist him by flying afresh for refuge to the Cross and Blood of Jesus; for even though all the past had been fleshly excitement and delusion, He is still "able to save to the uttermost all that come unto God by Him." Wherefore, "Unto whom coming," even as that Syro-Phœnician of old : and though, for a while, "He answered her never a word," yet did she follow after Him, crying, "Lord, help me," and at length came the wondrous answer, "O woman, great is thy faith; be it unto thee even as thou wilt." May the trial of your faith, being much more precious than of gold that perisheth, though it be tried with fire, be found unto praise, and honour and glory at the appearing of Jesus Christ, "even though now for a season, ye are in heaviness through manifold temptations."—With much warm love, your ever affectionate   RUTH.

Isa. xxv. 4 ; Deut. xxxiii. 27.

XXXI.

Sympathy in suffering.

"O Lord, I will praise Thee"

TO E. M.

August 1856.

My precious Friend, It has given me a new song to hear that you are really improving. I have been suffering much of late. I know that "He doeth all things well," but we may *feel*, since the immaculate Jesus wept at the grave of His friend. I felt constrained to pray for your precious life, yet also felt it cruel to hold you back from perfect bliss in the open vision of the Lamb. Most bitter to this heart would have been the pang of parting with you. Yet I think I could not have held you among thorns for my own sake; but those close dear ties in the flesh, for their sakes I did cry, "spare." How earnestly I long too that you may be a bright living witness for Jesus in the family and Church. Oh! that this purging may be to bring forth more fruit, and this chastening to yield the peaceable fruits of righteousness, "which are by Jesus Christ unto the glory and praise of God."

I trust it is light in your tabernacle, and that the glory of the Lord is filling the house; or, if not, that you are coming up from the wilderness leaning upon your Beloved. He is the apple tree among the trees of the wood, while His Bride is the lily among thorns. With me it has been emptying from vessel to vessel, and finding plenty of dregs, but not sensibly finding Him whom my soul loveth. I am

G

willing to suffer anything, so that the wood, hay, and stubble may be consumed, and Christ be all. I commend you to the Brother born for adversity. May He draw you near to Himself,[1] and open His stores of love.—With much tender love, your ever affectionate   RUTH.

Heb. ii. 14 to end.

XXXII.

The fulness of Christ revealed by the Spirit.

TO E. M.

HIGH PAVEMENT, *April* 30, 1857.

MUCH BELOVED FRIEND, My heart rejoices that the glorious Testifier has been again taking of the things of Jesus, and shewing them unto you; for it is in His days that "the righteous flourish;" and as He is exalted in the soul, self is abased.

I confess, some things you mention in your letter I had not before seen in that way. My soul longs more than ever for an increase of this spiritual knowledge of Him. Thorns within and thorns without I often keenly feel; but in Him is also found such rest and refreshing as to make one sing, even while feeling the smart.

May we cleave unto Him with full purpose of heart, that it may be with us as with Paul, "I live, yet not I; but Christ liveth in me." Thus, too, will it come to pass that we shall not seek our own things, but the things which are Jesus Christ's; and whether we live we shall

[1] Gen. xlv. 4, 5.

live unto the Lord, or whether we die we shall die unto the Lord, and so living or dying, we are the Lord's.

Truly, my dear friend, we should be learning more and more how completely He has saved us in Himself,[1] and how constantly He delights in us with all His heart, so that we have no need to seek for anything in ourselves to make us more entirely accepted or more beloved,—" He cannot love us more, nor will He love us less ; for in loving her (His Church, His Bride,) He loves Himself." The experience of this union releases the soul from a host of cares and anxious thoughts. Living in His love, that same love flows back to His own dear Person, and being satisfied with Him and His goodness, the heart has "leisure from itself" to seek His glory.

The things which I taste and handle declare I unto you, my beloved ; and most ardently do I long to grow in willingness to be poor in self, that I may be learning experimentally more of His unsearchable riches, who will be all or nothing. When He is ALL, there is no complaining in our spiritual streets ; much of our complaining shews a desire to be something which He will never gratify ; but viewing us in Himself, He ever says, " Thou art all fair, my love, there is no spot in thee ;" and the response of faith and love is, " Thou art all fair, my Beloved," " Thou art fairer than the children of men."

You will see where I am, just delighting in the same dear object ; yea, I think more absorbed in Him than ever, and more desiring to be so. When I hear any one speak against so much preaching and talking of Christ, I can only think— Well, if this is to be vile, I must be yet more vile, and will

[1] Isa. xlv. 17.

be base in mine own eyes that He may be more and more exalted. I do not wish to conceal this, for it is the truth, and I would always be honest. Moreover, to His praise I must confess, that the more I am taken up with Him, the more blessedly do I realise His grace to be sufficient for me, and that amidst many trials and temptations, and through all the plague of indwelling sin. This I find is more subdued by looking at Him than looking at it, because our Father hath laid all our help upon this mighty One. I humbly conceive, too, that much heartburning would be enjoyed, if pilgrims were to meet to search for Him in all the Scriptures,[1] and to ask for the Spirit of wisdom and revelation in the knowledge of Him.

You will remember what a blessing I had in tracing His sorrowful footprints under the pain of unanswered prayer in Psalm xxii. It is rather singular that my own steppings since have been in the same path, and thus He sometimes says, "Follow me." But He has given sweet encouraging words, and He is a precious sympathising companion in tribulation. Yet little did I think, when telling you of my Good Friday feast, that I was going to follow the Lamb in the sharp exercise of unanswered petition, and *that* when thinking I had the promise of an answer. I believe all is for the further abasing of self, and for the lifting up of my precious Jesus on high. How true is that word, " I will lead the blind by a way which they know not."

I want also to tell you how I have been enjoying those words, " The fire shall ever be burning upon the altar ; it shall never go out." You know I have often enjoyed them in an experimental sense—the fire of love burning on the

---

[1] Luke xxiv. 32.

altar of our heart, and kept alive by Him who kindled it.
Now the ever-burning fire on the Jewish altar seemed to
set forth the unsatisfactory nature of those sacrifices; for,
though thousands of goats, of bullocks, of rams, and of
lambs were consumed, still the fire burnt on, crying, as it
were, "Give, give." And as that flame was kindled from
heaven, how did it shew that sin remained unatoned for,
the law unfulfilled, justice unsatisfied; and that in all the
multiplied offerings the Divine Lawgiver had found no pleasure. They were only like promises of payment; and the un-
extinguished fire seemed like that word, "In burnt-offerings
and sacrifices for sin thou hast had no pleasure. Then said I,
Lo, I come (in the volume of the book it is written of me) to
do thy will, O God." And oh, what a glorious contrast: "It
pleased the Lord to bruise Him;" because every stroke
brought payment of the debt. He *did* find pleasure in that
sacrifice, because it brought honour to His Divine attributes,
and salvation to His people. Thenceforward the altar fire
burns not again; the fire of justice has gone out as regards
the Church, for the blood of the Lamb has quenched and
extinguished it. And "this is the covenant that I will
make with them after those days, saith the Lord: I will put
my laws into their hearts, and in their minds will I write
them, and their sins and their iniquities will I remember no
more." Oh, what fathomless depths of grace and love are
in those words! The sins were remembered against Him,
but they shall not be remembered against them; for them
waits no unquenchable fire. When their Surety said, "It
is finished," justice said, It is enough. He quenched His
Father's flaming sword in His own vital blood.

I know not whether you will get any of the savour of His

sacrifice through my weak words; but my endless, blissful theme is ever new, and it is a very feeling one—Jesus and salvation will never wear out. Oh, what will it be to see Him face to face while foretastes are so blissful? "In whom, though now we see him not, yet believing, we rejoice with joy unspeakable and full of glory."—I remain your tenderly affectionate (in Him, though in self unworthy)

RUTH. *

Isaiah xli. 14-17.

XXXIII.

Faith's view of Christ as the Chiefest amongst ten thousand.

TO E. M.

BETHEL COTTAGE, *Aug.* 1857.

MUCH BELOVED IN JESUS, I was delighted with your short line, and its sweet enclosure. Dear Miss C., I do rejoice with her, how the Lord does think upon the poor and needy, and visit them in their most needy times. She can say, "He hath done all things well." May this be only as the earnest of greater things, leading her to press after yet fuller revelations of Jesus. I would never have any sit down satisfied, but still press on after what is beyond; for there are heights and depths in the love of Christ of which the most favoured have no conception; and there are beauties and glories in His person which none have yet beheld. Oh! I would have none rest short of the revelation of His person. His benefits indeed are all precious; His atoning blood and sacrifice, His justifying righteousness, and the effects flowing therefrom, pardon, justification, peace in the conscience, &c., &c.; these are essential to salvation, and we seek them first, but it is a further and sweeter privilege to know and enjoy Himself. Salvation is sweet, but the Saviour crowns all; and when He is revealed in us, we bless the Lord and do not forget His benefits. Having once been brought to enjoy Him, may we be more and more jealous of felt distance or absence. Absent He never is, but He is at times silent, and we do not feel His presence. Oh! to make immediate and diligent search, and not go even a day's journey merely supposing He is in the company, for then will follow a sorrowing seeking for Him, as in Luke ii. 44-48, of which I have thought much to-day in this experimental sense. It is poor, heartless work when we can be quieted by "supposing" He is near; and how vainly we may seek Him amongst kinsfolk and acquaintance! Very often we find Him not there, *but* in Jerusalem, the place of sacrifice. "Ye shall seek me and find me, when ye shall search for me with all your heart."

I must now tell you how much I have been enjoying Lev. xiv. 18. The oil, as a type of the blessed Spirit, to be poured upon the head, and only think of whom—of the poor leper just healed. Who could enjoy it so much as he who had been so afflicted; shut out from the house of God; separated from His people; being so polluted that he must dwell alone, without the camp, and if any were coming near him, he must warn them by the sorrowful cry, "Unclean, unclean." Now he is to have the oil poured upon his head. Oh! would not such an one most joyfully sing, "He anointeth my head with oil, my cup runneth over?" Yes, indeed he would : I know it, and you know it too, for you have felt the same. "Sing, O ye heavens, for the Lord hath done it ; shout, ye lower parts of the earth." He hath said to the leper, "I will, be thou clean ;" and as the true Priest, He hath poured on that healed, pardoned one the true anointing ; and now no longer shut up and shut out, he comes up to the house of the Lord, to see the beauty of the Lord and to inquire in His temple. Precious, all precious Jesus! I feel the truth of what I write, and like the poor stranger of old, would fall at Thy dear feet, giving Thee thanks. [1] My soul does "give thanks to the Lord, for He is good, for His mercy endureth for ever." "Let the redeemed of the Lord say so, whom He hath redeemed from the hand of the enemy. [2]

My heart is full, and cannot half express what I would in praise of my Beloved. The chief sinner, the chief and only Saviour, have met and embraced again and again, and she sweetly finds that by Him she is justified from all her own evil things, from which she could never be justified by the law of Moses. In believing, she apprehends and enjoys the justification, for by faith we have experimental access into this grace in which we always stand before God. In short, this chief sinner finds such fulness and freeness in the salvation, such love and loveliness in the Saviour, that she can hardly leave off extolling and praising Him in whom she is justified, and in whom she may glory. Oh, come and "magnify the Lord with me, and let us exalt His name together." May He fill us with His love, and use us for His glory. May He so reveal Himself to us and through us, that it may be like oil from vessel to vessel ; for thus

[1] Luke xvii. 15, 16.　　　　[2] Ps. cvii. 2, 3.

"sweet to my heart is communion with saints" through communion with the King of saints.

I must cease, though I seem to have said nothing of the endless, blissful theme, the love and lowliness of our dear Redeemer, the Redeemer of worms. May He favour you all who know Him with His precious presence, and may many new Ebenezers be set up!

A warm adieu, with best love, from your tenderly attached but unworthy   RUTH.

XXXIV.

A meditation upon the triumph of faith over difficulties.

TO E. M.

I had a nice time this wet evening in musing on the subject of living faith, and the Word of the Lord. It is a true Word, but also a tried Word. When a promise is given, it certainly will be fulfilled; but we are sure to come into circumstances to try it, and try our faith in it. The Lord promised a son to Abraham and Sarah, but what years elapsed for the trial of faith before his birth; and when the son *was* given, what a fiery trial to take him up to Mount Moriah for a burnt-offering. Could faith live upon its prospects through such a trial? And could the promise stand sure amidst such apparent contradictions? Yes, indeed! "He was faithful who promised;" and He enabled faith to rest in the promise, even when the shadows of death had fallen so heavily upon it : and we know that faith was not disappointed.

Again, He promised the land of Canaan to Abraham's seed ; but see what came between, what bondage and hard service in Egypt, what ups and downs in the wilderness. But faith was kept alive in some hearts : see Joseph's command concerning his bones,[1] and Joshua and Caleb's noble testimony in the face of all difficulties and opposition.[2] What their faith expected came fully to pass : see Joshua xxi. 43-45.

Again, David was anointed king, and the kingdom was promised to him ; but see how faith was tried when he was hunted by Saul like a partridge upon the mountains, when he was a stranger in Gath, and, when like a homeless wanderer, he was sheltered with his men in the cave of Adullam; yet he was still a king in the Divine purpose, and at the set time he possessed the kingdom. And thus throughout the Word and in our own experience, we find how faith and the promise have been sharply tried, providentially and spiritually. The Lord may seem to have given us a promise ; faith and hope may have been drawn out to expect it; and the Word may quite warrant it ; but it has to go into the fire before fulfilment, as it was with our fathers. If the case be a spiritual one, the soul hopes for deliverance, watches for it, and has at times a sweet earnest thereof ; but yet it comes not, and again seems to be as far off as ever. The soul looks for light, but beholds darkness ; for peace, but beholds evil. This is a hard lesson, but it is the way of faith, and leads to the city which hath foundations. See what apparent contradictions the worthies of old had to endure; how contrary to flesh and

[1] Gen. l. 25.   [2] Num. xiv. 8, 9.

sense were the Lord's dealings with them. But as surely as the promised seed was born unto Abraham; and as surely as his children inherited the promised land ; and as surely as David sat upon the throne of Israel, so surely shall the soul which the Holy Spirit is exercising with the hard things of its nature's evils, find the end better than the beginning. Having had the face of desire turned toward the land of Canaan, it shall, in due time, surely enter there, and prove the difference between bondage and liberty, though now all these things seem against it.

XXXV.

The Believer " cast down " by the power of indwelling sin,
" yet not destroyed."

" He will not always chide, neither will he keep his anger for ever."
" But though he cause grief, yet will he have compassion, according to the
    multitude of his mercies."

TO E. M.

1857.

MY VERY DEAR FRIEND, and now companion in tribula-tion, My heart yearns towards you, and will indulge itself a little, because we are both in the same low place—feeling our vileness, and mourning after our Beloved. Surely there never was such an one as I, so weak and wicked; so wilful, not full of *His* will, but of *my own*. How I need the emptying from vessel to vessel. I need to have my purposes and enterprises broken that I may learn that His purposes shall stand fast, and that He will do all His pleasure. I can

say, as the repenting thief did, I am " in the the same condemnation," and "indeed justly," receiving but the due reward
of my deeds. I have been walking after the sight of my eyes.
" The legs of the lame are not equal;" so when we act from
sight and sense, our walk is not consistent; it is only when
walking by faith that it is so. Vile, ungrateful worm that
I am, what has it cost me in bitter anguish; yet the sorrow
is nothing to the sin. And, as I said to you, the ill savour
will come up continually, until the blessed Comforter bring
the savour of rest, even the fragrant sacrifice for sin which
was once offered, and which is now pleaded by Him who is
the sinner's surety and the sinner's friend. Well, I can only
lie at His feet and continue confessing all. I dare not
promise to do better ; I am in self-despair; but to Him will
I look for pardon of the sin, and power against it.

And shall it be in vain? Is His mercy clean gone for ever?
No, dear friend, we will speak well of Him: He is faithful:
He rests in His love, nor does it cool in the least in the
midst of all our treacherous dealings. " He will turn again ;
He will have compassion upon us; He will subdue our iniquities," having cast all our sins into the deep red sea of His
own blood. Where sin hath abounded, grace shall much more
abound ; and again we shall sing of pardoning mercy and
restoring love. How vain is the help of man. We may
listen to the song of some, and join in the mourning of others,
but none can lift the burden off save Himself. He is the
Physician of value who says, " I have seen his ways, and
will heal him, and restore comforts unto him and to his
mourners." Indeed, I do expect it ; faith is looking again
towards His holy temple, and love is stretching out for the
first sight or sound of the Beloved's approach. " Look unto

me, and be ye saved "—saved from the sin and from the punishment: "Is anything too hard for the Lord?" Nothing, nothing; we will hope in Him, for we shall yet praise Him for the help of His countenance.

Since writing the above this word has come to me with sweet encouragement, "Thine enemies shall be found liars unto thee; and thou shalt tread upon their high places."[1] The very things which Satan and the flesh cast up as hindrances, faith shall tread upon in the name of the Lord. Oh, this is the victory, even our faith. Sweet have I found that verse also, "For with God nothing shall be impossible;" wherefore I would say to myself and my friend, "Cast not away your confidence, which hath great recompense of reward." His blood shall cleanse, and His power shall conquer: I feel a sweet assurance of it, though with an aching heart. Flesh shall not prevail against Him, for He hath that mighty power "whereby He is able to subdue all things unto Himself." What then is better for the poor Esthers than to be still going in unto the king with the venture of faith—"if I perish, I perish." "*She* fell down at his feet, and besought him with tears to put away the mischief of Haman the Agagite." Yes, this is what *we* want, to have the devices of the flesh frustrated and brought to nought, when, like Haman, they seem most powerful. Shall Esther thus press her plea against the enemy; and shall the earthly king yield to her suit, devising means to put away that which seemed to be irrevocable? and shall we have worse success with Him who waits to be gracious, and is exalted to shew mercy? No, no; He will arise to deliver.[2]

Wherefore, though shame and confusion of face belong

---

[1] Deut. xxxiii. 29.   [2] Ps. xii. 5.

unto us, we will, by the Spirit's help, keep crying to the King against sin and self; and if for a long time He answer us never a word, we deserve it,[1] and must still follow Him with "Lord help me." This sowing in tears will be followed by a harvest of joy, love, and praise. Yes, Thou gracious near Kinsman, Thy treacherous one does heartily believe that love will bring Thee back, and that we shall flow together, and sing together for Thy goodness, for wheat, for wine and for oil, and for the young of the flock, for in Thy feast are royal dainties. A little waft of Thy fragrance comes now and then, which betokens Thee near; though the cloud has hid Thee out of our sight, and it is not yet blotted out of the conscience with precious blood, yet it is all blotted out of Thy book. Nothing stands against us there; the debt is paid; and Thou canst holily and honourably come and receive us afresh to Thine embrace, and shew us every black item put away by the sacrifice of Thyself. "Even so come, Lord Jesus."

Thus have I written to you, dear friend, in hope; and I scarcely know why; only as I have often sent you a song from the mount, I thought you should hear also the low note of the valley, from whence only at times the heart could pour itself out to the Lord.

Take courage. The precious blood of the Surety is more powerful for us than sin, flesh, and all the foes against us.[2] Whether at your worst, or at your best, do not be looking more at yourself than at Jesus. He is the way of escape, and He is the strength to endure; and we shall be helped in all, though we sometimes faint.—Warm love from the weakest and worst of all, your very affectionate   Ruth.

John xxvii. 13, 14; Zech. ix. 11, 12.

[1] Ps. cxix. 75.   [2] Rom. viii. 37.

XXXVI.

The suffering sympathy of Christ.

"In all things it behoved him to be made like unto his brethren ; that he might be a merciful and faithful high priest, in things pertaining to God."

TO E. M.

Good Friday Morning, 1857.

MY TENDERLY-BELOVED FRIEND, This morning you are much on my mind in connexion with our precious suffering Head, and I must send you a few lines.

"Jesus has shewed Himself again" to His poor worm it was in Ps. xxii., especially in the first part, where He is described as suffering the anguish of experimental forsaking, and also great conflict from unanswered prayer. This I never realised so fully before. Oh how He has left His precious footprints in every thorny path—"The footsteps of the flock" are thus so prepared, that

"No thorns can harm, for Jesus went
Before to tread them down."

We feel that He, having suffered before us, is able both to sympathise and to succour. How touching to hear Him compare the deliverances of His people with His own un-succoured condition—"Our fathers trusted in thee : they trusted and thou didst deliver them. They cried unto thee, and were delivered : they trusted in thee and were not confounded." Then stooping to the lowest place of abasement, as if less than any of them, He says, "But I am a worm,

and no man ; a reproach of men, and despised of the people."
It was as though in that degraded position which He had
taken for His people, He must not expect to be dealt with
so tenderly as they,—

> "O love ! of unexampled kind,
> Which leaves all thought so far behind."

My soul was also deeply humbled in the depths of verse
2, "O my God, I cry in the daytime, but thou hearest not ;
and in the night season, and am not silent." It was a
night season indeed, even darkness which might be felt.
For what agony of soul did our Beloved not endure when
He had no answer from God. It is wonderful to see how
"He was in all points tempted like as we are ; " not only
tempted with evil by Satan, but tried by His friends, tried
by His Father, and tried in all the sensibilities of the nature
which He had taken ; yet, in all He endured without sin.

His sorrowful utterances were to shew that He had the
tenderest susceptibility of feeling in all His sufferings. But
there was not one murmur or rebellious feeling, or one hard
thought. He pitied His disciples—"the flesh is weak ; "
and though He knew they would all forsake Him through
fear, He even made a way for that escape in His matchless
love : "If ye seek me, let these go their way." His Father
He fully justified in all His dealings with Him as the Surety ;
for while crying with anguish, "Thou hearest not," He
directly adds, "But thou art holy, O thou that inhabitest
the praises of Israel." He was indeed a Lamb without
blemish. His Father, His enemies, and His Church, have
to say, "I find no fault in Him." This precious, spotless
One gave Himself for us to the sorrows of death and the
pains of hell, which bitter cup of trembling He drained,

even to the very dregs; so that He could triumphantly say, "It is finished." Ah! but never will He say, either of the love or the glory, "It is finished." Oh, no! while eternal ages roll on, love will be ever inflowing, and glory ever unfolding, and all coming to us through that rich medium—His sufferings and death. We read of "the sufferings of Christ, and the glory which should follow." The sufferings are past; He has entered into the glory; but the full revelation of it, in and to His Bride, is yet to come. O wonderful Bridegroom, reveal to us more of Thy wonderful love, in Thy humiliation and exaltation. Let us live in that undying flame, that in our joys and sorrows we may be a sweet savour of Thee to Thy loved ones—

> "Bruised Bridegroom, take us wholly ;
> Take and make us what Thou wilt ; "

only continually draw us out of self into Thee; and cause us to grow up in Thee in all things, while many winds and storms and heart-achings cause us to root down in Thee also. Oh do Thou shine more and more brightly in us, to the perfect day.

It is blessed, dearest friend, to spend Good-Friday under His shadow as the crucified One ; there His fruits are sweet to our taste. It is precious to be led on by His Spirit to His joy as the glorified One, for then our joy is full. They that "dwell in [this] secret place of the Most High shall abide under the shadow of the Almighty." It is a secret place for the hidden ones, of which He says, " There is a place by me ; and I will put thee in a clift of the rock." This hallowed place is kept secret from all those who are " alive without the law ; " they want not this blessed hiding-place. No carnal eye ever saw it ; no carnal heart ever enjoyed the rest. It is the secret chamber for the secret life, where He who is our life says, " There will I give thee my loves."[1] He gives all in Himself. At Calvary we see how He the Living Rock was cleft, that His dove might be spared ; and how lovingly He says, " O my dove, that art in the clefts of the rock ; let me see thy countenance, let me hear thy voice."[2]

My dear heavenly Boaz has made this a GOOD Friday to His unworthy gleaner. I had feared I should not find Him whom my soul loveth, and have fellowship of love in His sufferings ; but where mine enemies dealt proudly He has been above them.[3] Praise to the worthy Lamb. " Praise is comely for the upright :" " I made thee go upright ; "[4] and then follows your Ps. lxxxiv. 12.

This is not like a letter ; but if the Spirit will breathe of Jesus' fragrance through it, you will rejoice with me in Him.—With dear love, your own worthless, but in Him ever affectionate,   RUTH.

XXXVII.

Christ, our substitute, the consolation in time of trial.

TO E. M.

3 MELVILLE PLACE, *Sept.* 24, 1857.

MUCH-LOVED AND TENDERLY-REMEMBERED FRIEND, I was delighted to receive your note. The Lord has been gracious,

---

[1] Song vii. 12.
[2] Song ii. 14.
[3] Ps. lxvi. 10, 13.
[4] Lev. xxvi. 13.

He has had mercy, and I do praise Him. May all have to say,—" It has been good for me that I have been afflicted." No doubt there is in this trial some special message to each. May our language be,—I will hear what God the Lord will speak."

I have this morning much enjoyed those words, " I will sing of mercy and judgment: unto thee, O Lord, will I sing." Judgment to JESUS, and mercy to vile worthless ME. Mercy flowing warmly through His pierced heart and precious veins. What a channel wherein to flow! Oh! what love of our Father to lay upon Him all our iniquities, to number Him with the transgressors, and then to give Him judgment without mercy, saving all the mercy for us rebellious younger children. Oh! what a loving Elder Brother, who for the joy of our release and blessing, was content to be judged, condemned, and executed; and what a blessed Comforter who takes of these wonders and reveals them to the soul, making it to sing for joy, like that word, " Awake and sing, ye that dwell in dust." At times we do sadly cleave to the dust; but the power of love revives us again, causing us to awake and sing. The Lord bless you all, and pour out His Spirit upon you! Fresh oil prepares for all we are called to.—And now adieu. Soon the shadows of time will be past, and we, through free grace, shall spend eternity together in the open vision of the Lamb. In Him, your own warmly-affectionate

RUTH.

XXXVIII.

Written after seeing a microscope.

TO E. M.

Thursday, Jan. 1858.

VERY DEAR FRIEND, I have been musing with delight upon the wonders developed by the microscope. What perfection is there in every part of the works of our God! All creation sheweth His handiwork, His wisdom, and His goodness. Dr. Carson beautifully says, "The works of God and the Word of God bear the same testimony of Him as far as they go together; but the Word goes far beyond His outward works. It testifies of salvation, on which subject His works of creation say nothing."

The bank-note in miniature rests vividly on my mind, and reminds me of that word, "The things which are impossible with men are possible with God;" and "all things are possible to him that believeth." The Lord gives a promise, and faith receives it in sweet assurance; but anon, all things seem against it. The fogs of sense, flesh, and carnal reason arise, and so veil the promise that it appears as unreal as that almost invisible speck on the glass looked unlike a £20 note. But when faith is again brought into lively exercise, every line and letter is sweetly discerned, with the Divine "yea and amen" upon it. Oh, to look more through the glass of faith, and less with the blinking, deceiving eye of sense and reason.

I have been thinking further (the thought may well make

one blush) that even the beauties and loveliness of Jesus, which have so ravished our souls, do at times look only like that diminutive speck, which can scarcely be discerned. How we, then, look all ways to get the clear views of Him which before so enraptured us. But no,—our efforts are vain until the blessed Spirit again sets the glass of faith, and takes of the things of Christ and shews them unto us; in other words, until our Beloved manifests Himself afresh in endearing communion, constraining us to exclaim, "Thou art fairer than the children of men ; the chiefest among ten thousand, yea, altogether lovely." But if it be with us that "now we see Him not," yet having once beheld His beauty, no lower charms can satisfy, no other object fill the vacuum in our soul. Oh "make haste," our Beloved, and "be thou like to a roe or young hart upon the mountains of spices." Oh come, and "cause *the mountains* of Bether" (division) to flow down at Thy presence. Blessed Author and Finisher of faith, call into lively exercise that grace, that it may truly be "the substance of things hoped for, the evidence of things not seen."[1]—Wishing you the renewings of the Holy Ghost,[2] I remain, with best love, your unworthy but affectionate

RUTH.

XXXIX.

The suitability of Christ to the sinner.

TO E. M.

1858.

MUCH-BELOVED FRIEND, I must begin with saying, "Is it well with thee ?" When did you see the King ? Are

[1] Heb. xi. 1.   [2] 1 Cor. ii. 9, 10.

you free at court? Can you venture in the name of another? Have you sweet access by the faith of Jesus, and by His blood? The Father is pleased when the Son is honoured. Oh! for faith in exercise by the operation of the Holy Ghost to live in the fulness of Jesus in constant self-emptiness.

I have been sweetly seeing how the needy sinner suits the Saviour; for what would He do with His fulness of grace if He had not these dependants to receive it? and what should we do, who cannot call one mite our own, if we had not such a Saviour, full of grace and love, to bestow it? We should not match together half so well if we were not so needy and helpless, and we cannot put more honour upon Him than by living upon His royal bounty. He is the Covenant-Head, in which all covenant blessings are treasured up for the covenant children, who are always to be poor as poverty in themselves, but are freely welcome to all this store, which is the ordained medium of communication. Unbelief is the great barrier by which Satan works to keep us out of our privileges, and to rob God of His glory. We may well cry out with tears, " Lord, I believe, help thou mine unbelief."

I had a sweet season at the Lord's table yesterday. My soul was touched to see my precious Jesus, the Lord of glory, in all His suffering circumstances; to see Him crowned with the curse, nailed on the tree of curse, and that between two thieves. What degradation! Oh! I could hardly bear it. "They shall look upon him whom they have pierced, and they shall mourn for him." It is very humbling, but very sweet to meditate on the deep humiliation of that royal Sufferer; and there it is that hope springs up, mercy breaks out, and love flows to a vile sinner like me.

" Oh ! the sweet wonders of the cross,
  Where God my Saviour loved and died ;
  Her noblest life my spirit draws,
  From His dear wounds and bleeding side."

Remember "the blood is the life." Seek to have much of it, that it may not be with the soul "just alive," but "life more abundantly."

I have been much delighted with those words, "He healed all manner of sickness, and all manner of disease among the people." May the power of the Lord be present to heal you, if you have need of healing.

In the warm love of our unchanging Friend and Lord, ever yours most affectionately,

RUTH—a debtor to mercy and love.

XL.

The subjugation of self through the cross of Christ.

TO E. M.

THE CLIFF, CLEETHORPES, *Aug.* 1, 1858.

VERY DEAR MRS ——— . . . The notes you sent me of the sermon about Jacob were very nice. The expression " unselfing " was striking. Do you not think the revelation of Christ is the quickest of all means to effect this ? St. John says, "When I saw him I fell at his feet as dead"—typical of the bringing down of self. I do humbly believe that the more we know Him in union, love, and power, the more zealous we shall be against " self " in all its varied forms. Unbelief sets up self—what I do, what I do not do, what I ought to have done, and so on, till there is only a corner in the thoughts for the dear Surety, who has done all, and done it well too. But the more we receive of Him and His—or, in other words, the more Christ alone is exalted, the high towers of self are laid in the dust. When unbelief and self are predominant it is sad work. May the Lord tread these abominations under His feet, even as straw is trodden down for the dunghill. Oh! my loved friend, we long for the days of the Son of man in our souls, for in His days the righteous flourish.

I have been enjoying those words—"I will love them freely; for mine anger is turned away from him." It seems to me to be the language of the Father, who, having laid upon Him the iniquities of us all, then and there visited our transgressions with the rod, and our iniquities with stripes, till not one was left unatoned for; then His anger was turned away from the Surety, and He could love the poor debtors freely, because He was well pleased for His ʻrighteousness' sake. He had magnified the law, and made it honourable ; and He, the Father, blessed them there. In Him, "the Lord our righteousness," we may glory and rejoice ; and in Him find power to do so, for He is the power of God to every one that believeth. In believing we take hold of that power, and can say with David, "My soul shall make her boast in the Lord : the humble shall hear thereof, and be glad." Indeed, my dear friend, we only want to know more of our Law-fulfiller, and of the unsearchable riches which He has for our use ; then the love of Christ would constrain us to glory in Him, and praise Him. Oh! let us cry mightily for the Spirit of wisdom and revelation in the knowledge of Him. Oh! to know Him more. Oh! that He always eclipsed everything else. I have been thinking of the philosopher, whose only request to the king was, that he would stand from between him and the sun ; and so I would that all things, even the most lawful, should stand from between me and the blessed Sun of Righteousness. I have seen enough in Him to ravish my heart, and make the brightest things below look dim. But I want to see Him again, for I know that there are in Him infinite glories of which I have had yet no conception : " After these things Jesus shewed himself again to his disciples." Amen, so let it be.

The Lord bless you and yours ; and may Jesus shine warmly in your heart, and you be constrained to speak warmly in His praise.—With dear love, ever your affectionate but unworthy   RUTH.

John i. 14 ; 2 Cor. iv. 6.

XLI.

The preciousness of Christ unfathomable and ever new.

Zech. xiv. 17.

TO E. M.

HIGH PAVEMENT, *Sept.* 23, 1858.

MUCH-BELOVED IN JESUS, I rejoice to hear you have been guided to such a good pasture, and favoured with such a good spiritual appetite. Though we have had so many feasts upon a precious Jesus, we find each time as much freshness as though we had never partaken before. This has been very striking to me ; things of earth often repeated grow stale, but the same view of a precious Jesus a thousand times over is ever new. How often has the Divine Spirit testified in our souls " of the sufferings of Christ, and the glory that should follow." How often have we by faith beheld His bloody sweat in the garden, and spent sweet solemn moments at the foot of the Cross. Yet, when Jesus shews Himself again to us in either of those sacred positions, is He not as a lamb newly slain? and is not His sacrifice as an odour of a sweet smell, as fragrant as though but just offered, without spot unto God? Oh yes, He is ever the same, without sameness, and will be to all eternity. The glories, beauties, and excellences of His person are infinite. And from these boundless sources our finite minds will be feasted for ever and ever. We shall be abundantly satisfied with the fatness of Thy house, and Thou shalt make us drink of the river of thy pleasures.

Oh that my poor contracted heart were more enlarged into this our fathomless ocean of love and loveliness! Oh to abide in Him for ever! "One thing have I desired of the Lord, that will I seek after; that I may dwell in the house of the Lord all the days of my life, to behold the beauty of the Lord, and to inquire in his temple." Christ is our true temple; in Him we may inquire of the Lord concerning all our hard cases, and have an answer of peace. In Him we see the beauty of the Lord, even all his Divine attributes harmonising and glorified in saving poor sinners. This is seeing the King in His beauty; and beauty indeed it is in the eye of a sin-sick soul to see the holy Jehovah " a just God, and a Saviour" too. He was most just in punishing our sin in His most holy person: He is most just also in letting us go free; yea, accepting us in the Beloved. The ministration of condemnation was glorious, when it pleased the Lord to bruise Him; but the ministration of righteousness exceeds in glory, when the blessed Spirit brings near His righteousness, yea, puts it on the soul, saying, "Bring forth the best robe, and put it on him." It is also exceedingly glorious when the righteous Father welcomes the prodigal with the kiss of everlasting love, being well pleased for His righteousness' sake; and when "the Lord our righteousness sees of the travail of his soul and is satisfied," saying, "Thou art all fair, my love; there is no spot in thee." Then also is the poor soul richly satisfied, saying, "In the Lord have I righteousness and strength;" "I will make mention of thy righteousness, even of thine only." This is, indeed, a glorious ministration of righteousness, and is part of the fatness of Thy house, my King and my God. Here is food for hungry souls who have long been starving on the husks of self; and here is clothing for the naked soul, who has been into the "stripping-room," and had the filthy rags, and all the adornments of self stripped off.

O my precious friend, it is a mercy to be made and kept poor enough for Jesus to be *all.* You know how fond I am of Isaiah xxix. 19, "The meek also shall increase their joy in the Lord, and the poor among men shall rejoice in the Holy One of Israel;" and "Blessed are the poor in spirit; for theirs is the kingdom of heaven." Lord, make us inwardly poor, and keep us so, that Christ and nothing else but Christ may reign for evermore. O Lord, increase our faith; and increase its lively goings forth on the precious person, work, and love of Jesus; so shall we inherit substance, in the midst of our own felt poverty, and be content to have nothing in self, yet possess all things in Christ, which is one of the dear secrets of love, "The secret of the Lord is with them that fear him."

I have been much enjoying Hosea xii. 9, " I that am the Lord thy God from the land of Egypt will yet make thee to dwell in tabernacles, as in the days of the solemn feast." We know that in the days of our spiritual feasts we feel the tabernacle nature of all below, and feel ready to depart, and be with Christ, which is far better. Coming out of self, we dwell in that true tabernacle which the Lord pitched, and not man. May He fulfil His promise, and bring us so to dwell. That word also has been very sweet to me, "He shall come down like the rain;" and I trust it has been fulfilled in my dry soul. How welcome the showers on the dry land, or on the mown grass! The waters from our smitten rock run in His dry places like a river. The Lord grant us daily the renewings of the Holy Ghost, and cause His Word to do us good like a medicine, that we may be kept from a dry, barren spirit, though feeling that in ourselves we are very dry. May the blessed Spirit exalt Jesus more and more in your experience, that all your casting down may be for His lifting up.—With much tender love, your warmly-affectionate but unworthy　　　　　Ruth.

XLII.

A New Year's greeting.

TO E. M.

Jan. 1859.

My beloved Friend, I wonder if you got a new-year's portion yesterday. Last night, while seeking Jesus, these words came to my mind with sweetness : " The soul of the diligent shall be made fat." [1]　Wherefore I conclude they are to be

---

[1] Prov. xiii. 4.

my motto for the new year. I feel them to be very reproving to my sluggish heart; but there is such sweetness in the mouth of our Beloved, that even a reproof from His dear lips falls like a honey-drop into the soul. Oh may the blessed Spirit inspire us with true spiritual diligence which brings us to more than wishes and desires, for we may possess these and be slothful still; for " the soul of the sluggard desireth and hath nothing." But " the hand of the diligent shall bear rule," while "the slothful shall be under tribute:" under tribute to the world and the flseh, instead of in the liberty of the Spirit. Gracious Lord, do make us diligent, and keep us so by the renewings of the Holy Ghost.

But my main object in writing was to give you a word which melted my heart on Friday night, from Isaiah l., a favourite chapter of mine, and in reading which our precious Lord shewed Himself lovingly through the following verse : " I gave my back to the smiters, and my cheeks to them that plucked off the hair : I hid not my face from shame and spitting." No, He would hide us by not hiding Himself. He would be smitten, that by His stripes we might be healed. Our living balm-tree would have the fearful incisions in His own flesh, that His balsamic virtues might flow out to our diseased souls. Our well of Bethlehem was opened on Calvary. There may we poor sinners be gathered to-day, and clustering round His cross, drink freely of the best wine, drink away our sloth, and drink till we are wide awake in holy diligence, seeking for more of the living stream, and so feeding upon Him experimentally, live by Him. [1] Oh that holy, loving face, not hid from such indignities for our sakes! I wonder and adore !

[1] John vi. 56, 57.

May *your* meditation of Him be sweet, and may *He* bring His prisoner the bread and the wine.—Your warmly-affectionate
Ruth.

XLIII.

Christ our near Kinsman.

"A Brother born for adversity."

TO E. M.

Jan. 1859.

Under this character has my faith embraced our glorious Emmanuel this morning, and found Him very precious. Oh! I wonder not that the ancient Church so longed for His incarnation, and breathed out her desires ardently, saying, "Oh that thou wert as my brother, that sucked the breasts of my mother! when I should find thee without, I would kiss thee; yea, I should not be despised." She had not the happy privilege of finding Him without, but had to go to the mountain of myrrh and the hill of frankincense to behold Him through the shadowy sacrifices. But we can say,

"Our next of kin—our Brother now,"

"That He might sanctify us with His own blood, suffered *without* the gate." Let us therefore "go forth to Him *without* the camp, bearing His reproach." "For we have no continuing city here, but look for one to come." Oh! may we daily embrace Him "without," cleave to Him in all His humiliation, and walk with Him in the lowly path of suffering as the "Man of sorrows," who, in all our tribulations, has a heart to sympathise and a hand to help us!

I know as one wave rolls over another, our precious Elder Brother looks through the cloud to comfort us. This morning I was struck with Exodus xiv. 24, the Lord looking through the pillar of fire and of the cloud to trouble the Egyptians. It sweetly came to my mind, that as God manifested in the flesh, He looks through the cloud of His humanity, upon His people, with the tenderest love; while the same look troubles their enemies, for He overcame them by the blood of His cross. Oh! that was looking through the cloud and fire indeed, when by enduring the cross, and drinking the fiery cup of wrath, He so troubled the hosts of hell, "Spoiling principalities and powers," and triumphing over them in His cross. That look was darkness and destruction to them, but it gives "light by night" to His travelling pilgrims. Let us for ever bless this precious Brother, born for adversity.

Wishing you His blessed presence and guidance now, and at every future step.— I remain, with warm love, your ever-affectionate, unworthy RUTH.

XLIV.

This letter was received by a mother at a time of severe trial, when her husband and her five children were ill with measles.

The presence of Christ in a time of affliction.

TO E. M.

March 1859.

MUCH-LOVED FRIEND, I sincerely wish you the exercising of the Holy Ghost in the afflictions through which you are passing, that you may have the full benefit thereof; for it has been truly said, that "sanctified afflictions are great promotions." And those promotions come neither from the east nor from the west, but from the Lord alone, by whose power

> " Trials make the promise sweet,
> Trials give new life to prayer,
> Trials bring me to His feet,
> Lay me low and keep me there."

Many a visit of love has the Lord paid, and many a secret of love has the Lord revealed in the time of affliction, and some of the sweetest communings in the wilderness have been with the thorn in the flesh, or the cross on the back. Does not your soul respond to the truth of this? Is not Jesus a precious companion in tribulation? Are not His sympathies most tender? Has He not drawn near in the day when we cried unto Him, and said unto us, "Fear not"? Oh yes, the fruits of the valley are very choice, but yet we fear to go down thither; forgetting who has said, "I will go down with thee, and will also surely bring thee up again;" "As a beast goeth down into the valley, the Spirit of the Lord caused him to rest; so didst thou lead thy people, to make thyself a glorious name."[1] Are we not brought down into the valley of trouble or humiliation to cause us to rest only in Jesus? "These things [these afflictive things] I have spoken unto you, that in me ye might have peace. In the world ye shall have tribulation: but be of good cheer; I have overcome the world." At times trials seem to overcome us, yet "in all these things we are more than conquerors through Him that loved us." "This man shall be the peace, when the Assyrian shall come into our land;" "This is the

[1] Isa. lxiii. 14.

rest, wherewith ye may cause the weary to rest, and this is
the refreshing." So you prove it, so I prove it; and the
rock of His faithfulness is a blessed retreat, when our heart
is overwhelmed within us. The honey of His love dropping
from that rock does sweetly revive our fainting souls, and
make us joyful in tribulation, so that we sing even in the
trial, "He hath done all things well."

The measles have come at the right time, and have taken
hold of the right persons ; they are the Lord's messengers
and are not the sound of their Master's feet behind them ?
"Take away the dross from the silver, and there shall come
forth a vessel for the Finer." The Refiner is with you ; trust
Him with your dearest treasures, and may you feel Him
dearer than all. I am very fond of these words,—"So
Daniel was taken up out of the den, and no manner of hurt
was found upon him, because he believed in his God!" May
we have like precious faith.—Adieu ! with dear love your
affectionate, but unworthy companion in tribulation,

RUTH.

Deut. xxxii. 10-12.

XLV.

An important anniversary.

EBENEZER.
"Hitherto hath the Lord helped."

TO E. M.

Oct. 31, 1859.

DEARLY BELOVED FRIEND, In the dear Name, "which is
above every name," I once more greet you on this memorable

I

day. May the blessed Spirit so shed abroad the fragrance of that name in both your souls, that you may regard the day in the Lord and to the Lord, while you review the goodness and mercy which He has caused to pass before you.

You, dearest friend, commemorate a birthday and a wedding-day together; and oh! the mercy that though that was not first which is spiritual, but that which is natural, yet that which is spiritual hath followed. You are born of the Spirit, and you have had a second marriage. "Thy Maker is thy husband, the Lord of hosts is his name, and thy Redeemer the Holy One of Israel; The God of the whole earth shall he be called." These are personal favours of the first order, but innumerable other benefits are this day brought to mind, especially that the Lord provided one of the precious sons of Zion for your companion through life. One with whom you dwell as a fellow-heir of the grace of life, assured that though death will sever the natural union, it can never touch your oneness in Jesus; but that, having eaten together of the Paschal Lamb below with bitter herbs, you shall surely sit down together at His marriage supper above, where bitter herbs shall be tasted no more. Oh! praise Him who hath dealt wonderfully with you, and said, "My people shall never be ashamed." May He grant you much sweet communion in Himself, and abundantly bless you and your dear children, so that not a hoof shall be left behind.

You will recount many mercies to-day, but must end by saying, "How great is the sum of them," for the total amount of the sum you can never find out. "Praise ye the Lord."[1] May our precious Jesus shine on you, and in

[1] 1 Thess. v. 18; Rom. xi. 36.

you, that your souls may be as a watered garden, and as a
well of water whose waters fail not. And may your beloved offspring be by the Spirit gathered, one by one, into
the inner circle below, and every one of them appear in
Zion above, with us also to sing the new song, "Unto Him
that loved us."—So prays, with tender love, your warmly
affectionate but unworthy   RUTH.

1 Thess. v. 23, 24; 1 Chron. xvii. 27; Eph. iii. 20, 21.

XLVI.

Christ in everything.

TO E. M.

1859.

DEAREST MRS ——, Thank you most affectionately for
the grapes kindly left for me. How the Lord does load me
with benefits, and gives me Himself too, which is best of
all. He is heaven's rich grape. He has been in the wine-
press of divine wrath for us, and hence it is we drink "the
pure blood of the grape." I wish you much of it; for
truly it cheereth the heart of God and man.[1] What a
wonder of love, and what a cordial we find it when weary
and faint in the wilderness. We drink, and forget our
own poverty in the unsearchable riches of Christ.

RUTH.

[1] This is according to Judges ix. 9, 13.

XLVII.

The riches of Christ for the poor in spirit.

TO E. M.

1859.

. . . Oh for more faith, living faith, to draw largely upon our royal Banker, who has issued such large promissory-notes for time and for eternity as exceed our utmost conceptions. For time—"All things are yours" in Him. For eternity—"He hath blessed us with all spiritual blessings in heavenly places in Christ Jesus." In contrast to present "light afflictions," He hath placed "a far more exceeding and eternal weight of glory;" and that we might now enjoy strong consolation, He hath given us "exceeding great and precious promises." Far larger notes are these than the richest banker ever issued, and much more certain to be honoured; and, what is better than all, they are for the poor—the very poor—the mean of birth and having nothing, even for beggars found upon a dunghill.

Oh, wondrous grace, free love, royal bounty! It melts my heart this very moment, for it has come even unto me in the richest of Divine liberality. Oh for Spirit-enlargement into our possessions and His promises. We are not straitened in Him, but in our own bowels. Truly our Father has prepared of His goodness for the poor.— With warmest love, your ever affectionate

RUTH.

XLVIII.

Warnings to an unconverted friend.

" How long halt ye between two opinions ? if the Lord be God, follow him :
but if Baal, then follow him."

TO MR J. A.

High Pavement, *Dec.* 1855.

Dear Mr J——, What will you say to me for taking
the liberty of writing to you ?   Perhaps you will feel in-
dignant and offended ; but I hope that will soon pass away,
for Jesus says, " Blessed is he whosoever shall not be
offended in me."   It is in His name, and for His sake I
write to you, and for your soul's sake also.   I feel constrained to write to you to remind you that He is " the
friend of sinners."   He still " receiveth sinners, and eateth
with them."   He says, " If any man thirst, let him come unto
me and drink;" and, " Come unto me, all ye that labour and
are heavy laden, and I will give you rest."   Now I am sure
you have not found rest; you are not happy.   You have too
much light on spiritual subjects to be easy in a course of
vanity and worldliness.   You may drink the poisoned sweet,
but it leaves a sting and void behind.   You may think that
if you had a home, and some one to love in it, the void
would be filled up ; but no; it would still be left.

" And let you try whate'er you will ;
  Believe me, while you live,
A something will be wanting still,
  This world can never give."

That something is Jesus. He only can give true happiness. He is the one thing which is needful to put all else into the right place. If you did but know His preciousness, you would think it worth forsaking all to find Him. He gives just what you need, a heart to love Him, His ways, and His people; for He says, "A new heart will I give you, and a new spirit will I put within you." He also gives true repentance and free pardon; for He is exalted "to give repentance to Israel, and forgiveness of sins." He gives deliverance from the power and love of sin, saying, "I will put my fear in their hearts, that they shall not depart from me." He washes crimson sins white as snow in His own precious blood, for hear Him say, "Come now, and let us reason together, saith the Lord : though your sins be as scarlet, they shall be as white as snow : though they be red like crimson, they shall be as wool." He puts the best robe on prodigals who have been vainly trying to find satisfaction in the husks of this world's pleasures. By His Spirit He bringeth them to their right mind, cleanses them in His blood, and clothes them in His righteousness.

Perhaps you will say, "And what is all this to me?" Why, it is *this* to you, beloved,—without these things you must perish for ever. Should you ask, "What have *you* to do with it?" I answer, "I have a great concern for your soul's salvation." But you may object, "The things you have spoken of are for God's chosen people, and I do not know that I am one." You do not know that you are *not* one, and should rather say, "Why not, my soul ? Why *not* for Thee ?" And though they are a free gift not to be obtained by any creature power, yet ask God to give them to you. Ask Him to give you the Holy Spirit to make you feel your need of them.   Oh may that Holy Spirit

> " Convince you of your sin,
>   Then lead to Jesus' blood ;
>   And to your wondering soul reveal
>   The secret love of God."

That you may have an experimental knowledge and en-joyment of these things, is the earnest and affectionate desire of yours very sincerely,   R. BRYAN.

Jer. vi. 16, but I hope not the last clause.

XLIX.

Warnings to an unconverted friend

" But one thing is needful."

TO MR J. A.

HIGH PAVEMENT, *Jan.* 19, 1856.

DEAR MR J——, I must thank you for your very kind reply to my note.   When I wrote, I had not the slightest thought you would answer it, and your letter, therefore, was doubly welcome.   The candour and honesty of its contents much delight me ; while at the same time I truly mourn over your present state of soul.   Yet I do not sorrow with-out hope ; for I humbly trust the Lord has a purpose of mercy towards you, and that ere long He will make you " see " and " feel " those things which, at present, you say you only hear of.   I beg to say that what you hear is " true report;" and it is solemn to remember that the things of eternity are stern realities, and will be proved to be so whether you realise it or not. The " broad road" will "lead to destruction," however carelessly persons may walk therein; and the threatenings of God's Word against sin will be executed, however indifferently persons may hear or read of them. It will not stand as an excuse before Him to say, "I did not feel the force of the threatenings, or did not see any evil in my pursuits." What God has declared to be evil is so; and those who do such things will be judged by Him as evil doers, just as His Word declares, "He will render to every man according to his deeds." Now the pleasures of the world are not only empty and unsatisfactory, but they destroy the soul and displease God, as the Scriptures declare; and all who persist in them are His enemies, as we read, "The friendship of the world is enmity with God; whosoever therefore will be a friend of the world is the enemy of God." They are called "lovers of pleasure more than lovers of God." What a true description !

You say that before any one can give up the fascinations of the world he must have a dread of the consequences, and that to this point you are not yet come. But I would now bring before you the certainty of those consequences, even if they are not believed or dreaded. They do not hinge upon the perception or feeling of the creature, but upon the truth of Him who has said, "The end of those things is death." This is a real matter of fact; and, however unfelt, the truth of it will follow you into every party of pleasure, yea, into every one of those streams which are truly called, "The pleasures of sin ;" for "whatsoever a man soweth that shall he also reap."

You will perhaps think me harsh, but "faithful are the wounds of a friend." These things are so; I see them, and see your danger, and cannot but say—

> "Stop and think
> Before you further go;"

and would ask with the prophet, "Lord, I pray thee, open (the young man's) eyes that he may see."

But perhaps you will say, "I have no other sources of pleasure; would you have me quite miserable?" O beloved, there is not a blood-redeemed sinner before the throne but was miserable once; and I well remember a time in my early days when I was miserable too. I could not enjoy the world as some I knew seemed to do; there was something wanting. I could not enjoy religion and the things of God as believers did. I felt unlike everybody else, and as if I never should find happiness either in the world or in the church. But though I knew it not, the Lord's hand was in it; and He drew me by a strange way, till at last He brought me to the foot of the cross, to find true peace and happiness in the love of a bleeding Saviour. I should not, therefore, be sorry for you to lose your present poor pleasures, and feel "an aching void," for in my Saviour's heart there is yet room, and He can fill it all. I find His love so precious that I long for others to enjoy it, and cannot help saying, "Oh taste and see that the Lord is good!"

I am delighted that you *do* seek, if it is only sometimes, and ever so feebly. May the Holy Spirit enable you to pray more earnestly and seek more diligently; it will not be in vain. You little know what are the joys of His salvation. It is well worth being miserable half one's life to attain such substantial enjoyments which are for ever.

I have been sorry to hear that you are out of health; and yet a hope sprang up in my heart that the Lord might thereby speak to your soul with power, saying, "Seek ye my face." He called Samuel many times before he knew whose voice it was; and He will make you willing in the day of His power."

I fear you will think I am taking too much advantage of your kindness by writing again; but I could not let your note remain without a reply, because I am affectionately watching for your soul.

The Lord bless you.— With much interest, I am yours very sincerely,

R. BRYAN.

1 Chron. iv. 10.

L.

Warnings to an unconverted friend.

" What is your life ?   It is even a vapour, that appeareth for a little time, and then vanisheth away."

TO MR J. A.

HIGH PAVEMENT, *Aug.* 1, 1856.

DEAR MR J——, I was truly surprised that you should take the trouble to answer my note, and since you have thus encouraged me, I must again venture a few lines upon the same all-important subject—viz., the salvation of your never-dying soul. It *is* all-important; and now is the time to consider it; for though you are young your life is not insured, and you have already had a serious warning in that affliction, which might have opened the gate into an eternal world. Oh! had it been so, where would you now have been? and what would have been your portion? Would you have been "present with the Lord," beholding the beauties of Jesus, and singing in the ever-new song the praises of the Lamb which was slain? Or would you have been banished from His presence, cast into outer darkness, to receive the wages of sin, that eternal death which never, never dies? These questions may be unpleasing; but it certainly is worth while to ask them, and to answer them, because one of these states must before long be yours as well as mine. There is no medium state; with every soul of man it must be joy inconceivable, or woe unutterable; and whichever of these be our portion, it will be for ever, and ever, and ever. There will be no fear of the happiness ending,—no hope of the suffering terminating or even abating; for in that darksome prison, never, never will be heard those precious words, "It is finished!" Sin will never be made an end of, and therefore the consequences of sin can never cease; but while eternal ages roll, it will be "wrath to come," "wrath to come."

Perhaps you will think me more gloomy than ever, but this I cannot help; I have eternity in near prospect, and solemnly feel it will profit a man nothing if he should gain the whole world and lose his own soul. My heart says with Moses, "Oh that they were wise, that they understood this, that they would consider their latter end." The fact is, it will come whether it is considered or not; for the Scriptures say, "It is appointed unto men once to die: but after this the judgment;" and Jesus has declared of those that die in their sins, "Whither I go ye cannot come;" "Cast ye the unprofitable servant into outer darkness : there shall be weeping and gnashing of teeth."

But perhaps you will say this is too severe, and only belongs to great sinners, such as have been profane and immoral in their conduct. Nay, beloved, mark—this last Scripture does not speak of any openly wicked sinners, but only of an unprofitable servant. Now, have not you been to God an "unprofitable servant," even though you may have been outwardly moral and correct? Again, it is written, "The wicked shall be turned into hell, and all the nations that forget God."[1] You see how the sentence runs; not only to the wicked, but to all who *forget* God. This reaches the very thoughts of the heart, and shews that God's holy law passes judgment on them as well as on words and actions. Yea, indeed, its first great commandment searches the heart, for it is this, "Thou shalt love the Lord thy God with all thy heart, and with all thy soul, and with all thy mind, and with all thy strength."[2] Now, under this law we were all born, and by it must be judged. Nor can we say it is unreasonable that we should be required to love the holy God who is our Creator and Preserver. But have we loved Him supremely? Have we remembered Him in His ways? No, not one of us has done it by nature ; but, as He says, "My people have forgotten me days without number;" "God is not in all his thoughts;" "Every imagination of the thoughts of man's heart is only evil continually;" and, "Shall not God search this out; for he knoweth the secrets of the heart." Surely your kind and very candid note confesses the truth of these things when you say, " It is my thoughts that lead me astray." So, then, we need go no further than the thoughts of the heart to prove

---

[1] Ps. ix. 17.   [2] Mark xii. 30.

that we have all gone astray from God; that we are guilty
under His law; and its condemning sentence is againt us,
for it says, "The soul that sinneth it shall die;"[1] and "the
thought of foolishness is sin."[2]   These are God's own words,
not mine; you can turn to the Bible and read them.

But if it be true that we are by nature in such a fearful
state, how is it that we can be so indifferent about it?   And
how is it that while under the sentence of death, and with
the wrath of God already on us, we can be merry and sport-
ive, and care for none of these things ?   It is because we are
not only "shapen in iniquity and conceived in sin," but "we
are dead in trespasses and sins;" that is, spiritually dead, so
that we cannot know God, or love Him, or feel our real state
before Him, any more than those who are literally dead can
see, or hear, or feel the things that are going on around
them.   And because of this state of spiritual death we may
tell persons over and over again about their lost and dangerous condition, but they do not feel it, and they never will
until they experience what the Lord spoke of to Nicodemus,
John iii., " Except a man be born again he cannot see the
kingdom of God ;" " Marvel not that I said unto thee, ye
must be born again."   This new birth is entirely of God; it
is the being quickened by the Holy Spirit, and made to feel
that we are sinners and enemies to God by wicked works.
When this new birth takes place we feel many things to be
evil, which before we thought nothing of.   The Spirit convinces us of sin, makes us know what sin is, and that we are
full of it; as it is written, " When he [the Spirit] is come,
he will convince the world of sin."   When this takes place
we no longer try to excuse ourselves, because we are not so

[1] Ezek. xviii. 4.   [2] Prov. xxiv. 9.

bad as others—have wronged no one—and have done the best we can. We cannot rest here, but feel that we have done enough to banish us for ever from the presence of God; and the great anxiety now is how we may get salvation.

I fear I shall weary you, but yet I should very much like to tell you the account of a little heathen girl which has much interested me, and will show you what I mean by being born again of the Spirit, and how He can quicken without outward means.

A little Hindoo girl was stolen from her parents, taken to Calcutta, and sold for a slave. She was a sweet girl, and the lady who bought her, having no children, took a fancy to her, and thought she would not make her a slave, but bring her up to be a companion, and she grew very fond of her. The lady was a Mohammedan, and taught the little girl to be the same. This went on until she was about sixteen years old, when all at once it came into her mind, she knew not how or why, that she was a sinner, and needed salvation. She was in great distress of mind, and went to the lady for comfort; but she could not give her any, she could not tell her of a Saviour, but tried to amuse her, and make her forget her trouble. So she hired rope-dancers and jugglers, and tried all the sports they are fond of in India, to give her pleasure. But all were of no use ; she remained as miserable as ever. The lady then sent for a Mohammedan priest; but he could not understand her distress. However, he took her under his care, and taught her many prayers in Arabic, which she did not understand ; told her to repeat them five times a-day, and always turn towards Mecca when she said them. She tried in vain to get comfort from these things. She felt there was no forgiveness, no salvation there. After three long years, the thought struck her, that perhaps all her sorrow of mind was a punishment for having left the faith of her fathers. So she searched out a Hindoo priest, and entreated him to receive her back to his church, but he cursed her in the name of his god. She told him all her distress, but he would not listen till she offered him money, and then he undertook her case. He directed her to take an offering of fruit and flowers to a certain goddess, and once a-week to offer a kid of the goats for a bloody sacrifice. For a long time she did all he told her, but got no relief; she found that the blood of goats could not take away sin, and often cried in deep distress, "Oh I shall die! and what shall I do if I die without obtaining salvation?" At last she became ill through distress, and the lady watched her with deep sorrow, fearing she would sink into an early grave. One day as she sat alone in a room, thinking and longing and weeping, a beggar came to the door; her heart was so full that she talked of what she wanted to all she met, and in speaking to the beggar used a word which means salvation; he said, "I think I have heard that word before;" she eagerly asked, "Where? tell me where I can find that which I want, and for which I am dying. I shall soon die, and oh, what shall I do if I die without obtaining salvation?" The man told her of a place where the poor natives had rice given them, and "there," he said, "I have heard it; and they tell of one Jesus Christ, who can give salvation." "Oh, where is He? take me to Him," she said. The beggar thought she was mad, and was going away, but she would not let him go without telling her more. She dreaded missing the prize which now seemed almost within her reach. "Well," he said, "I can tell you of a man who

will lead you to Jesus," and directed her to a part of the town
where Marraput Christian lived, who was once a rich
Brahmin, but had given up all for the sake of Jesus.   She
set out that very evening in search of him, and went from
house to house inquiring of those she met where lived
Marraput Christian, the man who would lead her to Jesus,
but none could tell her.   It grew late, and her heart was
nearly broken, for she thought she must return as she came,
and die without obtaining salvation.   She was just turning
to go home when she saw a man walking along the road
and thought she would try once more, so she asked him
where Marraput Christian lived, the man who would lead
her to Jesus.   To her great joy he shewed her the house,
and she met Marraput coming out of the door.   She asked,
with tears and anguish, " Are you the man who can lead me
to Jesus ?   Oh, take me to Him.   I shall die, and what shall
I do without obtaining salvation ? "   He took her in, and
said, " My dear young friend, sit down and tell me all."
She told her history, and then rose and said, " Now, sir, take
me to Jesus ; you know where He is, oh, take me to Him !"
For she thought Jesus was on earth, and that she might go
to Him at once.   Marraput knew that though He was not
here, He was just as able to pity and welcome her at the
mercy-seat ; so he only said, " Let us pray."   As he prayed,
the poor Hindoo felt that she found that which she so long
wanted,—salvation, pardon, and peace.   This simple narrative
touched my heart.   It does so shew the work of the Spirit
in one who had never seen a Bible, nor heard of the gospel,
or of Jesus the sinner's friend.   There she was in the midst
of heathens, mourning for sin and seeking for salvation.
The good Shepherd was seeking this lamb before she sought

Him, and He appointed the means to bring her to His fold and His feet. Oh, that it might be thus with you! May you by the Spirit be wounded under a sense of sin, then will you, with like earnestness, seek to be led to Jesus, the Saviour; for you *must* die, and, oh, what will you do if you die without finding salvation?

I must cease. Excuse the length of this; my heart is in it. I long for your salvation, and still mention you to the King to whom power belongeth.—Believe me, with much affectionate interest, your sincere friend,

R. BRYAN.

LI.

An introductory letter to Miss F., written to her Mother.

TO MRS F.

Saturday Afternoon.

MY VALUED FRIEND, Will you give the enclosed to your dear H—— at a suitable opportunity? The Lord preserve your going out and coming in, and, if it be His holy will, revive your drooping, fragile flower; but, above all, bring her into His garden enclosed below, and then gather her as His lily to wear in His own bosom above. Oh! the happiness of being enfolded in His love for ever, where clouds and storms can never come.

Well we are on the sure way—the King's highway—you and my dear brother are journeying therein amidst the many cares and storms of wilderness life, and I amidst the pains and weakness of decaying mortality. To each the promise stands good,—" As thy days, so shall thy strength be."

K

" Thine enemies shall be found liars unto thee, and thou shalt tread upon their high places." In passing through life the interests of time have their claims, but we often give them sadly too much importance. How secondary do they look in the light of eternity, for in one moment our breath may fail, and we have done with them for ever. The Lord bless you both with sweet communion with Himself, enabling you to cast all your care upon Him, for He careth for you. He clothes His lilies, He feeds His doves, He makes a way through the sea for His ransomed to pass over.— With warm love, your own unworthy RUTH.

LII.

Heart-searching suitable to a birthday.

ECCLES xii. 1.
" The Lord bless thee, and keep thee."

TO MISS F.

March 31, 1859.

MY BELOVED H——, I have been told that you this day attain your twenty-first year. Will you accept an affectionate greeting from a pilgrim friend ? and will you allow me to express the feelings of my heart, though they be not so lively or so congratulatory as may seem to comport with a birthday.

You have reached another milestone on the pathway of life, and where does it find you ? In a medium path between the world and Christ ? Ah ! there is no middle path. Consider it, and then " consider your ways ; " for either you are serving the Lord or serving His enemies—the world, the flesh, and the devil. I do think you *sometimes* long to be on the Lord's side, and that your heart says of His people—

> " Number'd with them may I be,
> Here and in eternity."

My heart says— Amen ; and may it be soon, that I may have joy over you in the Lord, and that He may have the cream of your life, the flower of your days, for He is worthy. He who bled and died for sinners such as you and I, is worthy of all our powers, and of a thousand hearts if we had them. May the blessed Spirit make you feel deeply your need of Him, and this very day, if it be His holy will, may your language be—

> " Here's my heart, Lord, take and seal it,
> Seal it in Thy courts above."

Most heartily I desire for you a spiritual birthday in the fulfilment of that precious promise,—" A new heart will I give you, and a new spirit will I put within you." Then will you say, " My Father, thou art the guide of my youth ;" and only then will you find true happiness, for

> " Fading is the worldling's treasure,
> All his boasted pomp and show ;
> Solid joys and lasting pleasure,
> None but Zion's pilgrims know."

Though not with you, I am bearing you on my heart before the Lord. May He guide you every step in life, and grant you the blessings of the upper and the nether springs. Forgive the intrusion of these poor lines from one who watches for your never-dying soul ; and, with tender love, remains your affectionate friend, R. BRYAN.

Psalm xc. 12-16.

LIII.

Encouragements to one afar off, to come unto Jesus.

TO MISS F.

Saturday, May 12, 1860.

MY BELOVED H——, You do not know how much I have thought of you since you have been poorly, and how I have hoped this cough might be as the rough messenger, by which the Lord would effectually touch your heart, making you feel yourself a lost, helpless sinner, and bringing you to sue for mercy at the foot of the Cross, where no needy sinner ever perished yet. No, my beloved young friend, there is no perishing at the footstool of mercy. You cannot be too sinful, too hard, too cold, too powerless for Jesus to save.

If you feel your need of Him, it is His gift, "'Tis the Spirit's rising beam." Oh that it may be so! My heart yearns after your soul, travails in birth till Christ be formed "in you the hope of glory," and I grudge every year and month that you and your dear brother and sister continue far off from God, and strangers to "the peace that is made by His blood."

> " Oh that the time of love may come !
> When you shall surely see,
> Not only that He shed His blood,
> But each shall say, *for me.*"

For you, dear one, I have been thinking of this word, " I have refined thee, but not with silver, I have chosen thee in the furnace of affliction." And if it be so, you will say, "It is good for me that I have been afflicted," for "before I was afflicted I went astray." I sometimes long for a peep into your heart, for I cannot think your thoughts and desires are all after the empty things of this world. I think there is under all a longing to be "*found*" by the Good Shepherd, and marked for His own.

Perhaps you sometimes think, "If I am not chosen, it is of no use desiring and praying." So I thought once, and it lay like a stone on my heart, choking and chilling each little sigh for mercy, when the cry would have risen, "Lord, save me." But I have found it was one of Satan's devices to keep me from prayer—and so it is with you, if such are your feelings. Even as it was with the young man whom Satan threw down and tare when they were bringing him to Jesus.[1] But he could not hinder the blessing, and that is comfort.

The question with you should be, not whether you are chosen, but what are the characters whom Jesus came to save, and invites to come to Him? "The Son of man is come to seek and to save that which was lost." "I am not come to call the righteous, but sinners to repentance." This man receiveth sinners and eateth with them. "Come unto me all ye that labour and are heavy laden, and I will give you rest." Jesus is a *great* Saviour, and you are a *great* sinner, therefore you are the very case for Him. It is true, with all your endeavours you cannot repent, but " Him hath God exalted to give repentance and remission of sins." Neither can you pray, but He gives the spirit of grace and supplications. You cannot mourn for sin, but He makes the "heart soft." "They shall come with weeping, and with supplications will I lead them." You cannot believe but He is the Author and Finisher of faith. So all these are things not to

[1] Luke ix. 42.

keep you away, but just to bring you to Him, even though
you do not know assuredly that He has chosen you. He
says, "Him that cometh to me I will in no wise cast out."
The Spirit says, "Come." The Bride says, "Come," and
"whosoever will, let him take the water of life freely."
May you, dear H——, come, and come again, you will not
be cast out; but perhaps in this very furnace the Lord will
say to you, "Yea, I have loved thee with an everlasting love,
therefore with loving-kindness have I drawn thee. I will
bring the third part through the fire, and will refine them
as silver is refined, and will try them as gold is tried; they
shall call on my name, and I will hear them : I will say, It
is my people : and they shall say, The Lord is my God."
Amen, so let it be with thee, my dearest friend.

I have been writing mentally all the week, but was too
ill to pen my thoughts. I am rather better to-day, and so
have done it freely. Perhaps my thoughts may not have
touched yours ; all depends upon the Spirit of power. Oh
breathe, celestial Dove, in that dear heart the breath of life
divine. Move upon the dark waters of that soul, and say,
"Let there be light," and the light of life shall burst forth.
Be in that loved one the spirit of supplication, that she may
pray and not faint. The Lord preserve you in journeying,
restore your health, and bless your soul, that you may
heartily say,—

> "Gladly the world's poor toys I leave
> For those who know not Thee."

I know you will excuse the many imperfections of these
poor lines, written from the bed of pain and weakness.—
With much love, I remain your affectionate friend,

RUTH BRYAN.

LIV.

Pleadings with a soul.

Lam. iii. 22.

TO MISS F.

MY DEAR FRIEND, It grieves me to hear you are come back so unwell. How gladly would I see you and try to soothe and comfort you ; but though I cannot come to see you, as I am very weak, and fast going down to the last valley, yet I am with you in spirit, and can speak to the King for you as the blessed Spirit enables me. For what would you make request ? Is it for life and health ? He can give them, for "He bringeth down to the grave, and bringeth up again." So do not be too much cast down. But do you cling more to life than you would wish? Ah! it is only salvation applied, and Christ enjoyed, that can loosen our hold of things seen, and of those earthly attractions which have long entwined themselves around the heart, for then we have found something infinitely better. But is it your chief desire to find that salvation, and hear that blessed Saviour say, " Fear not, I have redeemed thee, thou art mine " ? Oh, then, my heart will rejoice, for such desires will surely be granted. "Your heart shall live that seek the Lord."

> " Those feeble desires, those wishes so weak,
> 'Tis Jesus inspires, and bids you still seek."

I do hope and trust the Lord has a purpose of love to you, and that He has put these rough cords of affliction round you to draw you to Himself. Oh, blessed Spirit, convince that dear soul of sin, and then say to her, "Behold the Lamb of God, which taketh away the sin of the world." Break her heart, and then bind it up with the love and blood of Jesus. O Jesus, manifest Thyself to her as her own precious Saviour. O my covenant God, save her for Thy mercy's sake, and if it be Thy holy will, spare her to shew forth Thy praise. Amen, amen.

The Lord bless you, and turn the water of affliction into the wine of consolation.—With tenderest love and ardent longings, your warmly affectionate,

R. B.

LV.

A counsel of love.

TO MISS F.

My dear H——, I hope a little line of love will not fatigue or excite you. A line from the blessed book to encourage you in looking for manifested pardon and love, "Come now, and let us reason together, saith the Lord: though your sins be as scarlet, they shall be as white as snow; though they be red like crimson, they shall be as wool." "The blood of Jesus Christ his Son cleanseth us from all sin." "He will turn again: He will have compassion upon us. He will subdue our iniquities, and Thou wilt cast all their sins into the depths of the sea." The sea of Immanuel's blood! Oh! what love to poor sinners, to pour out His precious blood for their cleansing. He is a precious Saviour, a loving Saviour, a free Saviour. He saves without money or price, without merit on our part or even one good thought to plead, and He waits to be gracious; nor will He let one poor sinner perish who is crying to Him from the heart for mercy and pardon. No, not you, my loved one. " He will be very gracious to thee at the voice of thy cry.—With tender love, your affectionate,   R. B.

LVI.

A letter is now introduced to Mrs B——, preparatory to the series of letters addressed to Miss M——. During a visit of Mrs B—— to the sea-side in Kent, she read it to Miss M——, who was in bad health and soul distress, and it proved so seasonable that, on returning to Nottingham, Mrs B—— requested Miss Bryan to open the subsequent correspondence, which extended over some years.

TO MRS B.

The power of the precious blood of Christ.

1849.

MY DEAR SISTER IN OUR PRECIOUS LORD JESUS, Many, many times have I thought of you since you so tenderly leaned over my sinking frame, almost thinking to see me no more in the flesh, unless it were to pay the last kind attention to my sleeping dust. But, beloved, we parted with a bright prospect beyond, and a sweet assurance that we should meet again to part—*no never*, never ! Since then I have gone near, indeed, to the gates of the grave, and the shadows of death seemed closing thickly around me; but there was no harm, dear sister. Jesus has been through death and through the grave, and He has left them stingless, to those for whom He died. "O death, where is thy sting? O grave, where is thy victory?" Thanks be to God which giveth us the victory through our Lord Jesus Christ. May He bless you, and give you many heart-burnings while He talks to you by the way, and opens to you in all the Scriptures the things concerning Himself, which will make you for a season forget the things concerning yourself; and while you are lost and Jesus found, you nothing and Jesus all, you will step on lightly, even with a heavy load in the flesh.

I hope Mr B—— is anxiously seeking the Pearl of great price. Perhaps his sun is near setting, and then comes a never-ending eternity. Oh, that he may not enter it without the blood of Jesus; that is the only way by which a poor sinner can enter into heaven itself. Coming with that precious blood, the vilest shall not be shut out, for it "cleanseth from all sin." Secret sin, open sin, old sin, long-continued sin, sins against light and knowledge, sins against judgment and mercy, known sin, unknown sin;—every kind and manner of sin which a poor trembling Spirit-convinced sinner feels, does this powerful blood take away. To this many now before the Throne, and many also on earth, can bear honest witness, and I for one would lift up my feeble voice to encourage every sin-burdened soul to put their whole confidence in that blood of which I have felt the benefit. My sins were as scarlet, my guilt of crimson dye, but blood of a richer hue which flowed out from the veins of my precious Saviour has made me white as snow, and I long for poor fellow-sinners thus to be brought nigh to

God, for "now in Christ Jesus [we] who sometime were far off are made nigh by the blood of Christ."

I know not how Mr B—— is feeling, or where he is looking for salvation, but I have much concern for his soul, and a desire that he may "behold the Lamb of God, which taketh away the sin of the world." One sight of Him by faith would be as powerful to his soul as looking at the brazen serpent was to the body of the bitten Israelites ; for as Moses lifted up the serpent in the wilderness, even so (has) the Son of Man (been) lifted up, that "whosoever believeth in him should not perish, but have everlasting life." So Jesus says Himself, "Come unto me, all ye that labour and are heavy laden, and I will give you rest." "All that the Father giveth me shall come to me, and him that cometh to me I will in no wise cast out." Oh that this precious "shall come" may draw your earthly husband to your heavenly One ; for they shall come who are ready to perish, who have no eye to pity, no hand to save or help them ; who feel hopeless and helpless, they shall come. Oh that the Lord may find him, then will my soul rejoice to know that he is one of those lost sheep, whom the Good Shepherd came on purpose to seek and find.

Now, my dear sister in Jesus, the God of love and peace be with you, bruise Satan under your feet shortly, cause you to triumph in Christ, and make you exceeding joyful in all your tribulations, through the love of God shed abroad in your heart by the Holy Ghost, which is given unto you.— Accept affectionate love in Jesus, from yours very sincerely,

R. BRYAN.

LVII.

The tenderness of the Good Shepherd.

TO MISS M.

January 19, 1850.

A stranger takes the liberty of sending greeting in that dear Name of Jesus, that Name so precious to the believing soul, precious to the seeking soul, precious to the wounded spirit and to the broken heart, precious to the lame and the lost, to the bound and the bruised, to the leprous and the filthy ; yea, to every spirit-touched soul does this loved Name sound sweetly, either as that which is known to be precious by enjoyment, or that which is estimated precious as being just what is needed. His name was called Jesus because He should save His people from their sins; and those seeking, trembling souls, who dare not yet say they are of His people, do feel painfully that they want saving from their sins, that such a Saviour would suit them well, and to be able, under Divine anointing honestly and lov-ingly to add the little word "my," would be more to them than possessing mines of gold and crowns of earthly glory. The very thought of saying and feeling "my Saviour," sets their hearts longing; and the glow of a little hope that it will come, almost makes their lame feet leap and their dumb tongue to sing.

There is a blessed, holy attraction in this altogether lovely Jesus which acts powerfully upon all quickened souls, draw-

ing them out in desire, and drawing them on in pursuit,
till the set time comes to favour them more manifestly;
then the meeting between a sin-sick soul and a sin-bearing
Saviour has in it such secrets of love and sweetness, that it
seems as if a thousand years of the most painful waiting,
would be richly repaid by one moment of such bliss. But
oh, it is not for a moment and then away; the Saviour and
the saved shall never really part. He "hateth putting
away," and though darkness obscure, and clouds seem to
intervene after the first meeting, yet union remains, communion shall return, and a glorious eternity consummate the
bliss. Of every sheep and every lamb the Good Shepherd
will take care, and fold them all safely above. They shall
surely pass under the hand of Him that telleth them, and
not one be missing; however faint, or feeble, or fearing, or
unworthy any one may be, they are all bought and paid for,
and the flock must be as complete as the price was satis-
factory. The wolf may howl, the dog may bark, the way
may be dreary, and the poor heart may often tremble, but
the Good Shepherd will not be out of hearing, even if He
seem to be out of sight. He will rescue even out of the
paw of the lion, and out of the paw of the bear.

Perhaps Miss M——'s heart is saying, " I know all this,
but fear I am not one of His flock." Is sin hated, self
loathed, the world forsaken, Jesus longed for, His people
loved, His ordinances and Word prized and sought unto to
find Him in them, and the good old way inquired after with
a desire to walk therein? If so, these surely seem like the
breathings and bleatings of the sheep; and let Miss M——
be encouraged into the assurance that the Good Shepherd's
heart is so loving and tender, it is as easily touched by the

half-uttered "baa" of the weakling lamb as by the full-toned "Abba" of the sheep that knows its fold and its owner.

It may be, He is now saying to this fearing one, " I have refined thee, but not with silver, I have chosen thee in the furnace of affliction." It may be, He is trying, and will ere long bring forth as gold; and if He has fixed upon the furnace as a meeting-place between thee and Himself, it will be worth enduring a seven times heated flame. It may be, at present thou hast not seen Him, but He sees thee, and is regulating all the fiery process. It may be, that as yet thou hast but fallen down bound into the midst of the fire. Well, so did some before thee, who afterwards, in glorious company with the Son of God, walked loose and unharmed in the flames. Think it not strange concerning this fiery trial, which is to try you, as though some strange thing had happened unto you, but consider that as a father chasteneth his son, so thy God chasteneth thee ; and though at present it seem not joyous but grievous, yet afterwards may it yield the peaceable fruits of righteousness, through the divine " exercising " of the Holy Ghost thereby.

Your case is too hard for yourself, but bring it to Jesus, and He will hear it. Surely mine was harder, yea, the hardest of all, so helpless, so hopeless, so sinful, so unbelieving, so hard, so cold, so ignorant, yea, so everything I would not be, but Jesus undertook, and to the uttermost He saved. I was a five hundred pence debtor, but every farthing He paid, and now by Him made free, I live to praise Him, and to encourage all poor, convicted sinners to trust Him with the worst of their bad case. He will not send such empty away. He will in no wise cast them out. None need despair, since He has saved such a worthless, hell-deserving one as myself. May the Holy Ghost enable you to make the venture of faith, and it shall not be in vain. [1]

The Lord bless you, sanctify your affliction, grant you manifest forgiveness of sins, and an inheritance among all them that are sanctified through faith that is in Jesus. You are seeking Him, perhaps sometimes sorrowing, but "they that sow in tears shall reap in joy." My heart desires He may soon be found of you, and though entirely strangers in the flesh, yet for His dear sake, I venture to subscribe my self yours very sincerely, RUTH BRYAN.

1 Pet. v. 10.

LVIII.

The wounds of sin and the healing power of the good Samaritan.

" This man receiveth sinners and eateth with them."

TO MISS M.

Feb. 27, 1850.

DEAR MISS M——, Do not be alarmed at again seeing the handwriting of an unworthy stranger, thinking you will be constantly subject to these intrusions. Indeed, I do not intend it; and you need not have one anxious feeling in the thought that you must reply. I shall not think it the least breach of politeness, or the least want of Christian courtesy, for you to be entirely silent. I well know what weakness and nervousness is, and it would much grieve me

[1] Esther iv. 16, and v. 2.

to add to that burden ; therefore please to read these lines in perfect ease and freedom from all such feelings.

On reading your note my spirit was strongly impelled to commune with you again, and the contents of it touched my heart to tears, for in your dark picture I find the very counterpart of myself. Yes, indeed ! though now enjoying the sweets of union,[1] and the love of my beloved.[2] Yet for years I walked where you now walk, and felt as you now feel. Though preserved in outward morality and propriety, yet I was often horrified at my own inward vileness, and loathed my corrupt self more than words can express. I also sinned against light, and knowledge, and privilege. Thoroughly do I know what you mean by secret sin,[3] and depths of iniquity, such as, if known to your dearest friends, would make them abhor you for ever. I have felt it, and under the awful power of hateful temptation, have been sure that if the workings of my vile heart could be seen, the dear saints who then noticed me would spurn me, and cast me out of their society. Yet I did not wish to deceive them ; I could tell no one what I felt, but always declared myself the vilest of the vile ; and when they tried to encourage me by saying that my spots were the spots of God's children, I just thought it was only because I could not make them know how really black and bad I was. You describe me to the life when you speak of short periods of reviving, then relapsing into apathy, and only being aroused by some fierce temptation. I had gleams of light and tastes of sweetness, and then I could hope. But these soon passed away, and general carelessness and indifference gradually succeeded, with conscience-reprovings and heart-smitings. I had no

[1] Song vi. 3.   [2] Song ii. 3, 4.   [3] Ps. xxv. 7, 8.

power, or even hearty will against this state, till some new
form of abomination startled me, or some old easily besetting sin made head against the careless daughter. This
roused me to bitter groans and cries for mercy, with deepest
shame and remorse, and I thought surely the Lord would be
at length provoked to cast me off for such seeming mockery,
in thus crying out against sin, and yet being so much the
subject of its awful activity. Ah, indeed! I felt there never
was such a wretch, such a living mass of putrefying sores
and corruption. Others might be worse outside, but I felt
the sin was not less my own, or less polluting, because it
worked chiefly within; and I thought if the Lord ever saved
me, I should be the greatest wonder in heaven, and that
there never could be such another trophy of redeeming love.
I think so still, and am in nowise disposed to yield that
point even to you, bad as you think yourself, for my guilt
has many aggravations which I cannot enumerate. I used
to say that nothing less than sovereign power and irresistible grace would ever be sufficient for such a hell-deserving
one as myself. That has been granted,—power whch broke
down my will, and grace which melted my heart; and I,
even unworthiest I, can sing of "Sovereign grace o'er sin
abounding."

I would again draw near to you, beloved, in that wilderness of fear and sin where you are travelling heavily, and
which I trod with sorrowful steps before you. I would encourage your heart in God, "who regardeth the cry of the
destitute, and will not despise their prayer." You are not
expecting too much in desiring to lose the spirit of bondage,
and to have the spirit of adoption, crying, Abba, Father; to
go on from the convincing of the Spirit to the comforting of

L

the Spirit,—from His leading through the chambers of imagery and increasing abominations, to His testimony of the altogether lovely Jesus as your Saviour.

I used to say, I want individuality and personality put into all that Jesus did and suffered, to have it just made my own; and I believe no Spirit-touched soul can be satisfied without it. The Spirit-convicted must be Spirit-comforted, the Spirit-wounded must be Spirit-healed, and that will always be with precious blood. "I wound, and I heal; I kill, and I make alive." "Not by might, nor by power, but by my Spirit, saith the Lord of hosts." Like you, I sighed for this sure testimony, and all the voices of all the saints, I knew, could not persuade me that I was a child, till the Spirit revealed relationship, and then, though some thought me presumptuous, they could not stop the cry, "Abba, Father, my Lord and my God, my Beloved and my Friend." It is God persuades or enlarges poor Japheth to dwell in the tents of Shem, and he dare not for his life presume to go there without; but he is often on the way thither before he can believe it, and when he finds himself really there manifestly in Christ, it is something like the disciples, "they believed not for joy, and wondered;" and like the Church, "When the Lord turned again our captivity, we were like them that dream." Thus it was with me; it seemed too good to be true, that I, who deserved the lowest hell, and had felt so long as though I were hanging over it, should be delivered for ever from it. "Deliver [her] from going down to the pit, I have found a ransom."

May the Lord cheer you, dear Miss M———, or I am sure my poor words will not; but as the first features of our case are so truly similar, I doubt not that ere long we shall come to a fuller recognition of family likeness. I doubt not that you also having sown in tears shall reap in joy, though you do not now to your own apprehension seem to be bearing precious seed. Well, I do firmly believe that the same good Samaritan who found me after I had fallen amongst thieves, —sin, Satan, the world, and cursed unbelief,—found me stripped, wounded, and half dead,—I believe this same compassionate One will ere long purposely pass by where you are, and do as He did for me ;—bind up your wounds, pour into them oil and wine to cleanse and heal.

Perhaps you say, " Lord, I would believe, help Thou mine unbelief." So be it. I know from woful experience what a subtle, mischief-working foe unbelief is, and that we are prone to listen to it, and parley with it too. None can have been more unbelieving than I. But He whose love was stronger than death would not be turned aside. May your heart be encouraged, and your eye turned from yourself to Him, then, like the serpent-bitten Israelites, you would be healed and live. May the Spirit of the Lord give the look of faith, the touch of faith, that your sighs may be turned to songs.

I long after your soul in the bowels of Jesus Christ. To Him I commend you. Having myself obtained mercy, I can assure you, for your encouragement, that your case cannot be too hard or too bad, and I have no doubt He has already undertaken it. "If any man sin, we have an Advocate with the Father, Jesus Christ the righteous." And He pleads according to law, for Himself is the propitiation for our sins. Adieu, dear Miss M——. May the Lord, whom you seek, come speedily to His temple, even your heart.—Accept affectionate regards for Jesus' sake, from yours very sincerely,

RUTH BRYAN.

LIX.

Christ able to save to the uttermost.

"Peace be unto thee ; fear not : thou shalt not die."

TO MISS M.

April 1850.

MY DEAR MISS M——, Grace and peace be with you, and may the God of consolation shortly fill you with joy and peace in believing. May He turn your eyes away from the mystery of iniquity within, to the great mystery of godliness, God manifest in the flesh, stretched upon the cross for you, redeeming you from the deserved curse of the law by being made a curse for you, bearing your very sins (which seem to you greater than any other) in His own body on the tree. This is the only sight which can heal your wounded heart and bring rest to your weary, labouring spirit. You are bowed down with the burden of sin, even as the poor woman was with the infirmity wherewith Satan had bound her for eighteen years, and, like her, you can in nowise lift up yourself. It must be a power out of yourself that shall loose you from your heavy burden and bitter bondage.

Poor heart ! you are hopeless and helpless unless "the Deliverer" appear on your behalf; and He will do it, for He never said to the seed of Jacob, "Seek ye me in vain." You are seeking Him and His favour, and you think you shall never find it ; but "His thoughts are not as your thoughts," for "as the heavens are higher than the earth," so are His thoughts and ways above yours. You look at your own deservings, and judge by things seen and felt. He judges righteous judgment, and has found a wondrous way in which He can honourably deal with you according to the deservings of another.

O my beloved friend, how will your heart leap and your tongue sing when this secret is opened to you in power! How will your burden fall off when you get a faith view of the cross and of the precious Sufferer there! These words, perhaps, seem now to you like idle tales as regards your personal experience, and you believe them not with any comforting application. "Power belongeth unto God," but truly I can believe on your behalf, and have no doubt you will be as a brand plucked from the burning, a trophy of redeeming love, a jewel in my Saviour's crown, and that as chief sinners we shall ere long sing together, "Where sin abounded, grace did much more abound."

You may perhaps say, "You cannot know how bad I am, or you would not feel so sure." And *you* do not know how bad *I* am, or you would not think yourself worse. The arm that reached me (low indeed in the pit of corruption) can reach you, the blood that cleansed me can cleanse you, the love that sealed my pardon can seal yours. Notwithstanding all you can say concerning your bad case, 1 fully expect that in the Lord's time you will send me an Ebenezer stone inscribed with pardon free and full. Thereon we will sit down together, and, taking the harp from the willow, sing, "It is the Lord's doing, and marvellous in our eyes." "Grace, grace unto it." What! do you think you have outsinned the blood, the love, the power, or the will of Him who is able to save to the uttermost all that come unto God by Him, and who said, "Him that cometh to me I will in no wise cast out?" Nay, do not so wrong your own soul and the sinner-receiving Saviour. His invitation, His promise is to you, "Come unto me, all ye that labour and are heavy laden, and I will give you rest."

I was thankful to hear you had some alleviation of bodily affliction, and sincerely hope it will prove permanent, if that will be for your good. It must be distressing to suffer acutely in body and soul too. You kindly mention my health. Through mercy it is considerably established, so that I can engage again in the activities of life. Perhaps you know that this was very contrary to my wish. I was very tired of my wilderness-school, and longed for my glory-home, having such bright views thereof as bedimmed earth and all in it. Yes! I, who once lay trembling at the mouth of the pit, and felt that by my own corruptions I was pre-paring for those everlasting burnings, have, by sovereign grace, been taken thence into Beulah's happy land. I have been in the very suburbs of celestial bliss, have felt joys un-utterable, and desired to drop this fettering clay, and to be for ever with my Lord. But He denied my pressing suit, and sent me back to tell His wondrous love to sister sinners. Oh, would that it might reach your heart, and that mercy-drops of precious blood might take your guilt and grief away!

It seems your affliction came upon you contrary to human probability, and when you were on a pinnacle of worldly ease and honour, and perhaps of fleshly pride. So did Ne-buchadnezzar's. He was suddenly brought down from his greatness, lost his human understanding, his mental powers, so that he might well say, "I was as a beast before Thee." Yet I verily believe the Lord had a favour towards him, to do him good in his latter end; for at the end of the days

" he lifted up his eyes to heaven," and spake like one chastened, but not killed, as one judged in himself that he
should not be condemned of the world.   Read his humble
praise and confession,—Dan. iv. 34,—and pick up a crumb
of encouragement, if the great Master will let it fall thus
from His table for you. You know it is not a new or strange
thing He is doing with you ; for He has said, " The loftiness
of man shall be bowed down, and the haughtiness of men
shall be made low ; and the Lord alone shall be exalted in
that day."   It is one thing to read this in words, but quite
another to come under the discipline of it, to find all our
ornaments taken away, and truly discover, instead of our
imagined beauty, the loathsomeness of our corruption ; instead of a girdle keeping all in order, a rent; instead of
well-set hair to please ourselves and others, baldness ; instead
of a stomacher, a girding of sackcloth ; and burning in the
conscience instead of beauty.[1]   Ah, to go through all this
is fearful indeed !   I have known it, you now know it, and
the poor heart fears that such an abased, polluted creature
must only be " a vessel of wrath fitted to destruction."
But this is only the spirit of judgment and the spirit of
burning, praying the daughters of Zion that the branch of
the Lord may be beautiful and glorious, and the fruit of the
earth excellent and comely ; and these very poor creatures
shall be called holy, and found written among the living in
Jerusalem.

You speak of the rising of your heart in independence
against the Lord's dealings to make you dependent.   This
is exactly His way.   Just where we would not have the cross,
it shall be laid on; and where nature is the most sensitive,

[1] Isaiah iii. 17, &c. ; compare Revelation iii. 17, 18.

it shall least be spared. The reason is plain—the deeply-rooted evil needs the caustic or the knife. Your independence might have passed with you for a virtue, had not close dealing with it by a skilful hand brought out its hidden hideousness, and now you stand aghast at the discovery. But remember you do not now begin to be so vile, you always were so in God's sight, but the calm surface hid it from your own eyes. He has broken up the fountain of this great deep, and is discovering your iniquity to turn away your captivity, in which you have willingly been held by the very evil you now deplore. " Lo, all these things worketh God oftentimes with man " to " withdraw man from his purpose, and hide pride from man." He will give you a humble, thankful spirit, affectionately willing to be dependent, if it will glorify Him.

You speak of being thought obstinate in rejecting comfort. The very same thing was said to me, while truly my heart groaned for it, but I had no power either to believe or receive. However, when the day of His power came, I was made willing enough. This day is what *you* are waiting for, and you shall not wait in vain, as the mouth of the Lord hath spoken it—Isaiah xxx. 18 ; Lamentations iii. 25, 26. You speak of some sweet words and promises coming to your mind with comfort, and that afterwards you think it was presumption to take them as yours. This is the enemy trying to snatch the morsel from your hungry soul. He would have you reject everything because you do not get a full deliverance, but I pray you receive without fear those little hints of the Lord's kindness to thee, lest thou grieve His Holy Spirit, who thus helps thee with a little help.

And now I commit you to Him who is able to do for you

exceeding abundantly above all I can ask or think; who will perfect that which concerneth you, and it shall be to the praise of the glory of His grace, wherein He hath made us accepted in the Beloved. May the Holy Ghost witness it in your soul.—With deep interest, believe me, dear Miss M——, though very unworthy, affectionately yours,

RUTH BRYAN.

LX.

Balm in Gilead.

"But I said, How shall I put thee among the children, and give thee a pleasant land, a goodly heritage of the hosts of nations? And I said, Thou shalt call me, My father; and shalt not turn away from me." —JER. iii. 19.

TO MISS M.

NOTTINGHAM, *June* 3, 1850.

MY BELOVED SISTER IN JESUS, These "shalls" and "shall nots" reach even your hard case, for, wayward though you may be, you have not power to get away from them.

Nay, do not start at the appellation, for I must so call you, even though, like Ephraim of old, you should be "unwise," and "stay long in the place of breaking forth of children." Spiritual life in the first quickening by the Holy Ghost is as real and as sure of consummation as it is in the ripest growth thereof, though it is not always as easily discernible. Surely my spirit feels union with yours in the bonds of the Covenant; yea, I feel one with you in the indissoluble ties of love Divine, most truly believing you to

be part of the travail of my precious Redeemer's soul. For
you, with worthless me, He agonised in sweat of blood and
pangs to us unknown, and He shall see of the travail of His
soul and shall be satisfied. All your sins shall not be sufficient to prevent it, and, unworthy though I be, I do look in
your case to be partaker of His joy, and bid you welcome
into the land flowing with milk and honey. For as surely
as you are by the quickening Spirit passing under the rod in
conviction, felt bondage, and heavy groanings which cannot
be uttered, so surely shall you "pass again under the hand
of Him that telleth them," into the sweet bond of the Covenant, which is everlasting love—a bond which cannot be
broken by all the combined powers of earth and hell. Take
courage, then; "faithful is He that calleth thee, who also will
do it." Ah indeed, or it would never be done at all; for
one step you cannot take, one thought you cannot think, one
word you cannot speak to forward your own salvation. Poor
hopeless, helpless one, you just lie entirely at the disposal of
holy sovereignty; and if He save you not by His own power
for His own holy name's sake, perish you must and will.
But He has given commandment to save you, and ere long
He will pluck your feet out of the net which now entangles
your steps, will bring your soul out of prison, and you shall
praise His name who has indeed dealt wondrously with you.

You think my case was not half so desperate as yours, and
yet again and again you depict to the life the vile workings
of my abominably deceitful heart. These workings I would
never mention to glory in my shame, but only "for the lifting of Jesus on high," and for the encouragement of those
poor souls who are groaning in the pit of corruption, and
who feel that by every effort they only sink deeper into the

mire. Too well do I know what you describe when you
speak of yielding to temptation, feelingly crying out against
iniquity, and yet at the same time conscious of, in some sort,
regarding it in my heart. Easily-besetting sins I had, and did
really loathe them, yet I fell into them again and again, partly
in consequence of indulging them. Yet the outward surface
was fair, although I thought none on earth could conceive
what a monster of iniquity I was. The testimony of sin was
at times deeply stamped upon everything I did, said, thought,
or looked, so that I was a burden and terror to myself, and
would most gladly have exchanged with any of the brute
creation to get rid of my polluted but never-dying soul,
which trembled at the remembrance of the holiness of Him
before whom I must appear. I detested hypocrisy, but
feared it, because of being always kept outwardly moral
and nurtured amongst Christian friends and privileges. I
trembled at a name to live, while I was dead, and felt that
I could make none really believe what a sink of iniquity
was working within. This made the feelings and expressions of my more favoured moments seem to me like hypocrisy; for if they were really spiritual, how could I return
to my filthiness, like the "sow that was washed to her wal-
lowing in the mire?" True, I did hate the evil I was the
subject of, and yet I felt it had power over me, and also
that there was something in me which had a secret liking
for it. These things greatly cast me down, and made me
think my spots could not be the spots of God's children.

But how often since my deliverance have I seen cause to
bless the Lord that I learnt war in my spiritual youth,—
that He brought me into His temple by the north gate,—that
I felt so keenly the cutting blasts of a long dreary winter,

before basking in the beams of the blessed Sun of righteousness,—that the fountains of the great deep of iniquity in my
heart were broken up, and the flood of evil burst upon me,
before I was brought so blissfully into the banqueting-house,
and reclined under the banner of love. All the Lord's ways
are right ways ; but I do now esteem it a favour to have
been thus dealt with, because I observe those who have
made more slight discoveries of their own corruption before
their pardon is sealed, do appear often so astounded to find
the enemy still in the land, and are ready to die with fear
when the trumpet sounds them from the banquet to the
battle.   But, O thoroughly vile creatures, such as I have
felt myself to be, do know that the moment the sun goes
down the beasts of the forest will again creep forth, that the
richest feast is only just to strengthen for more conflict or
tribulation, and that there can be no long cessation of arms
while we carry about this body of death.   It may be, my
beloved, you cannot yet take any comfort from these
thoughts, because you are so severely feeling the painfulness
of the discipline, but the end of a thing is better than the
beginning.   They " that sow in tears shall reap in joy."
They who feel the heaviest load will prize deliverance most ;
they who are most beaten off from confidence in themselves
will be the least moved as they discover their own weakness ; and they who have the sentence of death most deeply
inscribed in their hearts will be most constrained to live
out of themselves, and trust wholly in another.

May the Lord cheer your heart, for in the midst of all
your casting down He is drawing near you, and giving you
cause to sing of mercy as well as judgment.   What are all
those little bedewings upon your spirit, and beamings of

light through the gloom, but drops of mercy betokening a
shower of blessings to come. Oh, seek to give the Lord the
glory due unto His name! give not place to the devil, who
would have you "lie against your right," and say your
wound is incurable. There is balm in Gilead that can heal
it, a Physician there that can reach it; He can cure your
body, He can bless your soul; and though the lion hath
roared so frightfully, yet out of this eater He can bring meat,
and out of this strong one sweetness. You are just fitting
for a marvellous display of invincible power and omnipotent
grace.

Shall Satan have you? No! you are none of his, though
so long disguised in black livery. The prey shall be taken
from the mighty, and the lawful captive delivered, not for
price or reward on your part. You shall come forth free
by a royal grant, without any demand made upon you; but
mind it is because another has paid the full cost of your
release. And on whom then will your admiring eyes be
fastened? Oh, on Him who not merely said He would
give, but really has given His own life for your ransom!
Eternal praises to this dear Deliverer who was anointed "to
bind up the broken-hearted, to proclaim liberty to the captives, and the opening of the prison to them that are bound;"
yea, bound in affliction and irons, like you and me, the iron
bonds of our nature's corruption and evil, and the iron grasp
of the law revealing iniquity, and saying, "Pay me that thou
owest." Oh, this does bring down the heart, indeed, with
labour and sorrow! we fall down, and there seems none to
help; then we cry unto the Lord in our trouble, and He
bringeth us out of our distresses. (Read the 107th Psalm,
which has been precious to me.) He has brought me out,

though encompassed with every improbability. I am free to praise Him and to encourage you, and I would have you know that His prisoners are as safe as His freed ones. He is judging and chastening you now, that you should not be condemned with the world.

As for writing to me "to give you up as a hypocrite," I should just have answered, "How shall I give thee up, Ephraim?" "My bowels are troubled for [thee;]" and if I should speak or think against thee, I should "earnestly remember [thee] still." I can only say of our correspondence,

> "God moves in a mysterious way
> His wonders to perform."

Your letters touch a most sensitive chord in my heart, and I weep tears of sympathy with you, and wondering thankfulness, that the Lord should in the least refresh you by my unworthy means. It is condescension indeed! I know not that any one ever so fully described my former self and feelings. You say you write selfishly; so you must and will while the case of your soul is, to your apprehension, pending in uncertainty : it is the sphere where self is all-important and all-absorbing; and it will often tend to produce an unkind fretfulness towards all around, which you deplore, while feeling and manifesting it. But you do not say enough about self. Do tell me about your health. I long to know of any improvement, and how far you are an invalid. The Lord blend your will into His ! Your letters are very precious to me, but never write to increase your suffering in mind or body. It is more pleasure and privilege to me to write to you than I can describe, and the freedom of spirit therein is wonderful as a stranger in the flesh, but not strangers now. I feel to know and love you, though I often think you would never love me if you knew me in person; it is all for Jesus' sake, and that is most sweet.

I am quite ashamed to write again so quickly to you, but the Lord our God seemed to bring the portion, and though I have had many misgivings, I felt such a flow of soul, that I feared to grieve or quench the Spirit if I withheld it.

And now, my dear Miss M——, I commend you to that tender Shepherd, who knows all your case and will meet it; and, with much love and sympathy, I am your truly affectionate   RUTH.

LXI.

A harassed soul pointed to the Blood.

TO MISS M.

HIGH PAVEMENT, *Dec.* 2, 1850.

VERY DEAR MISS M——, I do rejoice that He who comforteth those who are cast down has comforted you by the coming of His dear servant. The savour of his visit, I trust, still remains upon your spirit. Jesus "must needs go through Samaria" to meet with a great sinner, and astonish her by the discovery that "He knew all things that ever [she] did." How would she listen and wonder as He turned the black heart inside out, and set her secret and her open sins in "the light of His countenance;" but this was the prelude to His giving her the "living water." Many a "needs be" has there been since then, that He should go through certain places to meet with certain sinners, either to wound or heal. Methinks Mr D—— must needs go through D—— to meet with my poor sorrowful friend, and refresh her weary soul by the way, by giving her a cup of cold water in the name of the Lord. It seems at that time that all the water was spent in your vessel, and you felt ready to die with thirst in the place where you were. May you not then, with one of old, call the name of Him who thus spake unto you, " Thou God seest me ! " If these helps do not bring you out of bondage they revive you in it, and strengthen you still to wait and to hope, however appearances may seem against you.

From the tenor of your two notes last received, I fear you have some return of your illness; will you tell me more particulars when you write again ? My heart sympathises with you affectionately; but at the same time, if this painful dispensation be a net the Lord has cast upon you, to draw you out of the world into His living family circle, can I wish it otherwise ? Can you ? If now you might have restored health, associations, and all worldly ease and delight, without Jesus, would you accept them on such terms ? If with an interest in Jesus you must have bodily suffering, outward disappointment, frustrated hopes, and broken purposes, would you forego Him to get rid of them ? I trow not ! Satan provokes you sore to make you fret. He gets you to look *at* this undesired affliction, instead of waiting for the end of the Lord *in* it, and then you find it " hard to kick against the pricks." You smart under sin and under trial, and all these things seem against you; but the Lord is overruling all to give you an expected end of peace, and not of evil. He is by these means bringing down your proud heart with labour and sorrow, but He will deliver you from your destructions. "O Israel, thou hast destroyed thyself, but in me is thine help."

May the Lord give you true resignation of spirit, and a submissive will, which would greatly lessen the weight of your burden; and may He please to rebuke Satan, who strengthens the unbelief of your heart, resists you at the throne of grace, and accuses you of presumption for every movement of faith towards the promise or the pardon. This I learn from some remarks in your note; for, after some little taking hold and encouragement, you directly start back affrighted as if you had laid your hand upon a portion that did not belong to you, and the Lord would certainly come forth against you for it. This is the false insinuation of unbelief and Satan to keep your soul from peace. Beware you do not cherish it, because in so doing you dishonour Him who is the Author and Finisher of faith. He gives the " heirs of promise " faith to lay hold of the promise, and He is never more honoured than when they plead it against apparent rebukes, against the threats and taunts of the enemy, and against their felt discouragement and unworthiness. This is confidence in royal clemency, through royal blood ; and thus the Majesty of heaven is honoured by vile sinners on earth, for this is the work of His own Spirit in them.

Wherefore, my beloved, " grieve not the Spirit," "resist the devil, and he will flee from you." It is he who tries to choke prayer, hinder faith, and feed unbelief. Your only successful resistance is by the " blood of the Lamb ; " against that, Satan cannot stand, for it cleanses from all sin. He can bring plenty of accusations against us, and just ones ; but when faith can venture them on blood divine, each fiery

M

dart is quenched by that blood; and the self-condemned, hell-deserving sinner is " more than conqueror through Him that loved us." No wonder, then, that subtle foe strives so hard against the first buddings of faith, and will, if possible, nip the least putting forth thereof, to affright the poor soul from the only Stronghold when he cannot reach it. He shall not prevail ultimately; he shall not rob Emmanuel of one blood-bought jewel, not even of my dear hunted, harassed, desponding friend, for whom, I believe, He has paid the full price of ransom. He has said to law and justice long ago, " If [she] hath wronged thee, or oweth thee ought, put that on mine account; I have written it with mine own hand, I will repay it." [1] Having bought you, and paid for you, He will not lose you. And yet, though Satan shall not rob God of His right to you, he may rob your soul of present comfort; and by giving place to him, you will suffer loss experimentally. Therefore write I thus, that by the Divine blessing your weak hands which hang down may be lifted up, your feeble knees strengthened, and you, though so lame, may not be turned out of the way of faith; but rather have the sore of unbelief healed, and be enabled to say, " Though He slay me, yet will I trust in Him." "What time I am afraid, I will trust in Thee." May you be encouraged to look towards Jesus, if you cannot look at Him, —to hope in His salvation, if at present you cannot enjoy it, or triumph in it; and though your sins rise mountains high, presenting a new mountain every day, seek faith, more faith, in that precious blood, which, as a mighty ocean, will overtop them all. I humbly pray my precious Emmanuel to shew Himself to you through the lattice, to let you *see*

[1] Philem. 18, 19.

that you are graven on the palms of His hands; yea, that as the great High Priest He bears you on His heart, and on His shoulders, in the holiest place, not made with hands.

And now I commend you unto Him who will "perfect that which concerneth you," for He will have a desire unto the work of His own hands. I cease not to pray for you, and am looking out for the loosing of the prisoner. Adieu, my dear Miss M——.—With affectionate love, believe me, yours very sincerely, RUTH.

LXII.

Submission to the Lord's will under bereavement.

LEVIT. x. 3.
" And Aaron held his peace."

TO MISS M.

NOTTINGHAM, *Dec.* 31, 1850.

MY BELOVED FRIEND, It is with much hesitation and considerable delicacy of feeling that I now address you, fearing to add to the grief of an already wounded heart. But yet I know not how to be silent towards you, now that your troubled spirit is the subject of new sorrow from the loss of one much beloved. I know that sometimes anguish is too deep to bear the touch of human sympathy, and that there are cases which only He can reach who gave to the heart its sensibilities, and who can quell its most violent throbbings, or speak peace to its most agitated and distracted emotions.

This I once very sensibly experienced under a most painful bereavement. It was the death of a half-brother whom I loved, and that death occasioned or accelerated, it was feared, by his own imprudence. My feelings were harrowed because of the state of my poor brother's soul, and my heart was agonised with self-accusation for not being sufficiently faithful to him, though I had used my poor powers in the way of warning. But now he was gone without hope, I felt all was distraction; and nothing that was said could remove or soothe my anguish, till, with power never to be forgotten, these words were sounded in my soul, "Shall not the Judge of all the earth do right?" With them came a great calm and a solemn submission to the Divine sovereignty. It was something like Aaron's silence, when his two sons had been cut off by immediate judgment from the Lord. There seemed no alleviation to his natural feelings, but everything to aggravate grief; yet grace prevailed above nature, and, absorbed in the Divine will, his soul seemed to anchor on the Rock while wave and billow went over him. The Lord's wonders are seen in the deep, and He can do as great miracles by supporting under, as by preserving from, peculiar trials.

Excuse me for speaking thus. These things may be very inapplicable to your sorrow; but of whatever nature be the circumstances of our trial, nothing is so truly quieting as being enabled to bow to our Father's will, and take the cup immediately from His hand. No events take Him by surprise. "Shall there be evil in a city, and the Lord hath not done it?" When useful, amiable, and valued lives are unexpectedly cut off we marvel; but though deep the mysteries of Jehovah's permissive will, far too deep for us to fathom, yet these things do not happen by chance. We see this in the case of Job, whose children were all cut off by Satan's agency, but not without Divine permission. He, recognising as in a Father's hand the sword which had slain his earthly comforts, said, "The Lord gave, and the Lord hath taken away; blessed be the name of the Lord." While most puzzled by the Lord's providential movements, and writhing under the smart of bereavement, it is most soothing and blessed to be enabled by the Spirit to feel, "Father, Thy will be done." "Father, glorify Thy name." Oh that our precious Jesus may draw near and bind up your bleeding heart, yea, all your hearts; and may He administer His strong consolations and cordials, as He is wont to do in times of special need!

To yourself, my loved friend, may He be very gracious, giving you even this "valley of Achor for a door of hope." May He keep Satan from gaining advantage, and you from giving place to him. He will provoke to fretfulness, but may the Lord rebuke him, and give you to feel and say, "I know, O Lord, that thy judgments are right, and that thou in faithfulness hast afflicted me."[1] Very sweet is Heb. xii. 5-9. Finally, may the Lord sanctify this stroke, and "honey" yet "be found in the end of the rod;" and though the grape seem very, very sour, yet may there be "a blessing in it."

I would commit you to Him who can make all grace to abound towards you in support, comfort, and deliverance.

Kindly excuse this, and believe me, with tenderest sympathy, yours very affectionately,

R. BRYAN.

---

[1] Ps. cxix. 75.

LXIII.

The immutability of God's purposes in grace.

TO MISS M.

High Pavement, *Feb.* 21, 1851.

MY DEAR AFFLICTED FRIEND, I am sorry to hear that you are too ill to write. The Lord has indeed spread His net over you, and laid affliction upon your loins. He has added grief to your sorrow, and broken you with breach upon breach, till you feel but as a wreck, and as one "ready to perish." But "they shall come which were ready to perish." However lame, however lost, they "shall come;" however vile and base, however far off by wicked works, and further still by unbelief, they "shall come." Nothing shall hinder the accomplishment of the determinate counsel and foreknowledge of God; for "whom He did foreknow, He also did predestinate;" and "whom He did predestinate, them He also called; and whom He called, them He also justified; and whom He justified, them He also glorified." It is all done in God's account, and nothing in earth or hell can undo it. What has been done above on the sinner's account, shall be done below in the sinner's experience. Effectual calling, irresistible power, omnipotent grace, combine to accomplish the "shall come." They "shall come" to Mount Sinai, and amidst the thunders of the righteous law learn their own unrighteousness, by nature and practice. They "shall come" to judgment here, be made to plead guilty, feel condemned in heart and conscience; and wait with fear and trembling, expecting execution, till the great trumpet is blown. The jubilee sound tells of release; it chiefly affects those in debt, distress, and difficulties. Then, to their own astonishment, those prisoners which were ready to perish "shall come" out of a strait into a large place—from just condemnation to free pardon for all offences, past, present, and to come. They "shall come" to be washed in the fountain of blood; they "shall come" from wearing sackcloth and ashes, to be covered with the robe of righteousness, and clothed with the garments of salvation; they "shall come" from the spirit of heaviness to have the garment of praise, the ring of love, the crown of loving-kindness and tender mercy; they "shall come" from the mount of terrors to the mount of peace, and to all the blessings and blessed company there, of which you may read in Heb. xii. 22-24. They "shall come" thither by faith, while dwellers in mortality; and, moreover, when their wilderness days are ended, they "shall come" to Mount Zion above; and the Shepherd will rejoice over the sheep which was lost; and the sheep will tell, to the Shepherd's praise, how it wandered as far as it could, how it destroyed itself, how it was "ready to perish," how it was so lost and so helpless, that when it desired to return it could not; and then how the Shepherd found it, and through floods of guilt, mountains of fears, and hosts of foes, had brought it safe home to glory. Oh, then will not they all again sing Hallelujah! worthy is the Lamb which was slain! And the much sinning and much forgiven one will strive to be loudest in the song.

"Ah," say you, "what has this to do with me? I am more fit for the depths of hell than the heights of heaven!" Why, it *has* to do with you, my beloved; it is strong consolation that your vile sin, stubborn will, proud spirit, desperate unbelief, and *cruel*, powerful foe shall not prevail against God. His "*shall come*" will be stronger than all these; and I do solidly believe this "*shall come*" includes *you*, and that you "*shall come*," and are coming, as it is written, "They shall come with weeping, and with supplications will I lead them." Are you not weeping over your sins? Are you not supplicating pardon for them, and power against them? And do you not often feel as if none were like you, none could know how bad you are, and none help you but the crucified Saviour? And do you not mourn for a sight of Him crucified for you? It is said, "They shall look upon Him whom they have pierced, and shall mourn for Him." Surely this "*shall come*" will bring you to that sacred place, even the cross, where, gazing by faith upon the wondrous Sufferer, your burden will fall off into His sepulchre, never to appear before God again, for "their sins and their iniquities will I remember no more." Who is a pardoning God like unto Thee? "A just God, and a Saviour." Your hard case, my beloved friend, does not go beyond His "uttermost," to which He is able to save. What you are, cannot help your salvation; what you are, shall not hinder it; all is of free grace from first to last. Help is laid upon One that is mighty, whose own arm brought salvation, who trod the wine-press alone, and of the people there were none with Him. He finished the transgression, made an end of sin, and brought in everlasting righteousness. He is the end of the law for righteousness to every one that believeth.

Wander no longer, then, upon the dark mountains of your own doings, but "lift up [your] eyes unto the hills [of salvation,] from whence cometh [your] help. [Your] help cometh from the Lord, which made heaven and earth," and who says, " Come now, and let us reason together : Though your sins be as scarlet, they shall be white as snow ; though they be red like crimson, they shall be as wool." " I will pardon them whom I reserve." Surely you are a reserved one, and a preserved one too, that you may be a pardoned one. The inbeing of sin will be felt, and the plague of sin mourned, but the curse and condemnation are for ever removed from them whom He reserves; for " the iniquity of Israel shall be sought for, and there shall be none ; and the sins of Judah, and they shall not be found ; " for " who shall lay anything to the charge of God's elect ? It is God that justifieth; who is he that condemneth ? It is Christ that died, yea rather, that is risen again, who is even at the right hand of God, who also maketh intercession for us ;" so that " if any man sin, we have an Advocate with the Father, Jesus Christ the righteous : and He is the propitiation for our sins."

Oh that it would please the Holy Spirit to pour this spiced wine, this strong consolation into your trembling soul; that out of weakness you may be made strong, may wax valiant in the fight, and by faith turn to flight those armies of the aliens, which so proudly threaten you with destruction ! " Now I commend you to God, and to the word of His grace, which is able to build you up, and to give you an inheritance among all them which are sanctified ; " and He " is able to keep you from falling, and to present you faultless before the presence of His glory with exceeding joy." To Him be glory, both now and ever, Amen. I trust you have been restored to some degree of calmness concerning your heavy loss. The Lord's " judgments are a great deep ; " we must not attempt to fathom them. " His ways are past finding out ; " we must not expect to trace them. Quiet submission becomes sinful worms. The Lord give it you, and all your trials will be much lightened. "The cup which my Father hath given me, shall I not drink it ?"

The Lord "guide you by His counsel, and afterwards receive you to glory."—So desires, with kindest love and sympathy, your affectionate friend, RUTH.

LXIV.

Mercy for the chief of sinners.

TO MISS M.

HIGH PAVEMENT, *April* 23, 1854.

MY DEAR MISS M——, Grace be with you, my beloved, and mercy and peace from God our Father, and our Lord Jesus Christ. I write again to you as a companion in wilderness-tribulation, to inquire how you are getting on in your travels from the City of Destruction towards the Mount Zion above. Are you still compassing the mount which burneth with blackness and darkness ; from whence issues a fiery law which makes the convinced sinner tremble, and cry out, " I am vile ?" For " by the law is the knowledge of sin." Have you still the burden on your back ? and are your eyes still holden, so that you cannot see Jesus ; but only see mountains of guilt rising darkly before you ? Are your transgressions still increasing and accumulating ? and the arrows of the Almighty still sticking fast in you ? and does " hope deferred " often make the poor heart sick ? Ah then, surely, thou art the tossed with tempest, and not comforted ; whose stones shall be laid with fair colours, and thy foundations with sapphires;[1] for blessed are they whom the Lord chasteneth, and teacheth them out of His law. He will in due time have mercy upon these His desolate, and will comfort His afflicted; He will not always chide, neither will He keep His anger for ever; but will receive graciously, love freely, and heal through the stripes of His dear Son.[2] "He who has begun the good work in you," by the north wind of conviction, will perform it unto the day of Jesus Christ, when the south wind of His love shall blow softly, and you be filled with joy and peace in believing. Surely He will bring you on from the terrible Mount of Condemnation "to the place where is a cross;" and when looking up, by faith, you see "One hanging crucified for you," then will your soul dissolve in love; and you will feelingly understand how the holy Jehovah can be just and yet justify ungodly you; having had full satisfaction for all your sins in the person of His Son.

Why, my dear friend, the Prince of Life, the Lord of glory did not come from heaven to save little sinners, but chief sinners, lost sinners, helpless sinners, the vilest of sinners, such sinners as poor Ruth and her trembling friend. He did not come to cleanse from only moderate guilt, but sins red as scarlet and crimson; yea, sins black as hell does His blood take away. Oh, dishonour Him not by saying you are too bad, or your case too hard? there are now before the throne, and on the way to it, those as bad, as hard, as unlikely as ever you can be. What can resist Omnipotence? He who died for sinners has an omnipotent arm to pluck them from the burning, and bring them up from the pit, however low they may be sunk in the mire. This I have

[1] Isa. liv. 11.   [2] 1 Pet. ii. 24.

proved many a time. May the Holy Spirit testify of Jesus in your soul, and may that faith spring up which is the gift of God, so that with another unbelieving one you may cry out, "My Lord and my God." Is anything too hard for the Lord? Nay, verily, He is able of Gentile sinners, as hard as stones, to raise up children to Abraham; the more unlikely the material, the greater glory to His name in forming thereof a vessel meet for His use. Oh that your heart may be encouraged, and that you may see what honour He will have in forgiving and saving you and me, who owe Him, not fifty, or five hundred pence, but ten thousand talents! Oh, think what joy is in heaven over such sinners as we are, when our repentings are kindled by Him who is exalted to give repentance unto His Israel, and remission of sins; and think, when we reach the heavenly shores, how those bright angels who never sinned, will adore Him, while we recount to them the mighty sum He cancelled for us. Surely, with new ardour, they will cry, "Worthy is the Lamb;" and we respond, "For He hath redeemed us unto God by His blood."

Come, my friend, take courage; hate sin and loathe it as much as you will, but never magnify it above the efficacy and merits of the death and blood of Jesus. Forget not how great will be his glory in our salvation, in bringing those who were so very far off "nigh by the blood" of His cross. It may be your outward path is rough, and you are still the subject of thorny trials. Well, be not cast down on this account, for we know that it is through much tribulation we must enter the kingdom. This is not the pilgrim's rest, it is the place of his passage through which he must journey to a better country; but Divine love will make all things work together for good. The loftiness of man must be bowed down, and the haughtiness of man made low, that the Lord alone may be exalted. Seek a resigned, submissive will; it is the Lord's own gift, and a great lightening of the outward cross. Murmuring thoughts ill become worms who deserve the lowest hell; everything on this side hell is more than we deserve. The Lord grant that mercies may melt us as well as meet us. Oh, for a grateful spirit ! I long to dissolve in thankfulness for the Lord's great benefits to such an *unworthy* creature ; and I wish you, my dear friend, the same blessing. Your afflictions are heavy, but you must sing of mercy as well as judgment, and may your experience be as Ps. cxix. 50, 67.

Fare thee well. To Israel's Shepherd I do not fail to commend you; though He needs not my poor reminding, for Himself loveth you ; delays are not denials.—With sympathetic love, affectionately I remain your unworthy friend,

RUTH.

LXV.

Submission to the ways of God.

TO MISS M.

HIGH PAVEMENT, *June* 12, 1851.

MY BELOVED AFFLICTED ONE, There will be no true peace in thy bosom till thou art reconciled in the submission of faith to the Lord's righteous and providential dealings.[1] "It is hard for thee to kick against the pricks," as thy wounded soul and bleeding heart evince. Oh, judge not Him who is infinite in wisdom, all His ways are judgment, a God of truth and without iniquity; just and right is He. It is pre-

[1] 1 Samuel iii. 18 ; Job ii. 10.

sumption in vain man so to do.　Seek reconciliation to His will and His way; and though He blight thy choicest flower and wither thy most cherished gourd, say, say, my beloved, dost thou well to be angry?　Does it alter anything?　Does it alleviate anything?　Nay, verily, but it brings death in thy feelings and darkness in thy soul, and if there were a beam of hope arising it is thus beclouded again.　The enemy knows this, and therefore he provokes thee to murmur against the God of thy mercies.　" The Lord rebuke thee, O Satan; even the Lord that hath chosen Jerusalem rebuke thee: is not this a brand plucked out of the fire?"

Oh, my dear friend, "give not place to the devil!" "Whom resist steadfast in the faith." "Resist the devil, and he will flee from you:" "taking the shield of faith, wherewith ye shall be able to quench all the fiery darts of the wicked" one.　He works upon your weak frame, enfeebled mind, and painful circumstances; and from or by these leads you to draw wrong conclusions and unjust inferences, and thus tighten the cords of your bondage.　But oh, fly for refuge to the hope set before you in the gospel; fly to the shadow of the Cross, the shelter of the Rock!　There is pardon for the guiltiest, cleansing for the filthiest, safety for the weakest, and conquest for the most faint-hearted.　"Not by might, nor by power, but by my Spirit, saith the Lord of hosts."　" For when I am weak, then am I strong," said a captain in Emmanuel's army, who, like you, wanted the thorn to be taken out of the flesh; but his King knew better, the proud flesh needed the pricking thorn, and the buffeted soldier was brought to say, " Most gladly therefore will I rather glory in mine infirmities, that the power of Christ may rest upon me."　See what the grace of God can do, and presume not to think your case is beyond its power, while the same witness declares, " Where sin abounded, grace did much more abound." It abounds "to pardon crimson sins," to break the rebellious will, to stop the murmuring tongue, and take the guilt away ; and He who has all fulness of grace received gifts for the rebellious also, that the Lord God might dwell amongst them.

My heart sympathises with you in your afflictive bereavement. There is a veil of mystery thrown over some of the Lord's proceedings, and over the destinies of some we love. If we attempt to lift the veil, we add grief to our sorrow, and get sharp rebukes ; for " secret things belong unto the Lord our God," and "He giveth not account of any of His matters." Seek for absorption in His will. He seeth not as man seeth, but always judgeth righteous judgment. When the enemy cometh into your soul like a flood, with temptations and insinuations, may the Spirit of God lift up a standard against him. And I must again repeat that striking word, " Give not place to the devil." Parley not, listen not ; for, O my beloved, he is insulting your best Friend, your pardoning, long-suffering God, who has borne with your manners in the wilderness, and who still forbears ; to whom still belong forgiveness, though you have so rebelled against Him. True, He has, in the exercise of His royal prerogative of sovereignty, permitted that which confounds your reason and pierces your heart, but presume not to think Him " cruel." Wait the light of eternity, when you will see clearly that He has dealt unjustly with none. And surely, my dear one, He has not been cruel to you, for you are in the land of hope, and your trembling lips can yet cry, " God be merciful to me a sinner." Oh, may mercy dissolve that wounded heart into thankfulness and love! Truly, my soul is grieved for you, well knowing the dark, cold region you are cheerlessly traversing. Oh that the good Shepherd would take you to "the sunny side of the hill," that in His light you might look more at your mercies and less at your miseries!

How should I rejoice to know that you were feeling it—

> "Sweet to lie passive in His arms,
> And know no will but *His.*"

Your natural hopes and prospects are a wreck; but how short would have been your enjoyment, if they had had the brightest accomplishment! Our life is but a vapour, and all that concerns it is shadowy and fleeting; but the brightness might have beguiled you, the shadow deceived you; and your heart have centred its delights in creature good, instead of being set "on things above." Then cease regrets, my beloved, for that which is not. Remember Lot's wife; she looked back, and went forward no more. Oh, may a gracious God, by the power of His Spirit, say to your distracting reminiscences and forebodings, "Peace, be still," that there may be a great calm, and your soul be "quieted as a weaned child." You have long been as a weaning one —fractious and fretful. Forgive me; I do not speak unkindly, my heart is pained for you; but I see where you suffer loss, and your cruel foe is gaining great advantage, and love makes me speak. I myself am of a thoughtful, anxious mind, and the Lord has rebuked me sharply, and made me feel what a puny being I am. I cannot make one hair white or black, or by one corroding care avert what I most dread, or insure what I most desire. Why then waste time and energies in these fruitless and weakening anxieties which alter nothing? Moreover, my Divine Teacher shews me the blessedness of committing all to Him,[1] and being still; and then He often does wondrously, while we look wondering on. I am very slow to learn, and slower to practise, but I see the privilege of the lesson, and have felt a little of it in sharp trial, and I want you also to have the benefit of the instruction; and may the Lord bless you, and give you understanding in all things.

I have been staying at Great Malvern, in Worcestershire. I wonder if you know it? It is a beautiful place, very romantic; the air peculiarly pure and renovating; the water possessing excellent qualities, and flowing from many springs; the hills very majestic, and the vales as lovely: all fresh and fertile, in the beauties of spring; and the sweet love of Jesus enlivening the whole. Oh for deep-felt gratitude for preservation in travelling, the privilege of beholding the beautiful creation, and many other mercies!

> " I bless His name for meaner things,
> But they are not my God."

And now, farewell. May the Holy Spirit work in your heart the work of faith with power!—To know which, would much rejoice your very affectionate

RUTH.

[1] Ps. xxxvii. 5.

LXVI.

Faith the gift of God.

TO MISS M.

HIGH PAVEMENT, *Jan.* 12, 1852.

MY BELOVED FRIEND, Permit me to greet you affectionately this new year in the name of our glorious Emmanuel,
of whom it was truly said, "This man receiveth sinners,
and eateth with them." I know you feel yourself the chief
of sinners; be encouraged then, for He is Jesus, "the same
yesterday, to-day, and for ever." Sinners He still receives
graciously, loves freely, pardons fully, and justifies from all
things past, present, or to come. Oh! that this might be the
year of meeting between your soul and your Surety; then
would you find the glad release from all those heavy debts
which you feel to be hourly increasing. "The great trumpet
shall be blown, and they shall come which were ready to
perish." You know when the jubilee blast was sounded
every Israelite was free. They might not only have wasted
their inheritance, but have sold even themselves, yet it mat-
tered not, in either case they became free in the glorious year
of release. Mortgaged lands, burdensome debts, and toilsome servitude, all came to an end on that happy morn. The
spiritual Israel have their jubilee too—the general one,
when the Archangel's trumpet shall awake their sleeping
dust, and the purchased possession shall return in glory to
Him who redeemed it with blood; and the inward personal
one, when each soul hears for itself, " Fear not, for I have

redeemed thee : I have called thee by thy name, thou art mine." Ah ! then the mountains of guilt are cast into the depths of the sea—that red sea of blood, whose waves overtop them all. Then the mighty debt is known to be cancelled, so that the poor debtor can sing of "sovereign grace o'er sin abounding," for "where sin abounded, grace did much more abound." Who knows but this very year may be the one of jubilee in your experience, my beloved ? There is a set time to favour Zion individually as well as Zion collectively, and when the time of the promise arrives, nothing shall prevent its accomplishment. Sin, Satan, unbelief, shall all give way ; those gates of brass shall open, the fetters fall off, and the imprisoned soul come forth to the light of day, scarcely believing for joy and wondering.

The Lord lift up your head, and may your manifested redemption draw nigh, which all your sense of poverty and misery will make doubly welcome. My poor namesake had lost all, and was in great destitution ; but she found a near kinsman who owned the relationship, and was willing to redeem, though first she had somewhat boldly to make her suit for his kindness. "Spread thy skirt over thine handmaid, for thou art a near kinsman." This looks like the plea of faith and necessity ; when the poor soul feels its poverty and nakedness, and entreats the heavenly Boaz to cover it with His skirt—that justifying righteousness which alone can hide its shame. He is never offended with such apparent presuming ; and never rejects such a forsaken and desolate one. As surely as Boaz did redeem and marry the Moabitish damsel, so surely Jesus has redeemed and will acknowledge every coming sinner.[1] "Ah !" say you, "this

[1] John vi. 37.

matter of faith is one thing which troubles me; the blessings
of salvation are enjoyed by faith, but I cannot get at it.   I
seem shut up in unbelief, and I cannot come forth."

> " Oh ! could I but believe,
>   Then all would easy be !
>   I would, but cannot ; Lord, thou know'st
>   My help must come from Thee."

Well, my loved friend, I feel most incompetent to speak to
you upon the important but dear subject of precious faith;
and when I read your question upon Eph. i. 13, a sense of
inability to answer almost deterred me from writing at all.
But, however, I can speak from experience, that I once felt
exactly as I have described; seeing the importance of faith,
and that without it I could not be saved, and yet finding
it impossible to believe to the saving of my soul, so that
I said with deep feeling, " I thought that I could as soon
make a world as believe."   But, say you, "Is it thus still?"
Nay, truly.   I was then shut up, but not unto despair; it
was unto the faith which has since been revealed.   Christ as
the object of faith was yet to be revealed in His glorious
person, finished work, and amazing love; and power put
into the soul to receive, take hold of, and enjoy Him and His
benefits as its personal portion.   Living faith is, indeed, as
you say, something more than a " declaration of belief," or
mere " assent to the truth of the written Word," or belief in
the divinity of the Saviour.   All this I had many times
when painfully feeling I had not the faith which enters into
rest,[1] and is accompanied with joy and peace,[2] or I had it
not so in exercise as to be followed by those blessed effects :
for I humbly conceive all the graces of the Spirit (of which

---

[1] Heb. iv. 10, 11.   [2] Rom. xv. 13.

faith is one) are communicated in regeneration; but, like
the powers of an infant, they must have growth and development before they come to strong exercise. Moreover, when
living faith is implanted it must have an object; and the
effects in the soul will be correspondent to that object.
Oftentimes, at the first, faith has to do with the law, justice,
and holiness of Jehovah, and His threatenings against sin.
These it may fully believe with personal application; and as
the soul falls down condemned before Him, not only in the
judgment, but also in feeling, believing its own vileness, and
that He will be righteous in casting it out of His sight, faith
justifies the Lord, and ascribes righteousness to its Maker,
while the soul is filled with compunction, and abhors itself
in dust and ashes. Here is repentance towards God, and
here is faith, but not that faith in Jesus which has the sealing of the Spirit. No living soul is, however, left here.
Faith is caused to grow, in hearing[1]—in hearing that there
is a way of escape, that God can still be just, and yet justify
the ungodly who believe in Jesus. Faith, receiving this
report of the great salvation through a great Saviour, and of
the exact suitability thereof to the soul's case, there is a
growing confidence that if He will He can pardon the sin,
heal the leper, loose the prisoner, and forgive the arrested
debtor who has "nothing to pay." Now the soul begins to
feel a love and tenderness towards this Friend of sinners,
and says, "Oh, that He were my friend! Oh, that He
would save and speak comfortably to me! Oh, that I
could know He loves me! This would be heaven below!
There is now full faith in His ability and His suitability;
but there is not the spirit of adoption, or the sealing of the

[1] Rom. x. 17.

Spirit. There is not the venture of faith, casting the whole weight of soul and sins upon Him or believing in Him for the personal benefit of His blood and righteousness, His life, death, and resurrection, or, as Hart so expressively calls it in his 79th hymn, "Believing into Him." This is the "work of faith with power;" and they who thus believe are manifestly saved[1]—do know that they have eternal life, and by the renewings of the Holy Ghost are kept believing, for they live by the faith of the Son of God. The justified shall live by faith, and they are sealed by the spirit of promise unto the day of redemption; which redemption plainly refers to the resurrection of the body, see also Rom. viii. 23. By this sealing they have manifestly to their own consciences God's mark upon them as His property, and thereby they are assured of a glorious resurrection to life eternal. Though now they carry this body as a body of sin and death, and often groan under its burden, and though soon it shall be laid in the grave as a body of corruption, yet it is a " purchased possession." They are sealed unto the day of redemption. God hath wrought them for the self-same thing.[2] The Spirit witnesses to it with or in their spirits, and they joyfully look for their Redeemer, who is mighty, and "who shall change their *vile* body, that it may be fashioned like unto His glorious body, according to the working whereby He is able even to subdue all things unto Himself." Truly, this sealed state is an immense privilege, and a free one—the gift of Heaven—the work of God—a royal grant of grace and love, as all will most joyfully acknowledge who do truly possess it. True, the Spirit seals the soul[3] after believing,[4]

[1] 1 John v. 13.
[2] 2 Cor. v. 4, 5.
[3] Eph. i. 13.
[4] Gal. iii. 14.

but not *for* it. By the appointment of Heaven the seal is annexed to the faith, but in nowise conditionally, for both are a free gift—both the work of God. Faith honours God by its seal, and God honours faith by His. John iii. 33; 2 Cor. i. 22.

Let this make the poor heart cry more importunately, " Lord, increase my faith," for He who is its Author is its Finisher, and He will have respect to the work of His own hands. It is also true that the Spirit [1] witnesseth to the soul's adoption in believing, and thus we are manifestly children of God by faith in Christ Jesus.[2] This is not because faith is a creature work, and the witnessing of the Spirit a rewarding the creature for that work; but is because it is the pleasure of our heavenly Father that His children, while in the body, shall walk in the way of faith, not by sight and sense. He is much honoured in every believing soul who is brought by His Spirit, not only to felt need, but felt nothingness, and enabled to glory in His Son as the " Lord our righteousness;" and therefore He has in the written Word very abundantly set forth the spiritual blessings which are experimentally enjoyed [3] in this way of faith,[4] and in no other way, that His people may be the more encouraged to seek for this good old path, and inquire for it. Also, He has given abundance of "wills" and " shalls " to insure their finding it, and all are most needful, for it is a way most contrary to our fallen nature and legal minds. Everything that is in us by nature opposes it; and, when quickened by the Spirit, how do unbelief, self, and Satan, strive to hold us back. We might say, in the words

[1] 1 John v. 10 ; Rom. viii. 16.   [3] Gal. iii. 9.
[2] Gal. iii. 26.   [4] Rom. i. 16, 17.

of Job, " There is a path which no fowl knoweth, and which
the vulture's eye hath not seen : the lion's whelps have not
trodden it, nor the fierce lion passed by it." Ah ! indeed, in
the pathway of faith all nature's keenness, swiftness, and
strength are in vain ; but those ransomed of the Lord, who
feel themselves as " fools," shall find it, and shall not err
therein.[1] The promise is sure to all the seed,—" He that
believeth shall be saved;" "for by grace ye are saved through
faith, and that not of yourselves; it is the gift of God."

Wherefore, be not discouraged, dearest, because you cannot work faith out of your own barren heart; it was never
intended you should. Jesus gives it freely, and He will increase it. You cannot say you have not the buddings of it
as first described : you have faith in a holy sin-avenging
God; and you have faith in a holy sin-atoning Saviour, as
able to save you, and just the Saviour you want. Do you
want to believe in Him more fully and firmly, venturing the
weight of all upon His obedience and sacrifice ? What can
you do better than ask Him to reveal Himself more clearly
in your soul, like him of old, who said, " Who is the Lord,
that I might believe on Him ? " Hearken to the gracious
answer: " Thou hast both seen Him, and it is He that talk-
eth with thee;" and he said, "Lord, I believe ; and he wor-
shipped Him." Now I think this is just your case. Jesus
has been talking to you, and you know Him not, just as He
talked to the woman of Samaria, and told her all things that
ever she did. May He open your eyes and your heart that
you may receive Him, believe on His name,[2] and have privilege to know that you are a child of God. Faith is the very
outgoing of heart and soul upon the person and work, blood

[1] Isa. xxxv. 8, 10.   [2] John i. 12.

and righteousness of Jehovah Jesus, and that under a deep sense of unworthiness, guiltiness, and hell-deserving. Unbelief would put these things as obstacles and barriers in the way, but faith will not have it so, seeing such richness and efficacy in the blood and obedience of Him who is mighty to save, that it says, " Wherefore He is able to save to the uttermost all that come unto God by Him." I can only add 2 Thess. i. 11, 12. And now farewell; I trust the Lord will bruise Satan under thy feet shortly.— With much affection, I remain your unworthy friend,   RUTH.

LXVII.

Faith overcomes impossibilities.

" Behold the Lamb of God, which taketh away the sin of the world."

TO MISS. M.

HIGH PAVEMENT,
NOTTINGHAM, *March* 21, 1852.

MY BELOVED FRIEND, I am often thinking about you, and wondering how you are travelling. But wheresoever you are, the Lord is saying, " O Israel, thou shalt not be forgotten of me." You are safe in His keeping, whether the "door of faith has been opened unto you," or you are yet crying, " Bring my soul out of prison." Jesus knows all about you. He will not suffer you to pass the bounds He has appointed, but in the favoured moment will say, " Loose her and let her go." He is anointed to preach liberty to the captives, and the opening of the prison to them that are bound ; not for price nor reward. He wants nothing at your hands. You are to receive all from Him, not bring anything to Him. He bestows His gifts freely upon the empty, the needy, the destitute, and frankly forgives those His debtors who have " nothing to pay." Those who have spent all their living, " wasted their substance," and are " discontented " also ; these shall come to the spiritual David, in the cave of Adullam, and He will receive them ; neither their debt nor discontent shall hinder.[1] " All that the Father giveth me shall come to me, and him that cometh to me I will in no wise cast out." " He is exalted to give repentance unto Israel, and the remission of sins." These are precious gifts to such as know their own sore, and the plague of their own hard heart. They do even feel it a privilege to sit and weep at Jesus's feet, under a sense of " much forgiven," having proved, too, that without power from on high they " could not repent, though they endeavoured oft," nor exercise that faith by which the soul has experimental access into a justified state.[2] " For by Him all that believe are justified from all things from which ye could not be justified by the law of Moses." " He that believeth is not condemned."

O thou tossed with tempest, and not comforted ! He will keep thee ; He will enable thee to cast thy soul and thy sins upon the sin-bearing Surety, who will, with His own blood, blot out all guilt from thy conscience, and with His own righteousness robe thy naked soul. Believing in Him thou shalt not be made ashamed, but shall by faith " inherit substance," even " durable riches and righteousness." What a possession for a poor, feelingly unrighteous, law-condemned

[1] 1 Sam. xxii. 1, 2.   [2] Rom. v. 1, 2.

bankrupt,—inherit righteousness! This is good news, indeed, to one whose best righteousness is as filthy rags. Oh that faith might come in the hearing of it, and she that hath dwelt in the dust awake by the Spirit's power to her privilege, and put on her beautiful garments! Ah! indeed, "faith is a precious gift," which seems to apprehend and take hold of all that God has to bestow upon us in the wilderness. Unbelief puts the blessing away for want of creature worthiness, but faith pleads on in the face of unworthiness. "Truth, Lord! yet the dogs eat of the crumbs that fall from the master's table." Do not our hearts say, "Lord, increase my faith?"

But, perhaps, my beloved is travelling heavily, and though I talk of these good things, can hardly listen to me "for anguish of spirit and cruel bondage." Well, I once was there, and in my Bible, Exodus vi. 9, is marked,—and it was done feelingly, in bitter moments,—" But though we believe not, he abideth faithful, he cannot deny himself." The children of Israel were brought out of bondage according to promise, although their spirit was too heavy to receive the glad tidings; and I, though so unworthy, have also been brought from under the galling yoke; though at the time named I could not lay hold of, or hearken to, the hope set before me in the gospel. And deliverance will come to dear Miss M——, even if she also be as weak in faith, and as grieved in spirit. But oh! would that she might be able to receive the consolation, and not dishonour the Lord by unbelief, as I did; but in the face of all improbabilities, and human impossibilities, just say, "Behold the handmaid of the Lord, be it unto me according to thy word."

May you, my dear one, look expectingly to Him who is

able to do exceeding abundantly above all we can ask or think, and not look into yourself for encouragement to expect. "David encouraged himself in the Lord his God." May the Holy Spirit so testify to your soul of the glorious person and finished work of Emmanuel, that you may be encouraged there too. "He is able to save to the uttermost all that come unto God by Him."

We had an encouraging sermon last week from Mr H——, from Ps. cvi. 8. Mr H—— said, "We could not understand the sweetness of that word 'nevertheless,' unless we painfully knew the experience of the seventh verse." You will know the truth of this, and with all your crooked ways and crooked things, within and without, there is a precious nevertheless attached to you; such an one as verse forty-four, and the end will be, nevertheless He saved her for His mercy's sake, His name's sake, His love's sake, and we will unite to sing, "Grace, grace, unto it."

I fear you are much afflicted, as I have not heard from you. The Lord support and comfort you, and bring you to be passive and quieted as a weaned child; there is "a needs be," though unseen by us. May it be truly with you as Heb. xii. 6-11. And now farewell; peace be with you. Accept affectionate love from your attached but unworthy

RUTH.

LXVIII.

Strength equal to the hour of weakness.

" Look unto Me, and be ye saved."
"They look unto Him, and were lightened ; and their faces were not
  ashamed."

TO MISS M.

HIGH PAVEMENT, *May* 8, 1852.

MY MUCH-ENDEARED FRIEND, Grace and peace be with you
from God our Father and the Lord Jesus Christ ; and may
the God of patience and consolation make all grace abound
towards you amidst your varied trials, and the cruel efforts
of your unwearied foe, who, finding that the Shepherd of
Israel is taking you out of his mouth, a poor maimed thing,
like Amos iii. 12, does rage against you, and roar upon you,
to frighten you from Christ the stronghold, your only place
of help.   He points to your filthy garments, and resists the
outgoings of your faith upon Him who alone can cleanse
you; he tries to strengthen unbelief and carnal reason, that
your eye may be turned inward instead of upward ; he tries
to magnify unduly creature comforts in your esteem, that
they may steal your heart from Christ, and rob your soul of
peace.   But "the Lord rebuke thee, O Satan ; is not this
a brand plucked out of the fire ? "   May the Holy Ghost,
my beloved, strengthen your faith and hope in God.

" If all created streams were dried,
  His love remains the same ;
  May we with this be satisfied,
  And glory in His name.

> "There naught is in the creature found,
>   But may be found in Thee ;
>   I must have all things, and abound,
>   While Christ is all to me."

I myself have found in Jesus and His precious love more
than I ever lost in the creature.   May we through grace be
enabled to enjoy thankfully what He lends, and resign it
lovingly and submissively, though not unfeelingly, when He
recalls.   You have been, and are, tried on the most tender
points.   Your nearest and dearest on earth seem to droop
and wither ; but the dearer than all will never fade away
from your embrace.   It has been well said, " He *lends* all
lesser things, but He *gives* Himself."   May your sorrowful
heart be comforted in this "unspeakable gift," and while you
are trembling at the future, may the Lord graciously encourage you, as He did me.   I had long been dreading the
death of my precious mother, when our minister one day
read Romans viii., and spoke upon the 38th verse, especially
upon those words, " Nor things to come."   Oh, what a
cordial this was to my soul, that the " things to come,"
which I so much feared, should not separate from the love
of God, which would support me through all !   Those things
have taken place, the thing which I feared has come upon
me ; but has the Lord proved unfaithful, or have His arm
or His promise failed ?   Ah no ! I live His humble, unworthy witness of the truth of Isaiah xliii. 2.   " Ye are
my witnesses, saith the Lord, that I am God." [1]

I was thankful to find, in your last letter, an earnest
desire to be resigned to all the will of God.   You know
those sweet lines—

[1] Isaiah xliii. 12.

" Subdue my will from day to day,
  Blend it with Thine, and take away
  All that now makes it hard to say.
    Thy will be done."

The Lord fulfil these in your experience ; it is in this sense
" hard for thee to kick against the pricks ; " piercing and
smarting must be the result. You have painfully felt it :
you have known the fretfulness of a wean*ing* child, may
you be brought to the quietness of a " wean*ed* one." Whatever your heavenly Father calls you to, He will support
you under ; but He will not give the manna for to-morrow,
or strengthen you for the next trial, while you have it only
in anticipation. "Give us this day our daily bread." "As
thy days, so shall thy strength be." " Sufficient unto the
day is the evil thereof." And herein I read my own foolishness ; often wearing out present strength with fears and
forebodings of future trial ; thus far disregarding present
mercies, and rebelling against the Lord's will, because un-
lawfully forestalling it. A minister once said, " The Lord
gives each of His children a bundle of rods to carry, one
for every day, with strength apportioned ; but they will
strive to lift all at once, and thus are overburdened, because they have only strength given for the present one."
Being naturally of an anxious mind, I must say that thus
foolish and ignorant have I often been, and surprised when
brought to discover how much I was dragging into the present hour what did not belong to it. Have you ever been
caught in this snare ?

I am truly rejoiced that you discover your proneness to
look within for encouragement, instead of encouraging yourself in the Lord your God. This is one great bane of your
peace, and springs much from unbelief and carnal reason,

which rise no higher than feelings, making all their calculations from thence. True faith, on the contrary, looks only
at Christ, expecting all the soul needs in Him, and for His
sake. If worthiness is the question, "Worthy is the
Lamb;" and to make His worthiness our plea, is well-
pleasing to the Father who gave Him, to the Spirit who
testifies of Him, and to Him who gave Himself an all-
sufficient ransom. The Holy Three are honoured when
faith holds up Christ, His merits, and His blood; but dishonoured, greatly dishonoured, when the soul seeks or
wishes for aught besides, when we look within for any im-
proved feelings or experience to ground our hope upon, or
to increase our confidence before Him. We want to be
something, but our Father has determined to make and
keep us nothing, so that Christ may be experimentally our
all, and every plea, every expectation, every hope centre in
Him, His glorious person, His law-magnifying obedience,
His justice-satisfying atonement. This is the God-glorify-
ing way of faith.

Ah, my dear friend, how welcome, under a sense of guilt
and condemnation to find—

> " His blood a full atonement made,
>   And cries aloud, Forgive ! "

How safe to—

> " Venture on Him, venture wholly,
>   Let no other trust intrude ! "

But say you sin is so active and unsubdued that this *seems*
like presumption ? True; but if sin were conquered and
subdued, then there would not be a venturing on Him.
Jesus is honoured by such presuming of misery upon mercy,
of a real sinner upon a real Saviour. But, say you again,

faith is not in the power of the creature? Certainly not. But this is no discouragement, because it is the free gift of Him who, while He says, "Look unto me, and be ye saved," causes the blind to see; and while he says, "Believe, and thou shalt be saved," causes faith to come by hearing, and so enables the soul to venture itself and its sins upon Him. "Stretch forth thy hand," He said, not because there was innate power in the withered hand, for it was dead, but power was with His word: the hand was stretched out in the obedience of faith, and made whole as the other. So, dearest friend, though your soul be impotent as that withered hand, your poor friend must set before you the way of faith, and the object of faith, even Jesus, the sin-bearing, sin-removing, sin-pardoning Saviour, whose name was so called, because He should save His people from their sins.[1] And she does this, not because there is power in her, or power in you, but because there is power in Him, and because "there is none other name under heaven given among men whereby we must be saved."

To Him I affectionately commend you, that by the power of the Holy Ghost it may be unto you as John xi. 25.

Accept warm love and best wishes from one who longs much after you in the bowels of Jesus Christ, and remains most affectionately yours,

R. BRYAN.

[1] 1 Pet. ii. 24; Zech. iii. 9; Matt. ix. 6.

LXIX.

Superabounding grace.

TO MISS M.

High Pavement, *Aug.* 24, 1852.

My beloved Friend, ... I most sincerely wish you a blessed evidence of your own election of God. To others this evidence is already open, in many marks and tokens of the work of grace, although to you it is at present sealed.[1] Nor can you get at this comfortable assurance till the Divine Witness[2] of the evidence open and read it to the joy of your heart. May He be pleased soon to come forth in your soul as the Comforter, the Spirit of adoption, and the Testifier of Jesus. His witnessing all your unbelief shall not be able to gainsay or resist; for it is with demonstration and power; and though feeling vile, and utterly black in yourself, that will not invalidate His testimony at all, nor in the leastwise alter that adoption, which does not originate in the merit of the creature, but in the sovereign will of the Creator. "Of His own will begat He us,"[3] irrespective of anything in ourselves. Though all our blackness is fully known to Him, yet it has no influence upon His determination to put us amongst the children. Yea, He will cause even this our vileness to turn to His own glory. We may feel the very worst of all, and say, "I am not worthy to be called thy child;" but the relationship remains unaltered, and our Father will not make us as one of His hired servants. The Pro-

[1] Jer. xxxii. 11.   [2] Rom. viii. 16.   [3] Jas. i. 18.

digal must be brought in, and prove the bowels of a Father's tenderness,[1] though there be a time in experience when the child differeth nothing from a servant, " but is under tutors and governors till the time appointed of the Father." During this time he is instructed and chastened[2] out of the law, which "is our schoolmaster to bring us unto Christ." Its deep spirituality discovereth, by the light of the Spirit, our nature's deformity; for by the law is the knowledge of sin. It judgeth also our thoughts, words, and actions, and pronounceth condemnation upon them all. Meanwhile, the conscience is enlightened to see things as they really are; it fully joineth issue with what the law saith, and in the discovery of so much evil the poor soul judgeth itself unworthy of eternal life. Instead of finding proof that it belongs to the royal family of heaven, it feels much more like the servant of sin, like one who is led captive by Satan at his will; and yet all this time it is a child of God, though not as yet realising this by faith in Christ Jesus. But when faith takes hold of Christ by the Spirit's power, there will be the witness within[3] of adoption, of sonship, and then it will be, " Knowing, beloved, your election of God ;" and then you will stand astonished, both in time and eternity, at the riches of that grace which put you in the number of the Saviour's family.

On recurring to your letter, I am reminded of North Wales, which you mention. I must not say much about it, lest I revive in you a pining for what you have not; but I may just say, I did exceedingly enjoy that lovely locality so new to me, combining mountain and marine scenery, both which were constantly before our windows, but not always visible, for the majestic mountains were obscured days to-

[1] Jer. xxxi. 20. [2] Ps. xciv. 12. [3] 1 John v. 10.

gether, being enveloped in a dense fog, something like that
darkening unbelief which hides from the soul those hills
whence alone our help cometh. But as with renewed delight we hailed a returning view of the Welsh mountains, so
does the poor soul welcome a glimpse of those "lasting
hills," which contain the "precious things" just suited to
its case. But we not only enjoyed nature's loveliness and
grandeur ; we also found some gems of grace, such as the
Lord will own when He maketh up His jewels: dear Welsh
sisters, with whom we could take sweet counsel ; sweetly
proving that whatever be the country, or natural language,
the new heart beats the same in all. Though I do almost
extravagantly enjoy the wonders of creation, yet the wonders
of Redemption are to me the cream of all; and to find one
dear saint, though poor and mean, and despised of men, is
treasure to this heart. Such was our privilege in North
Wales, and amidst its many fascinations, this is the endearment of the remembrance. Forgive me, dearest friend, for
hinting above about your pining for what you have not ;
you will retrace from your own note whence the thought ori-
ginated, in your extreme disquiet for want of country air. I do
indeed think this is one point where your foe is gaining advantage, and adding much to your torture, in setting your
eyes and heart upon something pleasing and in prospect,
that you may fret for it; or upon something displeasing and
present, that you may fret against it; and thus between the
two you are kept too much kicking against the pricks, and
severe smarting is the consequence. I know your case is
deeply trying, and I do affectionately feel for you, and long
that it may be with you as Ps. cxxxi. 2, believing such a state
of passive resignation would much reduce the bitterness of

your suffering. I speak only in love, and hope you will not be pained. Tell me if you are. I like to know how you feel, and would not therefrom sharpen words to wound you; but I am thoroughly convinced it is as you say in another part of your letter, that " we often magnify our trials by fretting, and striving to resist them;" and anxiously do I desire that you may be brought to bow your shoulder to bear, and yield your flesh a servant to that tribute which the Lord sees fit to lay upon it.

I have lately been thinking that there is a great difference in experience between being compelled to bear the daily cross, as Simon was the literal one,[1] and taking it up as our Lord exhorts.[2] Oh, let us importunately seek grace of Him, that we may come to this daily self-denial. He only exhorts us to hard things in order to bring us to Himself for strength to do them, for " He giveth more grace," and, when brought to entire resignation, the thing which did most distress us becomes much more endurable. Naturally, I have a very strong will, and therefore, as you may suppose, it has been much crossed. Too well I know the misery of fretting, and a little the mercy of being brought down, and saying feelingly, with the thorn at my breast, " Thy will be done." " Though He slay me, yet will I trust in Him." Now do not say this is out of your reach : it is not, because " power belongeth unto God," and all who are brought to sweet submission under trials are brought to it by Him. Seek it at His hands, that you may glorify Him in the fires. The thing I am now seeking in my daily walk is a subdued will. Will you not join me ? I do painfully feel that I have a stubborn will; but the acknowledgment of it will not do. I want it con-

[1] Matt. xxvii. 32.   [2] Luke ix. 23.

quered, and for this, look to Him who has all power in heaven and earth. You speak of thinking yourself so much worse than I am. Oh, my dear friend, there is not under the canopy of heaven—there is not in the pit of despair—a viler sinner than I. This is a true confession. I may have been kept under more restraints than yourself; but if not open to such temptations, what merit in not falling into them ? Besides, there needeth not the outward act to constitute me guilty of any sin. When tried by heart-evil, I am indeed unclean, unclean, and this not only as knowing the seeds of all evil to be there, but as having felt the abominations—having sunk in the pit of corruption, and become "a burden to myself." You cannot go lower than I in guiltiness; but I have lately felt that if I had a thousand such guilty souls I could trust them all with my precious Saviour, so great is the efficacy of His blood, so rich the merit of His justifying righteousness; and He loves to get glory by such desperate cases. Indeed, I believe He suffers His redeemed to know so much of their nature's evil to magnify the riches of His exceeding grace in their esteem. I deeply loathe my evil, but do not regret that I have so deeply felt it; and I often thank the Lord for it, because those who have felt the heaviest load, " do prize forgiveness most." "I looked for hell"—I knew I deserved it, and felt almost there, but " He gave me heaven." Oh! should I not praise Him ? And should not you be encouraged to hope ? And now, farewell. The God of peace give you peace by the blood of the Cross. Excuse my defects.—With affectionate love, your much attached,

R. B.

Psalm cxxxiv. 3; cxlvii. 11.

LXX.

Entering into rest by believing.

" Mighty to save."

TO MISS M.

NOTTINGHAM, *Dec.* 27, 1852.

MY BELOVED FRIEND, It is said of Anna that after she had seen the Lord's Christ she spake of Him to all them who were looking for redemption in Jerusalem. You, in experience, are looking for redemption, personal and powerful. What can I do better than speak to you of Him with whom there is mercy and plenteous redemption ; who is made of God unto poor bankrupt sinners "wisdom and righteousness, and sanctification and redemption ;" who is the Redeemer of such, and will thoroughly plead their cause ; who is exalted " a Prince and a Saviour, to give repentance unto Israel, and remission of sins." And since, without shedding of blood there could be no remission, Himself became a fountain from whence poured forth the crimson tide—the cleansing flood :

" When justice call'd for sinners' blood,
The Saviour gave His own."

And since, too, the way of salvation is not by works but by faith, He gives that also, for He is the Author and Finisher of it, and thus He gives rest to those who labour—to those who are heavy laden with their sins, and weary with toiling in vain. When He sees their power is gone, and there is none shut up or left, He puts forth His power and enables them to believe. Believing, they enter into rest, and entering into rest, they cease from their own works, bad and good, and Christ alone is their all. Does not this suit you? All a free gift. " Thou, Lord, hast wrought all our works in us," and "this is the work of God, that ye believe on Him whom He hath sent," which work He hath wrought in whomsoever it is found. All such will freely acknowledge it, being saved by grace through faith, and this not of themselves, for it is the gift of God, that no flesh should glory in His presence. I can tell you that this precious repentance-giving, pardon-giving, faith-giving, rest-giving Saviour just suited me, when I said most feelingly, " I want not only a Saviour full of grace, and truth, and love to those who believe in Him, but also a Saviour full of power to those who long to believe and cannot." Such a Saviour have I found, and this because He first found me. His name is Jesus, and He is so called because He saves His people from their sins. He has received gifts for men, yea, for the rebellious also, that the Lord God might dwell among us. Faith is one of His precious gifts : He puts it into the heart, and sweetly manifests Himself as the object of it ; so that the helpless soul which is fearing it may perish for want of faith finds itself made a believer, and wonderingly cries, " My Lord and my God !" Its mountain of guilt is thus removed out of the way, being cast into the red sea of a Saviour's blood. It is no longer of doubtful mind, but, by the faith of the Son of God, can say, He loved me, and gave Himself for me. These are some of the wondrous works of Him who is "mighty to save ;" and I trust, my dear friend, that, with unworthy me, you will be made a witness of what He can do in hard cases, whenever the heart is brought down with labour—when they

fall down and there is none to help. You say you have no
power to believe. If you had, you would not be a fit subject
for this glorious One of whom I am telling you, for it is to
the faint He gives power, and it is to those who have no
might He increases strength. He once saw a poor creature
who had an infirmity, and had long lain in sight of a cure
but could not get at it; "but when he knew he had been a
long time in that case," He did not upbraid him for want of
effort, but brought him the blessing he could not fetch, and
that in an unexpected and hopeless moment, as we learn
from his own plaintive account of his state, John v. 7.
Now you have not been thirty and eight years groaning with
your malady, and learning your want of power; wherefore, I
pray you, do not despair: you know not how near the moment
is when He shall put strength into you and say, "Arise and
walk"—I mean in a spiritual sense. "Then shall the lame
take the prey," and "leap as a hart: yea, and the tongue of
the dumb shall sing." Remember, the time you have waited
and the misery you have suffered is all as nothing in comparison with the greatness of the blessing you are waiting
for. One moment's enjoyment of salvation will make amends
for all. Oh, then, "though the vision tarry, wait for it;"
"they shall not be ashamed who wait for Him." He will
regard the cry of the destitute, and not despise their prayer.
. . . I will answer your question about Hart's Hymns. I
have an old edition I much prize, containing his experience.
How striking it is, and how he was favoured with fellowship
in the Saviour's sufferings. "Erskine's Sonnets" I much
enjoy, and have also an old edition of them. You know my
dear parents loved savoury meat, and I reap the benefit;
though I am now brought to read little beside the "standard

book," as my loved father used to call it.   While I was in bondage I was much harassed with temptation while reading it, and could often get more from authors; but when Christ was revealed in my soul, the Bible became a new book and my blessed companion, of course not always enjoyed alike. I quite think as you do about "Nothing to Pay." I, too, have read it with a melted heart.   Adieu, with kind love.— Your ever affectionate   RUTH.

LXXI.

The power of temptation and the arm of deliverance.

" Take away the dross from the silver, and there shall come forth a vessel for the finer."

" And I will bring the third part through the fire, and will refine them, as silver is refined ; and will try them as gold is tried.   They shall call on my name, and I will hear them.   I will say, It is my people, and they shall say, The Lord is my God."

" Behold I have refined thee, but not with silver ; I have chosen thee in the furnace of affliction."

TO MISS M.

HIGH PAVEMENT, *May* 23, 1853.

My VERY DEAR FRIEND, How much I regret that my silence should have given you uneasiness, and that the enemy should have prevailed to afflict you thereby.   As usual, his suggestions are entirely false.   It has not been my heart, but merely my hand, that has been closed towards you, and the Lord has not shut me up from praying for you; wherefore take encouragement to resist Satan, unbelief, and carnal reason, and do not so easily yield to their disquieting sug-

gestions. You are often in great fear where no cause of
fear is, and I believe God hath despised those enemies which
have encamped against you, and they shall be put to shame.[1]
You are ready to say, I cannot resist, I am so weak, I have
no power or might against this great company that cometh
against me, and often know not what to do.

Well, my beloved, you cannot do better than tell the Lord
all that, and instead of holding parley with the foe, cry to
Him to fight for you. Read in the wars of the Lord, 2 Chron.
xix. 12, 24, &c.; xviii. 31; xiv. 11-13; 1 Chron. v. 20-22,
with many other places, and see what He has done for those
who were too weak for their enemies, all which literal things
are typical of the spiritual ; and the Lord has, over and over
again, done the same in the soul's experience at the cry of
faith, yes, even of " little faith."   It matters not at all how
weak you are,—the weaker the better; that shall in no wise
hinder your possessing the " good land," for " they got not
the land in possession by their own sword, neither did their
own arm save them."   And so it is still; but the difficulty
is, you, like the rest of us, are so proud, you cannot submit
to be " nothing at all," but will be making calculations and
drawing conclusions from what you are, what you do, what
you leave undone, and what you deserve.   Why, my dear
friend, there is nothing of the gospel in all this ; it is all
muddy water from your own corrupt fountain, and your
heavenly Father never intends you to get refreshment there,
but only from the living water which flows from the throne
of God, through the pierced heart of your crucified Surety.
Oh ! may that precious Surety say to you with power,
" Come unto me and drink;" thus will self be blessedly

[1] Ps. liii. 5.

put out of the question, and you will experimentally prove that this strength, His doing, His dying, His deserving, are sufficient without any puny productions of yours.

I have been interested in observing that when I walk with my face toward the sun, my own black shadow is cast behind me; but when my back is toward the sun, this black resemblance of myself marches on before me, full in view. This "I considered, and received instruction." So that I was made to cry, "Turn me again, O Lord God of hosts; cause thy face to shine, and I shall be saved." Ah! we do indeed want turning by Divine power towards the Sun of righteousness, that self may be out of view; for no precious fruits of humility, love, joy, peace, meekness, long-suffering, faith, will flow by looking at our own black self, but the hardness will grow harder, and the darkness more horrible, and pride will fret and grumble, because self can get nothing to glory in. All must be found in Jesus: "In Him shall all the seed of Israel be justified, and shall glory." How many years was I unwittingly going about to establish my own righteousness.[1] I was truly loathing myself, and ever seeing "greater abominations," but mourning and fretting daily because I could get no better. I wanted to be spiritual, and holy, and humble, to be melted into contrition and repentance, but was looking to the wrong place for it, and never thought that the cursed leaven of pride was working in it all, and that I was dishonouring my precious Saviour by not being willing to come to Him, empty, needy, naked, and filthy too; but how plainly I see it now, and therefore do I write freely in love to you, thinking you are tainted with the same malady. The Lord hasten the day of power in

[1] Rom. x.

your soul, when you shall look unto Him and be lightened,
and your face no longer be ashamed.[1] "And in that day
thou shalt say, O Lord, I will praise thee: though thou
wast angry with me, thine anger is turned away, and thou
comfortedst me. Behold, God is my salvation; I will trust,
and not be afraid: for the Lord JEHOVAH is my strength and
my song; he also is become my salvation. Therefore with
joy shall ye draw water out of the wells of salvation."[2]

I did quite understand your feeling of distress when Mr
D—— spoke so confidently of your state, well remembering how a friend frequently grieved me in the same way,
because I feared I had deceived her, though I tried much
to make her know what a vile, black creature I was. However, I have lived to know that she judged rightly, and
that I am indeed a vessel of mercy, though then I thought
it so unlikely. "Grace, grace, unto it."

I was thankful to hear from your last that you are a little
better. The Lord perfect that which concerneth you. The
spirit of prayer granted you after the severe buffeting of
the enemy rejoiced my heart, and is surely an earnest of
greater things to come. What a word is that, "Blessed is
the man that endureth temptation, for when he is tried he
shall receive the crown of life, which the Lord hath promised to them that love him." And then, again, "Though
now for a season, if need be, ye are in heaviness through
manifold temptations: that the trial of your faith, being
much more precious than of gold that perisheth, though it
be tried with fire, might be found unto praise and honour
and glory at the appearing of Jesus Christ." The Word is
full of encouragement to tempted souls, and God is faith-

[1] Ps. xxxiv. 5.   [2] Isa. xii. 1-3.

ful.[1] I believe He will arise for your help, and set you in safety from him that puffeth at you.

I myself have had some sharp spiritual exercise, and have been often on the battlefield, and had to cry for help to One who is mighty; for my enemies were too strong for me, but the Lord was my stay,[2] or indeed they had swallowed me up. He has not given me for a prey to their teeth, but has at times sweetly brought me into the banqueting-house to strengthen me for further conflict. I have indeed afresh proved what I am in my fallen nature. "Tekel"[3] is written upon it all; but "in the Lord have I righteousness and strength;" and it is a rich mercy to be driven from confidence in the flesh, though by roughest measures.

And now, may the Lord be very gracious unto you at the voice of your cry: when He heareth may He answer it.—Accept love and best wishes from your unworthy but affectionate friend,   RUTH.

LXXII.

Jesus the Brother born for adversity.

TO MISS M.

HIGH PAVEMENT, NOTTINGHAM, *Dec.* 7, 1853.

MY BELOVED FRIEND, I was pleased to receive a few lines from you, though you do not say much about yourself, and I fear from some remarks that your health is not materially improving.

---

[1] 1 Cor. x. 13.   [2] Ps. xviii. 17, 18.   [3] Dan. v. 27.

From the views you sent me, I should think the place of
your residence very lovely, but well know that no beauties
of creation can satisfy a soul breathing after Jesus, who is
the peerless Pearl, the matchless perfection of beauty and
love. Every lovely feature in creation is but to shadow
Him forth, and every sweet endearment in relationship just
the same; all that is lovely and loving He comprises in
Himself as He stands related to His Church. It is for her
He is Emmanuel, and to her, as such, the chiefest among
ten thousand, yea, the altogether lovely. He stoops so low
that she can lean upon Him in these lowlands of sorrow and
sin, and He is so exalted that He can bear her up in spirit
even above all heavens where Himself is ascended. He is so
condescending that He communes with her in her pilgrimage dress, though all dusty and disordered with the weary
way. He is so princely in His love that He has provided
for her a court-dress, with all the accompaniments suited to
His own dignity. Moreover, the beauty she now faintly sees,
and will one day fully see, in Him, the same beauty He will
yet see in her, for when He shall appear we shall be like
Him. And if now she feels too full of sorrow, and grief, and
sin, to look so high, she may behold Him "in another form,"
even in " the likeness of sinful flesh," "a man of sorrows and
acquainted with grief," in temptation, in poverty, in reproach.
She may behold Him even not having where to lay His precious head. She may see Him weep, hear Him sigh, and
hear Him groan, if she would know whether He can sympathise with her. Yea, further, in the days of felt evil, when
the iniquity of her heels doth compass her about, she may
hear how He was touched with the very feeling of her infirmity in those memorable words, " Innumerable evils have

compassed me about : mine iniquities have taken hold upon
me, so that I am not able to look up; they are more than the
hairs of mine head : therefore my heart faileth me." But,
you will say, He was holy and did no sin, neither was guile
found in His mouth. Ah, true; but it was her sin that took
hold upon Him—that very iniquity which is now pressing
her down, it pressed Him till His precious blood was forced
through His pores with agony intense. Here then is a companion in tribulation ; on this Beloved the feeblest, faintest,
vilest may venture to lean and to come up from the wilderness. His arm is power, His heart is love and tenderness.
It has been a bruised, broken heart; it has felt the shafts of
hell, the flames of wrath, and the bitter anguish of desertion
amidst it all.

Look, O tempted, sin-burdened one ! look and love, adore
and wonder, for there has been sorrow like unto thy sorrow,
and heavier too, and from the very same cause. Thy Lord
is so one with thee that He calls thine iniquities His own,
and He was dealt with as if He were the transgressor. He
was not a sinner, but He was made to be sin that thou
mightest be made the righteousness of God in Him. Though
a sinner in thyself or in the first Adam nature, He took all
thy guilt with Him to the Cross. Go there and learn that
God will by no means clear the guilty. Thy Surety was
accounted guilty for thy sake, and therefore thou art viewed
as guiltless ; and that same God who shewed Him no mercy
is to thee merciful and gracious, long-suffering, and abundant
in goodness and truth. All praise to a sin-bearing Saviour
—a sin-pardoning God, who can honourably blot out atoned
iniquity with atoning blood. May the Spirit give application, and then thy heart will rejoice, even thine. Then what

a keeping of Christmas it would be in company with the Lamb of God who taketh away the sins of the world, born for thee, obeying for thee, bruised for thee, bleeding for thee, dying, rising, ascending, all for thee, and pleading all on thy behalf. It is thus to us a child is born, to us a son is given, and we find it glad tidings of great joy, which brings peace to our souls and reveals to us the goodwill of Him that dwelt in the bush. The Lord hasten in thy experience the fulness of time when to thee personally He will send forth His Son, and thus visit thee with His salvation, that thy liberated soul may say, Now, Lord, lettest Thou thine handmaid depart in peace, for mine eyes have seen and my heart has felt Thy salvation! Once get a sight of the King in His beauty, and I know you would long to be with Him. You are now waiting for that sight, and He says, " They shall not be ashamed that wait for me."

Your letter contains pleasing instances of the Lord's dealings. "I will work, and who shall let it?" Like you, I long to have His sensible presence when called to cross over the Jordan of death. Many an invitation have I sent up to my dear Lord to meet me on the banks of that river and "let me breathe my life out in the arms of His Divine embrace." . . . You speak of your lovely retreat as being spiritually barren, but I trust you have some with whom you can take sweet counsel as you journey on; it is a privilege—"How dear to my heart is communion with saints." I shall be happy to hear from you soon, and wish you every blessing, and power to look up and see Jesus appearing in the presence of God for you. Adieu, my dear friend.—With kindest love in that precious Jesus who is our bond of union, I remain your very affectionate RUTH.

P

LXXIII.

Jesus, Jehovah Rophi.

TO MISS M.

HIGH PAVEMENT, *Nov.* 17, 1854.

My BELOVED FRIEND, I must first thank you for your last kind note, which was very sweet and refreshing. It is a privilege to hear of the triumph of faith, when flesh and sense would say, "All these things are against me." I do not know the lady you mention, but rejoice to hear of her testimony for the Lord, and am also thankful that it proved encouraging to you. All the ways of the Lord are right ways, and we lose much sweetness for want of resignation to His will in all things. While we fret against the Cross, it is felt the heavier. I believe, too, that we are losers by not receiving all events as from Him. By looking at second causes we come into great perplexity; and whatever creatures may intend against us, our Heavenly Father has some high purpose of grace in all that He suffers to befall us. He could prevent every apparent wrong, and He would, were not each bitter in our cup essential for His own glory and our real profit. The assurance of this has been very healing to my spirit many times under blights and losses, and also under mental wounds from those dear to me. I feel there is some personal lesson in all these things ; and often, when I would have felt ready to censure the instrument, I have discovered some pride or other lurking evil in myself, which the Lord aimed at by the untoward circumstance, intending by His Spirit to bring it to light and rebuke it. Thus has the mouth been stopped, and brought to kiss the hand which held the rod, however inexcusable in itself that rod might be. Also, when the heart is thus humbled, the wrong of others against us seems but secondary to our own, albeit ours may be against the Lord only. Oh, let us seek to be so instructed of the Lord that the rod and reproof may give wisdom. Let us aim at confiding love in Him, for He is infinite wisdom, and needs none of our interference.

If, too, the Lord severely tries our faith, it is only to manifest Himself afresh as Jehovah Jireh, or Jehovah Rophi, or Jehovah Tsidkenu, or under some other blessed covenant name, which is to be seen more brightly in the dark place. Moreover, if He takes away our Isaacs, it is only to make more room for Himself; and if He lessens our earthly store, it is only that we may live more immediately upon Himself. I want grace and faith to walk with Him when He walks against my flesh, not for destruction, but for salvation. " Whoso is wise, and will observe these things, even they shall understand the loving-kindness of the Lord." I am very fond of the word "understand" in that verse, because I am very sure we often misconceive the Lord's loving-kindness; and, judging by sense and carnal reason, think it is unkindness, when in truth He is in love drawing us nearer to Himself. And oh! is it not worth everything to be near Him, and to hear Him say, " Thou art ever with me, and all that I have is thine !" His heart of love, His life of obedience, His death and sufferings, His triumphant resurrection and ascension, His intercession, His glory, all are ours, and, what is best of all, Himself; for the glory of His person outmaches all that He has done, and to know for myself that "my beloved is mine" is a taste of the fulness of bliss.

Well, my loved friend, the dark steps we were noticing above are just the way by which the Lord often leads His children on to this blessedness; they do not generally reach it all at once, though some receive the white stone much sooner than others, but many have to travel the barren land of deserts and of pits, to wander in a solitary way, to have their hearts made desolate and their earthly substance blighted, ere Christ is revealed in them as their all—as the hope and the foretaste of glory. Well, it matters not how, if we do but come to know Him as *ours* in power and preciousness; and to this I doubt not you shall be brought, though often the way may seem long and your steps be weary. The cost and consequences of the journey rest not with you. All the weight of it is upon Him who has said to His Father, I will be surety for them, of my hand shalt thou require them : if I bring them not unto Thee, and set them before Thee, then let me bear the blame for ever. Ever precious Jesus, so able, so willing to bear all the burden of all who come unto Him! If you have nothing in yourself to encourage you, which I am sure you have not, there is plenty in Him, for with Him is mercy and plenteous redemption. May the Spirit enable you to be coming, coming, ever coming unto Him; so will your faith grow, and your great enemy, unbelief, be trodden down.[1] Fear not, the Lord will help you, He will strengthen you, He will deliver you. "God shall help her, and that right early."[2]

I had not thought of writing so much without mentioning dear Mr D——, but have been unexpectedly led on. I gave

[1] See Micah vii. 10.　　　　[2] Ps. xlvi. 5.

your remembrance to him, and his kind heart was grieved at your disappointment. He said how much he wished to see you, but could not; and he often trembled when made useful to any one, lest they should look to him, and then he knew something would come to disappoint and pain them. This is much what you express. The Lord seal the instruction, and teach us how to look through, and not to, the dearest instruments, that they may never come between our souls and Him!

I much enjoy what I have read of the ancient philosopher who declined the riches and honours offered to him by the emperor, saying, he " desired nothing so much of him as that he would stand out of the sunshine." And so would I say to every creature and every thing, " Pray stand from between me and the sun; eclipse not the glory of my Beloved, hide Him not in the least from my view, and let Him give or withhold what He pleases, so I may but enjoy Himself." This is the language of the new heart. The old heart is a very treacherous dealer, and when conferred with, brings on the doleful cry, " My leanness, my leanness;" but " the elder shall serve the younger," this is the cheering promise.

We have had Mr H—— here also. His testimony was clear, faithful, and savoury. I think you would have enjoyed much the Sabbath morning from " I am the Lord that healeth thee." Mr H—— spoke of the leprosy and its cure, as a striking type of our soul malady; also of diseases we are subject to *after* a sense of pardon and healing. Faith is subject to paralysis; it gets weak and shaky, the soul looking more at self than Jesus, but of this disease " I am the Lord that healeth thee;" our love sometimes takes cold, no warmth or fervour felt; a sense of His love is the healing of ours, "who healeth all thy diseases."

But I must close this long note. Like you, I feel more anxious for health of soul than of body, that the life I live in the flesh may be by the faith of the Son of God, and that I may not live upon evidences and feelings, but upon Him alone by faith. Thus will evidences and feelings be kept fresh and lively; whereas while we seek to rest in them they must be withholden, that so we may trust in Jesus only.— In Him and His precious love I am ever yours affectionately, Ruth.

!LXXIV.

The Sin-bearer and the sinner.

TO MISS M.

HIGH PAVEMENT, *February* 9, 1855.

MY BELOVED FRIEND, I hope you are a little more look-ing unto Jesus—a little more leaning upon Him amid your many weaknesses. He can bear all your weight, for He has borne all your sins, which are the worst part of your burden. Oh, that by the Spirit you may get a faith's view of a crucified Redeemer.

> " With your name upon His breast.
> In the garden bleeding, stooping,
> To the ground with horror press'd."

" Heaviness in the heart maketh it stoop," and that precious Sin-bearer had heaviness indeed when he said, "My soul is exceeding sorrowful, even unto death." The sins of His people, the curse of the law, the hidings of His father's face, all pressed His righteous soul as a cart is pressed under sheaves. His own self bare our sins in His own body on the tree, and bore them away from us for ever; and when we get the seal of it by the blessed Spirit in our conscience then we can say, "There is therefore now no condemnation" to me. "Who is he that condemneth? It is Christ that died." Here, in Christ's obedience unto death, is satisfaction for law, justice, and conscience. Here is that which has satisfied Jehovah himself. Here then rest thy weary soul, my beloved, and thou shalt not be ashamed nor confounded, world without end. "They looked unto him and were lightened, and their faces were not ashamed." Never was a sin-convinced, sin-wearied sinner cast off or cast out. This refuge is open for all such, and why, my friend, why not for thee? Who says thee nay? Only thine own fears, and unbelief, and Satan; but these are evil counsellors, and, like Ahithophel, they shall be frustrated. Our God will bring their counsel to naught. He will make the many devices of these crafty ones of none effect, for He has counselled to save thee. He has devised means whereby thou, His banished one, shall not be always expelled from His presence. "By the blood of the covenant" shalt thou be brought nigh, and by the Spirit's power. There is a cleft in the rock for thee, and as in purpose thou hast been there from all eternity, so in thine own experience shalt thou also be there in the appointed season. Would I might have to rejoice with thee and know that the Lord had taken off thy sackcloth, and clothed thee with gladness, giving thee "the garment of praise for the spirit of heaviness." Dearly beloved, you need not turn into yourself and say, "How unlikely." You are not in worse condition than the spendthrift prodigal. He was starving, helpless, and destitute when the gracious word was given— "Bring forth the best robe, and put it on him ; and put a ring on his hand, and shoes on his feet; and bring hither the fatted calf, and kill it; and let us eat and be merry. For this my son was dead, and is alive again ; he was lost, and is found." His own wilfulness and wickedness brought the misery upon himself, and yet that hindered not the flow of mercy and love, which comes all free to poor bankrupt prodigals. "O Israel, thou hast destroyed thyself, but in me is thy help." Our Father has "laid help upon one that is mighty," even upon Him who was red in His apparel, who travelled in the greatness of His strength for the salvation of His people, and who speaks of Himself as "mighty to save." May the blessed Spirit testify of your interest in these things, and so be to you the Comforter.—With affectionate love, I remain your unworthy friend, RUTH.

LXXV.

The tried and convinced sinner encouraged.

TO MISS M.

HIGH PAVEMENT, *June* 25, 1855.

MY BELOVED FRIEND, I am sorry to hear you have been so much out of health and spirits ; the latter is far the worst, for "the spirit of a man will sustain his infirmity ; but a wounded spirit who can bear?" Satan seems to have gained sad advantage over you in causing you almost to give up communion and correspondence with the living in Jerusalem. Ah ! how hard he strives to get us for himself, and to hinder us from anything which would tend to weaken his devices, and how we too often give place to him, and forsake our own mercies. But the Lord will not leave us in his hands. He may, when permitted, sift us as wheat, but our dear Redeemer says, "I have prayed for thee, that thy faith fail not." Faith indeed often seems to fail us as to the exercise of it, but the precious grace itself shall never fail from the living soul till sight and full possession make it no longer needful. Oh, that the Lord may be pleased to increase your faith, that you may resist the devil. He who has delivered you out of his kingdom of darkness can deliver you from the power of his cruel and cunning suggestions. He can teach your hands to war and your fingers to fight, and make you strong in faith giving glory to God. Oh, may He bruise him under your feet shortly, enabling you to overcome him by the blood of the Lamb.

You speak as though you had been under heavy trials. I can feel for you, having many crooks in the lot, and a sadly too susceptible and anxious heart which feels everything so much, but yet can say with David, " I know, O Lord, that thy judgments are right, and that thou in faithfulness hast afflicted me." I do not find bodily affliction the most painful part of tribulation ; many other things distress me much more ; but the Lord knows best what to send ; and a great mercy it is when He enables us quietly to take up the cross as it occurs, for everything is doubly bitter when our heart fretteth against the Lord, or even against our fellow-worms. They could not afflict us without His permission, and though that does not lessen their wrong, it may stop our murmuring,

and humble us before Him, like David, who looked away
from Shimei and said, " Let him alone, and let him curse;
for the Lord hath bidden him ; " and again, " So let him
curse, because the Lord hath said unto him, Curse David.
Who shall then say, Wherefore hast thou done so ?" Oh,
my beloved friend, whatever be the nature of your trials,
whether they arise from self, Satan, or any other creature,
there is but one refuge, one place of safe retreat, and that is
Jesus—He who is a hiding-place from the wind, and a covert
from the tempest, and from this cruel foe that has been
striving hard to keep you.

But, my dear friend, happy you who are brought now to
judgment, that you should not be condemned with the world.
Happy they who are now brought in guilty before God, and
their mouths stopped.   Their Redeemer is mighty ; He will
thoroughly plead their cause.   By the scars in His own precious body He will shew that their sins have been punished in
Him, and that therefore they cannot be condemned, sentence
having been executed upon Him in their stead.   Wherefore
it is written, "Cry unto her that her warfare is accomplished,
that her iniquity is pardoned : for she hath received of the
Lord's hand double for all her sins.'"   But am I, says my
friend, among those thus described ?   Well, have you not
been made feelingly to plead guilty ?   And if you have not
yet sensibly received the full release by the " double," are
you not waiting at that door, even the door of mercy ?   And
is not your only hope in the death of the Redeemer, the
King's Son ?   And are you not desiring that ere long you
may by faith find that you are really graven on the palms of
His pierced hands ?   Well then, if that be your position, I
can answer for Him that you shall not wait in vain.   I do

know enough of Him for that, and fear not to aver that in the pit of darkness, there is not one who perished hoping in His mercy, through His own blood, and waiting for His salvation. He is faithful, and what He says He means, and will perform, though earth and hell rise up against it. "Come unto me, all ye that labour and are heavy-laden, and I will give you rest." " All that the Father giveth me shall come to me ; and him that cometh to me I will in nowise cast out." " Seek, and ye shall find; knock, and it shall be opened." " Blessed are they that mourn: for they shall be comforted." "Blessed are they which do hunger and thirst after righteousness; for they shall be filled." The precious lips that spoke those words "were never known to lie;" but "thine enemies shall be found liars unto thee;" and "as the shepherd taketh out of the mouth of the lion two legs, or a piece of an ear,"[1] (a poor mutilated thing ;) so shalt thou be delivered, and stand upon the mount Zion above, with the harp of God in thine hand. Do not be alarmed, beloved, at my confidence: it is not grounded on you, but on Him who came into this drear wilderness on purpose to seek and to save that which was lost. I wonderfully like those words of David, " I have gone astray like a lost sheep; seek thy servant; for I do not forget thy commandments." He felt that he had got into a labyrinth, and cried to his Good Shepherd to come and seek him, for he felt quite lost, and the answer is as above, " The Son of man is come to seek and to save that which was lost." So you see, if you are so sadly off that you cannot come to Him, He will come to you, and find you, and bring you home on His strong shoulder with rejoicing.

You speak of fearing that what you have felt is a delusion,

[1] Amos iii. 12.

and your convictions only natural. If it be so, something from nature will quiet them and satisfy you, but if they be from Jehovah the Spirit, nothing but reconciliation to Jehovah the Father by Jehovah the Son will bring peace— nothing but Christ will satisfy your soul. Judge now, I pray you, and do not give place to the devil, but give the Lord the glory due unto His name, and praise Him for opening your blind eyes, even if you think you only see men as trees walking, for He will most surely perfect that which concerneth you, and He says, "Whoso offereth praise glorifieth me. Jeremiah xxxiii. 14, has just been brought home with sweetness to me. May the day of performing the promise draw near in your experience. I trust your health is again improving, and your mind more calm. In the winter there was every reason to think that I was just at "home," but in Divine sovereignty the Lord has rebuked the disease for the present, and I may have long to sojourn in Mesech. Moreover, since "home" has looked more in the distance, many other storms have arisen, and trials crossed the path, that patience may have her perfect work, and faith plenty to do at the "court of requests." But though we be at times like Hannah, who was a woman of a sorrowful spirit, yet the end is to see more wonders from Him who has given that sweet bill of promise, "Call upon me in the day of trouble: I will deliver thee, and thou shalt glorify me." Would I could honour Him more in the sunshine and in the storm, for He is worthy; but shame and confusion of face do indeed belong unto unworthiest me at all times. . . . . The Lord bless you, comfort you, set your feet upon the rock, and establish your goings there.—With kindest love, believe me, your ever affectionate　　　　　　　　　　Ruth.

LXXVI.

The snare broken.

"Cease ye from man whose breath is in his nostrils, for wherein is he to be accounted of ?"

TO MISS M.

MY BELOVED FRIEND, I am ashamed of my long silence. I think of you and grieve that your mind is still tried and perplexed by the inconsistencies of others, as I learnt from your last pensive note. But, perhaps, ere now that cloud has been dispersed. I earnestly hope that it is so, for, indeed, my beloved friend, there is so much crookedness, even in the living family, that we need to remember constantly the words of the Lord which head this page, and which were made powerful to my own soul a few days since. But how slow we are to obey this divine injunction. Even in this sense we may well say, " My soul cleaveth to the dust," while we should pray for quickening grace to cease from creatures, neither confiding in them too much for comfort, nor too much expecting to find all consistency within. Frail and imperfect are the best, and this is nothing new, for one of old says, " The most upright is sharper than a thorn hedge," and another, "I have seen an end of all perfection." Oh! that your tried, tempest-tossed heart may be led to find refuge in the perfect One, the Friend who loveth at all times, and sticketh closer than a brother, for this precious "neigh-

bour that is near, is better than a brother that is afar off."
A brother may look on our wound and pass by on the other
side, but this good Samaritan attends to our case from whatever cause be our sorrow, and whatever the hand that may
have wounded. His oil and wine do heal, and His sweet
words soothe the troubled heart, for He has got the tongue of
the learned, and knows how to speak a word in season to
him that is weary. He is merciful, and He can have compassion on the ignorant. The Spirit of the Lord is upon
Him, so that He is anointed to preach the gospel to the
poor, to heal the broken-hearted, and bring deliverance to
the captives, and to open the prison to them that are bound,
to set at liberty them that are bruised.

Did I tell you how much I had been profited sometime
since by St. Mark i. 18 ? The Spirit shewed me how many
things are as "nets" to entangle us, and to keep us back
from following Jesus, and also in how many ways we may
be using "nets" to catch some desire of our carnal hearts ;
but then how blessed when brought to that, " straightway
they forsook their nets and followed him." You know, dear
friend, that too much poring over the inconsistencies of
others may become as a "net" to catch our own feet, and
hinder us from looking to Jesus. A friend of mine was
once grievously annoyed by what was God-dishonouring in
another person. It fretted him much, though he had no
power to prevent it; but at length he heard the Shepherd's
voice, saying, " What is that to thee ? follow thou me,"
which broke the snare. It is vain to dwell upon that which
hinders our own souls and helps no one.

How is your health now, and how is the health of your
soul ? Have you been brought to the venture of faith, even

as one dear to me lately said in the view of the all-sufficient
Saviour, "I felt that I could venture the whole weight of my
soul upon Him, though vilest of the vile I felt I was." This
was my maid, who has been with us eleven years, and the
Lord has just sweetly sealed her for His own, which has
made me rejoice with exceeding great joy, for I have long
been watching for her soul. Oh, my dear friend, may the
blessed Spirit bring you to this. All your weight of sins,
sorrows, and cares the Burden-Bearer can sustain. "Casting
all your care upon Him, for He careth for you." And it is
no honour to Him to be carrying it yourself; it must sink
you into gloom and dejection. A minister once said, "The
Lord tells us to carry our cross and cast our care, but we try
to cast our cross and carry our care." I felt much self-con-
viction from the remark, but must say with the Psalmist,
"Nevertheless, he being full of compassion, forgave their
iniquity, and destroyed them not." So that, notwithstanding
my wilfulness and sin in many ways, I am still "the living,
the living" to praise Him, as I desire to do this day, and to
encourage you to put your trust under the shadow of His
wings, for there is healing there.[1] Do excuse this sad scrawl,
I hope you will write soon, if able; and, warmly wishing
you every covenant favour, I remain, with much love in our
precious Jesus, your affectionate friend,

RUTH.

Psalm cxlv. 14.

[1] Mal. iv. 2.

LXXVII.

Tribulation worketh patience.

"He hath said, I will never leave thee nor forsake thee."

TO MISS M.

HIGH PAVEMENT, *April* 21, 1856.

MY BELOVED FRIEND, I have been much longing to respond to your last welcome and cheering note. I do indeed rejoice that you had such a comfortable visit from the Lord's dear servant, Mr D——, and trust it was a lasting lift from the Lord Himself, and that you may not again sink so low as you did before, nor give place to unbelief and Satan, for these giant foes will raise questionings about the brightest manifestations and sweetest enjoyments. May the Lord rebuke them, and enable you to go forward trusting in Him, who will shew you greater things than these. I admire the Lord's work in the sweet effects you mention of being afraid to act to free yourself from trial, while you are kept waiting upon the Lord to see Him work and go before you in all things. This is very blessed and safe. One has well said, When we follow the Lord and keep His company, He always bears our expenses; if we run before Him or go alone, He may leave us to bear our own. The Lord may lead us round, but he will lead us right. Oh! may you, my dear friend, be kept in a waiting frame of spirit; it is most blessed, though very contrary to our flesh; and you know our time here is so short that if things of an outward kind be ever so disagreeable, it will soon, very soon, be over, and all that now annoys our flesh will, in the light of eternity, appear a very nothing. This thought reminds me of a dear young friend, who has only been married three or four years, but in that time has had a sea of tribulation to wade through. This has arisen from the sin of one who should have been her comfort, instead of which his attentions have been bestowed elsewhere, and she has had to bear neglect, contempt, personal unkindness ; and now for more than a year she, with her two children, has been deserted. But the Lord has sanctified the sorrow and drawn her to Himself ; and most moving it is to see her humbled, softened spirit— I mean spiritually softened, for she is naturally kind and amiable—and to hear her say she feels every step has been permitted, for if her path had been smooth, she might have rested in outward comforts, but now the world looks nothing to her, and things she once enjoyed have no charm. In speaking of probable future trial she said, " Oh, we have such a short time to stay here, it seems comparatively of little importance in what outward circumstances we are, so that the soul is right." This is a true testimony from a young disciple in deep trial. Oh ! may we live in the spirit of it, and our daily cry be, " Lord, lift thou up the light of thy countenance upon me." In company with Jesus, the heaviest trials are borne as amongst covenant blessings, even the sure mercies of David.

We call ourselves "pilgrims and strangers," but surely if we were quite satisfied with being so, we should not be so disconcerted by the annoyances of the road and of the inn— for what is any place here but an inn—just a lodging-place for a little season till our Father sends for us home. If our

Q

fellow-travellers are unkind, unreasonable, or aught beside, yet we shall soon part, and perhaps after all we may find how much self-love has been prevailing in us, and how often we are murmuring about the mote in their eye and neglecting the beam in our own. Oh! my loved one, may the Lord give us a meek, quiet, and patient spirit, which is, in the sight of God, of great price, though very contrary to our flesh. That has been a striking word to me, "We count them happy which endure." That word "endure" is worthy to be written in letters of gold. May the blessed Spirit set it in our hearts, and set our hearts steadfastly unto it in all the real or imaginary ills of life. To endure for Christ's sake breaks much of their force. Well, dear friend, we are both in the furnace; much, very much dross has in my case risen up, but my blessed and patient Refiner sits watching the process,—nor does all this, hateful as it is, make Him forsake the work of His hands. He will have me know a little what is in my heart, that I may know more of what is in His, even love, most invincible, unalterable, unquenchable love; love that endures to the end amidst all sorts of evil, and wandering, and ingratitude. It is indeed marvellous; and into the blessed depths of this love I desire to be daily sinking, in all the fresh discoveries of my utter worthlessness and vileness, that thus I may praise Him more who has redeemed me from it all. The Lord, you know, does not shew us how bad we are to cause despair, but to shew forth the riches of His grace in saving us, and to call forth new songs of praise to Him who loved us, and washed us from our sins in His own blood.

Oh, my dear friend, Jesus is worthy to be praised in the depths as well as in the heights. He is near, and dear, and precious in the hour of affliction, and in the path of tribulation, where He gives some of His choicest fruits and wines to revive those who are faint and weary in the wilderness. I am most thankful He gave you such a seasonable refreshment; and, like Manoah, you will be saying, "O my Lord, let the man of God whom thou didst send come again to us." But I mean especially the Lord himself, for it was His visitation that refreshed your spirit, and He sent His servant where He himself meant to come. Where He has been once He is quite sure to come again. "I will see you again, and your heart shall rejoice." Meanwhile it will be your mercy to be seeking for that excellent life of faith which is so strengthening to the soul, so glorifying to the Lord. Oh! may you be helped, yea enabled, "to trust in the Lord at all times;" not when you feel His love and have the shine of His countenance, but also in the dark and wintry day when clouds veil your sky, and sorrow invades your soul. "What time I am afraid I will trust in thee."—With kindest love and best wishes, I remain yours in Jesus most affectionately, RUTH.

LXXVIII.

The plausibility of unbelief.

"The Lord shall guide thee continually, and satisfy thy soul in drought.

TO MISS M.

HIGH PAVEMENT, *June* 10, 1856.

MY BELOVED FRIEND, It has been a pleasure to hear from you and of the Lord's dealings with you, for I cannot but hope that the gloom around you is not quite so dense as in days gone by. The bow of safety and peace seems to be more discernible in your cloud. Surely we will praise the Lord for any tokens for good, knowing He is so faithful, that where He gives the least item of covenant favour, it may be safely taken as a pledge of the whole. It is well when faith is watching for any kind word from Him, and does immediately take hold of it and echo it back again, as did the messengers of the king of Syria to Ahab.[1] But ah! is it not true that "the children of this world are in their generation wiser than the children of light?" They quickly take advantage for their own benefit in earthly things, but we are slow of heart in spiritual things—slow to believe what the Lord has done for us—slow to trust Him who has given us such exceeding great and precious promises, and ever ready to listen to Satan, unbelief, and carnal reason, instead of receiving His word with all readiness. What reason have we to cry, "Lord, increase our faith;" for really unbelief works at times so insidiously, it puts on the garb of humility and strives to make us consider it more humble and suitable for such great sinners as we are, to be doubting and holding back from the free promises of the gospel, instead of looking to Him, and expecting to receive of Christ's fulness. Oh! hateful dishonour to that able, willing Saviour who "receiveth sinners, and eateth with them." Many in this day who in their judgment reject all idea of creature merit are yet really stooping under this infirmity wherewith Satan binds them, and which is, in truth, looking at self instead of Jesus—looking for something in the creature, instead of all in Him. I was held so long in this specious snare, and do

[1] 1 Kings xx. 30-33.

now see it to be so derogatory to my precious Lord, that my
soul burns with indignation against this most hateful sin.
I rejoice to hear Bunyan call it "the white devil," and say,
"Oftentimes in its mischievous doings in the soul it shews
as if it were an angel of light; yea, it acteth like a counsellor
of heaven, for it is that sin which of all others hath some
shew of reason in its attempts, keeping the soul from Jesus
Christ by pretending its present unfitness and unprepared-
ness, pleading a want of more sense of sin, more humility,
more repentance, and more of a broken heart. It is the sin
which most suiteth with the conscience. The conscience of
the coming sinner tells him that he hath nothing good, that
he stands indictable for a thousand talents, that he is very
blind, ignorant, and hard hearted; and will you, says unbelief,
in such a case as you now are, presume to come to Jesus
Christ? It is the sin which most suits with our sense of
feeling: the coming sinner feels the workings of sin and
wretchedness in his flesh, and the wrath and judgment of God
due to sin, and often staggers under it. Now, says unbelief,
you may see you have no grace, for that which works in you
is corruption; you may also perceive that God doth not love
you, because the sense of His wrath abides upon you; therefore, how can you have the face to come to Jesus Christ? It
is that sin above all others that most suiteth the wisdom of the
flesh. The wisdom of the flesh thinks it prudent to question
awhile, to hearken to both sides awhile, to stand back awhile,
and not to be too rash or unadvised in a too bold presuming
upon Jesus Christ. It is that sin above all others that
weakens our prayers, our faith, our love, our hope, our diligence, and our expectations; it even taketh away the heart
from God in duty. This sin, as I have said before, appears

in the soul with so many sweet pretences to safety and security, that it is as it were counsel sent from heaven, bidding the soul to be wise, wary, and considerate, and to take heed of too rash a venture upon believing. Be sure first that God loves you ; be not sure of your salvation, but doubt it still, though the testimony of the Lord has been confirmed in you ; live not by faith but by sense, and when you can neither see nor feel, then fear and mistrust, then doubt and question all. This is the counsel of unbelief, which is so covered over with specious pretences that the wisest Christian can hardly shake off these reasonings." So says Bunyan; and these sayings have been very profitable to my soul. May the Holy Spirit make them so to yours, my dear friend. I do greatly long that the sly workings of this vile sin of unbelief should be discovered, and that we should do with it as Esther did with Haman—bring it into the presence of the King to plead against it, and get its schemes against us broken by His power.

I was rejoiced to hear that the Lord has guided you to the house of your Master's brethren, and that you are located in a pilgrim lodge. May the Lord grant you sweet communion, and bless the change to the benefit of your health. You mention our meeting face to face; it does not look likely, but we know not what is before us. I feel sure and certain you would be disappointed ; you think much too highly of me. I am reserved, have not conversational powers, and am altogether a very poor creature, but just fit for Jesus to save ; and by the grace of God I am what I am. The Lord bless you, and enlarge you abundantly in Christ.— With affectionate love, ever yours warmly in Him, RUTH.

Excuse the many defects.

LXXIX.

The bosom of Jesus.

TO MISS M.

High Pavement, *March* 10, 1857.

My beloved Friend, I hope you are finding comfort in being with your dear sister, though there is no nest below without a thorn; this you well know, and therefore will not expect it. But there is a bosom without a thorn, even where John leaned, and where, by faith, unworthy I often lean, and find sweet rest and refreshing; and in that dear bosom and in that dear heart "yet there is room," room even for thee, O weary one! There thou shalt find no rebuke, no spurning, no upbraiding. The invitation to the labouring and the weary is, "Come unto me," "and I will give you rest." Nor did those precious lips ever utter one unmeaning word. He means it all, and His ear and heart are open to all the sorrowful complaint of those poor and needy ones whom He invites to His rest. How many a long sad tale has He privileged me to breathe out to Him; oh! such as none else would have had patience to listen to or cared to redress. Others would have called it fancy or imaginary trouble; but He bore with it all, and either delivered out of it, or delivered in it—either made a way of escape, or gave strength to endure, through finding in Him enough to fill and satisfy under it all. Then at other times He has discovered the illusion of the enemy, kindly shewn me that I really was fretting under imaginary evil, and, without upbraiding, has set me on high from him that was puffing at me.[1]   When under deep and sore trials, His heart, and arm, and counsel have been for my support all-sufficient.   "Oh! what a friend is Christ to me;" and not less to thee, my beloved.   Oh! come then and magnify the Lord with me, and let us exalt His name together.   Do not let us be murmuring in these tents of flesh,[2] but by faith going forth to Jesus.   Our Father has not appointed us any portion in self, but He has given Christ, the true Manna, to be our portion for time and eternity; and the more we are brought to feed upon Him by faith, the less we shall need or desire aught beside.   Oh! may the blessed Spirit bring us to this dear privilege, that so we may grow up into Him our living Head in all things.

Mr W—— preached two Sabbaths.   The last was one of great power and blessedness to my soul.   I do love to hear of those eternal verities upon which he so constantly dwells, even love in its fountain and source, far back before the worlds were made,—the love of the Father, the love of the Son, and the love of the Spirit fixed upon the Church, well knowing all that would come to her in the Adam fall, but determining to bring her safe up to glory through and notwithstanding all.   Oh! it is good old wine of the kingdom, which strengthens my faith far more than endlessly dwelling on the changes in self and feeling.   Those changes we must have while below, for the decree has gone forth that while earth lasts, day and night, summer and winter, shall not cease; but the way to be strengthened under them is to consider Him who changes not, but rests in His love, and ever beholds His Church all fair in His own comeliness.

[1] Ps. xii. 5.   [2] Ps. cvi. 25.

May you be brought to rest in Him, my dear friend, for it is blessed indeed so to do.

I much enjoyed converse with the dear Margate friends. Jesus was our theme, and we were of one heart in desiring that He should be all and in all, and we have had an abiding blessing from it. . . . I hear Mr D—— is coming to England. I hope he may visit you, and that you may have as sweet a blessing as you did last time. The Lord sends His disciples where He Himself will come, and it is most sweet to converse of Him and with Him, and how the heart does burn while He opens in all the Scriptures the things concerning Himself. That is it, beloved friend, which is food to the soul, even the living Bread which came down from heaven ; and as we feed on Him we forget our poverty in the first Adam, because we have found such superlative riches in the second. Oh! yes indeed, He is full of fulness just suited to our needs, and He says, " Open thy mouth wide, and I will fill it." The more we receive the more we are yet enlarged to receive, and the more we know and enjoy of Him the more we see yet to be known and enjoyed. What our Father has bestowed upon us in giving Christ is wonderful indeed, and will be unfolding to all eternity. May we be learning more and more of His unsearchable riches now ; thus shall we be less affrighted at our own poverty, which we must also learn, but only to bring us to know more of the depths of His matchless love, and that we may rejoice and glory in Him alone. Ever praise Him, O my soul, who hath remembered and visited thee in thy low estate, for His mercy endureth for ever.

Oh, my dear friend, this lovely Saviour makes me so happy in Himself and with Himself that I sometimes think I must be going home, though perhaps it is rather a preparative for some trial; but all, however, shall be well; through the fire and through the water He will bring us safely to the wealthy place. I have had a precious baptism of love the last three weeks—a sweet foretaste of the fulness of joy, and of those pleasures which are at His right hand for evermore. I am most unworthy; but worthy, ever worthy, is the precious Lamb; and our Father has blessed us in Him; wherefore our own unworthiness is no barrier to the flowing of these heavenly streams; it has nothing to do with it. These streams rise in God, flow in Christ, and bear down before them all that is of the creature; yea in the ocean of His love and blood both self and sins get lost. For " of Him, and through Him, and to Him, are all things: to whom be glory for ever. Amen."

Do you know anything of the Orphan House at Bristol? I am deeply interested in it; it is so encouraging to faith. I am going to send you a report, hoping you may find it profitable, as I and many have done.—Your affectionate friend, RUTH.

LXXX.

The power of faith.

TO MISS M.

HIGH PAVEMENT, *June* 3, 1858.

MY BELOVED FRIEND, It is a mercy when we are enabled to deal openly with the Lord, and in child-like simplicity just to carry to Him every fresh perplexity, whether great or small. Nothing is too minute for His notice and counsel, nothing too mighty for Him to overrule and bring deliverance. Sometimes He brings deliverance *in* the trouble by blessed support and communion; sometimes deliverance *out* of the trouble by making a way of escape; but in whatever way He is pleased to work, He will answer those who call upon Him, for He has said, "Call unto me, and I will answer thee, and shew thee great and mighty things which thou knowest not." "Call upon me in the day of trouble, I will deliver thee, and thou shalt glorify me." May the grace of wrestling prayer be given, that you may put Him to the test of His own words, and may you look to His promises and not to your own feelings for encouragement to plead. Our ever prevailing plea is, the blood and righteousness of Jesus, in whom all the promises of God are yea and amen, and sometimes warm feelings are withholden that we may trust alone in Him and not to them. Faith can venture before the throne with "Jesus only," but sense wants the honey of sweet feelings to offer[1] *with* the Lamb, and thus to have more hope of acceptance; but we are accepted only in the Beloved, and our confidence before the Lord is to be by His blood alone through faith.[2] Oh, my dear friend, may you meditate on these things, for I feel sure that the living Church is, in the present day, much held in bondage by seeking to live more by feeling than by faith. The life of faith is not an unfeeling life, a cold life, a half-hearted life, a life of worldly conformity; it is faith that follows Christ fully, and forsakes all for Him, as Joshua and Caleb did when all the people talked of stoning them. They well knew their own weakness and the strength of the enemy, but

[1] Lev. ii. 11.   [2] Heb. x. 19; Eph. iii. 12.

rested all their trust in the love and faithfulness of the Lord, while those who walked by sight and sense looked only at the giant foes, and at their own weakness. Thus it is with us spiritually; when poring only upon what we are, we grow more and more discouraged; and seeking water from the creature cistern, our tongue faileth for thirst, for there is none *there*, but it is in the fountain of living waters, even our precious Jesus, in whom all fulness dwells for poor and needy souls; and when we are brought to this extremity, He kindly says, "I the Lord will hear them: I the God of Israel will not forsake them." How feelingly can my heart renew the cry, "Lord, increase my faith," for, alas! I often stagger through unbelief, not upon the subject of personal interest in Christ, but upon many others of less importance, yea and upon *that* also should I stagger if the Lord left me to the carnal reasonings of the flesh, "so foolish am I and ignorant." Well, may it please Him to bring us to say with the apostle, "The life which I now live in the flesh, I live by the faith of the Son of God." Faith humbly presses on through the tribulation path, looking unto Jesus, and fully understands that excellent saying of Hewitson, "The soul will be staggered even by loose stones in the way if we look manward; if we look Godward faith will not be staggered even by inaccessible mountains stretching and obstructing apparently our outward progress." Perhaps I shall weary you; but this subject of faith is dear to my heart, and I do long for your furtherance and joy of faith. Let not that which is lame be turned out of the way, but let it rather be healed. "Strengthen ye the weak hands, and confirm the feeble knees. Say to them that are of a fearful heart, Be strong, fear not: behold your God will come with vengeance,

even God with a recompense ; he will come and save you."
Yes, the feeble and the fearing He will save. Oh! may the
feet and ankle bones of faith receive strength to enter into
Christ the true temple, leaping and walking and praising
God. I wish you every blessing, and all needful grace, for
He is able to make all grace abound towards you.—With
kind love, ever yours affectionately, RUTH.

LXXXI.

Counsels to a young man entering the ministry.

(*Written by request, after a long conversation.*)

TO MR MACDONALD.

June 1855.

DEAR BROTHER IN THE LORD, You have set me a task in
again requesting me to write the substance of our conversation. You are surrounded with many deep streams in books
and in experienced servants of the Lord, and you have at
hand "the well-spring of wisdom, which is a flowing brook;"
also you have within the well of living water[1] springing up,
and the anointing to teach;[2] but as you have again expressed the desire, I must try, in humble dependence upon
the blessed Spirit, of whom our Lord said, " He shall teach
you all things, and shall bring all things to your remembrance, whatsoever I have said unto you."

I think we first spoke of preaching to dead sinners—that
they should be told of their guilty, lost condition, and entire
corruption, their sin set before them;[3] also the only way of

[1] John iv. 14. [2] 1 John ii. 27. [3] Acts ii. 23; and iii. 13-15.

escape, and that continuing in sin, they must perish.[1] Their responsibility must be appealed to,[2] and that not on the ground of their capability, but of God's rightful sovereignty, He not having lost His right to command, though they have lost all power to obey. Their complete helplessness must be stated, not leading them to think there is any power in the creature, and yet shewing how they are amenable to the Divine law, and that because of transgression the wrath of God comes upon the transgressor. We did not speak of the law, but surely its holy requirements should be set forth in their spirituality, in reaching to the thoughts and intents of the heart, in order to shew out transgression;[3] not because any can meet its demands, yet all are under it till released by the glad tidings of the gospel, coming by the Spirit's power. The law is for "the disobedient,"[4] and what it says is to them who are under it, to stop every mouth, and prove all guilty before God.[5] Also it is needful to set forth what must be fulfilled before any can be justified. Then comes in the great Law Fulfiller, who could lay His hand on both parties, giving to the Lawgiver rich satisfaction, and to the lawbreaker honourable salvation. Here is "a door of hope," and "as Moses lifted up the serpent in the wilderness, even so must the Son of man be lifted up," and when the Spirit opens the eyes, the sin-bitten look and live. Thus while the law shews out man's utter deformity,[6] it shews the Saviour's beauty, for He was fully conformed to its pattern.[7] By faith in Him the soul experiences full benefit of all He did and

---

[1] Psalm ix. 17.

[2] Acts xvii. 28-31; 2 Cor. v. 10, 11.

[3] Rom. iii. 20.

[4] 1 Tim. i. 9.

[5] Rom. iii. 19.

[6] Rom. vii. 8, 13.

[7] Matt. v. 17; John xvii. 4.

suffered, which is the only way of salvation,[1] and this faith is the gift of God.[2]

As to direct addresses to dead sinners, it has been said, "You might as well stand in a churchyard and call to a corpse to come out of the grave," which is most true as regards the state of a sinner, and the power of a merely human call. But God told Ezekiel to prophesy to bones dead and dry,[3] which was like preaching to dead sinners. The Lord's ministers speak to all dead in sin, warning and teaching every man, being at the same time quite sure that the word will only be used to gather out those who are chosen,[4] and equally sure that this can only be done by the power of the Spirit. They, feeling much for perishing sinners, "preach the word," and warn with great earnestness, yet place no dependence upon their feeling or their earnestness or their use of the letter of Scripture, but entirely on the Spirit, without whose power there will be no signs following, neither the quickening of the dead, nor the comforting, reproving, and edifying of the living; therefore, while warning and teaching in season and out of season, as Col. i. 28, 2 Tim. iv. 2, they continually recognise that God must give the increase.[5]

We spoke of exhorting dead sinners to pray. Prov. xxviii. 9, and Prov. xv. 8, seem to be against this, the sacrifice of the wicked being there said to be "an abomination to the Lord;" but it is evident that Peter did so exhort Simon Magus,[6] for he told him to repent and pray for forgiveness, even while plainly perceiving that he was "in the gall of

---

[1] Acts xiii. 38, 39 ; John iii. 36.
[2] Eph. ii. 8.
[3] Ezek. xxxvii. 2-4.

[4] Acts xiii. 48, and xv. 14.
[5] 1 Cor. iii. 6, 7 ; 2 Cor. iv. 4-7.
[6] Acts viii. 22, 23.

bitterness, and in the bond of iniquity." Also, he exhorts
the Jerusalem-sinners to repent,[1] yet not with any view to
creature power either in them or himself, for, in Acts v. 31,
he clearly states that repentance is the gift of Christ; but
while he so exhorted them, the Lord blessed the Word, for
we read that many which heard it believed.[2] Ministers
should so use the Word as the sower does the seed, knowing that the Spirit alone can prepare the heart and give it
entrance as well as cause it to spring up.

We spoke of the invitations of the gospel as being given
to character. Are not the hungry invited to the bread? the
thirsty to the waters? and the weary and heavy laden to
Christ for rest? And while the character is described, many
poor and needy ones will find their token. But, then, we
saw they are not to rest in being the character, but seek
relief and rest alone in the Saviour, as He says, "Look unto
me and be ye saved;" and it is written, "They looked unto
Him and were lightened, and their faces were not ashamed."
The Spirit does not direct to His own work in them, but to
the work of Jesus, as Jesus said, "He shall glorify *me*, for
he shall receive of *mine* and shall shew it unto you." The
Spirit says, "come," and the bride echoes His word "come;"
and why? "Come," because the fountain is so full and free
—the blood so life-giving and strengthening—the rest so
refreshing! "Come," because the blood is so efficacious to
cleanse, the righteousness to justify. Come to Jesus as
sinners, His benefits are for *sinners*. This encourages
seekers who do not know their "election" of God, which is
a glorious truth, but not the first step on the ladder,—they
have to do with "calling," and that is to sinners.[3] The Spirit

---

[1] Acts iii. 19.   [2] Acts iv. 4.   [3] 1 Tim. i. 15.

makes them feel that they are sinners, and the Spirit directs
them to the Saviour as crucified for sinners, and He often
does both by the preaching of the word.   And as the soul
is enabled to come to Jesus, and to look away from self
to Jesus, the Father is honoured who gave Jesus,[1] draws
sinners to Jesus,[2] and accepts them in Him.[3]   The Spirit
is honoured who testified of Jesus,[4] and Jesus is honoured
in what He has done and suffered.[5]   Thus the Triune
Jehovah is glorified, and the soul strengthened to "walk
up and down in the name of the Lord."[6]

We spoke a little of preaching personal experience.   Experience must not be put in the place of Christ,[7] nor encouragement from experience used instead of encouragement
in the Lord our God;[8] yet to tell somewhat, at times, of
personal deliverances may more reach the case of tried and
tempted souls, than only stating the Lord's power and willingness to deliver.   To describe the malady and tell the
skill of the physician may be the principal thing; yet for the
minister to mention occasionally some feature in his own
case, and how the efficacy was personally proved, may tell
home on the heart of those who are in soul-distress.

Paul did not scruple to tell what he had experienced
when cited before the rulers of his people,[9] though this may
not be considered as an example of preaching.   But may
not 2 Cor. i. 4-6 bear favourably upon some use of personal
experience ? You know we fully saw that some of the
Lord's ministers are more used for comforting and edifying
His people, and others for the calling of His dead—the
Spirit working in each severally as He will.

[1] 2 Cor. ix. 15.
[2] John vi. 44.
[3] Eph. i. 6.
[4] 1 Pet. i. 11.
[5] 1 Pet. ii. 24.
[6] Zech. x. 12.
[7] 2 Cor. iv. 5.
[8] 1 Sam. xxx. 6.
[9] Acts xxii., xxvi.

On personal experience we remarked, that while it is good to live in a constant sense of dependence, feeling that without divine power we cannot think, speak, or do anything to the divine glory, yet that it is making a wrong use of this, if therefrom we draw excuse for an inactive or unexercised state of soul, which rather betokens unhealthiness than true dependence.

The Lord having given us natural life, we look for Him to give power for the exercise of that life (when we are in health) in eating, drinking, walking, and working. And so being made spiritually alive in Christ Jesus, it is our privilege to look for divine power to exercise the spiritual faculties and the graces of the Spirit; not only to recognise that we have life, but that we may be feeding on Christ, rooting in Him and growing up into Him ; so that while deeply feeling the truth of His words, " Without me ye can do nothing," we may also come to the experience of His servant, who said, "I can do all things through Christ which strengtheneth me." Not only acknowledging that "in Him all fulness dwells," but seeking, by the Spirit's power, to have the exercise of faith thereupon, and be receiving of that fulness grace for grace. By exercise, faith is strengthened.

These were the points of our converse, and both our ideas are embodied, though many fresh scriptures have flowed in writing.

You must be sure to send me word wherever you differ, as it may tend to edification. Further search into truth is not labour in vain, and most sweet is the promise, John xvi. 13. The Lord ever bless you and set you apart for Himself by the Spirit's anointing. "Meditate upon these things, give thyself wholly to them."—Ever yours in Jesus,

R. B.

LXXXII.

Counsels to a young man entering the ministry.

To one who is as a "sparrow alone upon the housetop."
"Fear thou not, for I am with thee."

TO MR MACDONALD.

July 22, 1855.

MY DEAR FRIEND, I will tell you what I have just been thinking. You know our gracious Lord said to His disciples, "It is expedient for you that I go away ; for if I go not away the Comforter will not come unto you." It seems to me, that friend after friend, comfort after comfort, might also say to our foolish, clinging, sensitive hearts, "It is expedient for you that *we* go away ; for if we go not away the Comforter will not come unto you !" In other words, "If *we* remain, you will build on us part of your comfort, and then you will be a loser, not learning the height, depth, length, and breadth of the love, sweetness, and fulness which are in Christ Jesus. A pang may be felt as one by one is taken away; yet how blessed to be in the position of the poor sinner who was left alone with Jesus, when His gracious lips did drop as the honeycomb into her heart, saying, "Neither do I condemn thee : go, and sin no more." Oh, it is worth being stripped of all that is our own to hear this secret of divine love, and to enjoy Jesus as our "all in all."

Now, I know you will assent to this in your judgment; but I want you to have the full benefit and blessing in being brought nearer to Jesus; for I well know what creatures we are for self-hewn cisterns, and how when one is broken we seek for another, instead of turning to the Fountain. Look at your own heart, and see whether it is not so ; whether you are not often wanting a friend, a letter, or anything to break the desolate feeling. Am I speaking too closely? It is because I am so much of your own temperament that I thus judge you, and long to draw you to the full bliss of forsaking *all* for Christ. Then shall you most abundantly find all in Him, and praise Him for every stripping and emptying which prevented your resting in a lower source of enjoyment, or enjoying even Himself through the medium of others. Oh! it is most precious to commune directly with Himself, and receive lessons of wisdom from His own blessed mouth—

> " With Thee conversing, I forget
> All time and toil and care ;
> Labour is rest, seclusion sweet,
> When Thou my God art there."

This is the application of the subject. You are now in the very position to be learning the sweetness of being alone with Jesus; and if you feel a lack in outward ordinances, and a lack of Christian communion, it is to bring you in quiet retirement to open your heart more fully to the Prince of Peace, that you may not have to go *abroad* for your choice things, but find Him at *home* in the inner temple of the new heart; and thus shall your present wilderness blossom abundantly, and you shall rejoice even with joy and singing. Our dear Lord always gives us just what is needful for our present circumstances. Inasmuch as we are repining against them, we are "the rebellious, and shall dwell in a dry land;' but when we accept them at His hands, seeking therein for

Jesus, we shall find that there is a blessing in them, however painful they may be to the flesh. Your present trials are covenant discipline in covenant love, to teach you to live above self and creatures, to be less dependent upon streams, and to be drawing from the Fountain. You see how freely I write, just like an elder sister who has trodden the path before you. I myself have been deprived of blessings dear as the right hand and the right eye, that I might come to "Peniel," which I need not tell you means the "face of God." Just see how Jacob sent all over the brook, in Gen. xxxii. 22, 23, 30. Even the nearest and dearest must go away, and he must be left alone to see the "face of God;" then it is recorded "He blessed him there." Oh, that this might be written of you at M——.

I think much of the high calling which you are contemplating, and also of what is said to the tribe of Levi in the Old Testament, "Thou shalt have no inheritance in their land." Moses, in blessing that tribe, said, "Neither did he acknowledge his brethren, nor knew his own children," all betokening a peculiar separation to the Lord, and shewing that they should esteem everything secondary to His glory, and that He being their inheritance, their confidence and chief delight should be in Him. Blessed state of high privilege! May it be fully yours in the spiritual sense, and may all the changes and tossings to which you are subjected be a means used by the Lord to bring you to it. Press after it, for "the soul of the diligent shall be made fat." "Open thy mouth wide and I will fill it."

You will be soon moving away, I know not whither, but

"While place we seek or place we shun,
The soul finds happiness in none ;

> But with a God to guide our way,
> 'Tis equal joy to go or stay,
> My country, Lord, art Thou alone,
> Nor other can I claim or own,
> The point where all my wishes meet,
> My Law, my Love, Life's only sweet."

May the guiding cloud ever go before you to mark *where* you should encamp in the wilderness. Remember it *will* be a wilderness everywhere, and you in some sort or other must feel it to be so; but many a stream will gush out of the Rock, and many a refreshment be prepared when you are faint and weary; not to tempt you to sit down in peace, but to strengthen you to go onward.

I am glad you are at times happy in " The Hiding-place," although you do come back to the painful consciousness of self. Even while you are learning what you are, you are safe in what *He is*, and you shall at last be more than conqueror; yea, even experimentally so now while "looking unto Jesus." " Resist the devil and he will flee from you." " Walk in the Spirit, and you shall not fulfil the lusts of the flesh." Constantly come to the light of the Spirit, that your fleshly thoughts, words, and deeds may be reproved, and as He discloses to you the evil, beg Him also to subdue it. It is not enough to learn our sin and cry out against it; the blessing is promised " to him that overcometh." It is not merely in self-loathing, but in self-forsaking, that our victory comes. " Be thou," in this sense, " faithful unto death, and I will give thee a crown of life."

It is very probable that we shall meet no more on earth; but I trust that when the earthly house of our tabernacle shall be dissolved, we may have "a building of God, a house not made with hands, eternal in the heavens." When we have arrived there, it will be of no importance how roughly or how smoothly we have fared by the way. And now farewell ; seek close walking with God, yield yourself fully and continually to the Lord. "As ye have therefore received Christ Jesus the Lord, so walk ye in him," rejoicing that "ye are not your own."

The Lord bless you and keep you from evil, that it may not grieve you, and continually set before you an open door in providence, saying, "This is the way, walk ye in it." He is our Rock, following us all through the wilderness, where our bread is given us and our water is sure.—In our adorable Emmanuel, ever yours affectionately   R. B.

LXXXIII.

Counsels to a young man entering the ministry.

"Is it well with thee ?"

TO MR MACDONALD.

September 1855.

MY DEAR FRIEND, What will you have thought of me for being so long in answering your most welcome letter ? Perhaps you will consider it a fresh proof of human fickleness, and imagine that I am forgetting you. Well, I am sure, it is peculiarly needful for you ever to remember the Divine injunction, "Cease ye from man whose breath is in his nostrils, for wherein is he to be accounted of ?" I am sure a heart so sensitive as yours has often smarted, often bled, from wounds given by those you love; but it is all permitted in order to bring you to rest on His dear bosom, on which the favoured disciple leaned, for Him you can never love too much. I know, too, that my poor friendship would not be worth one regret; but I am far from forgetting you, and desire ever to plead for you before our Father who is in heaven. He knows your temperament, you situation, your conflicts, and all about you. His eye is upon you; His heart is toward you in all your wanderings; and because you are not walking closely enough with Him, He will sometimes send disappointing and trying providences to bring you nearer to Him. I long after you in the Lord, that you may know experimentally the full privilege and blessedness of union to Jesus, that you may dwell in divine love and drink deeply of the waters of salvation, for so you will be best qualified to commend them to others. For this you have need to be much in the closet, pleading much with the Lord to fill you with the Spirit, who shall teach you all things, and lead you into all truth. Some persons hold up one part of truth ; but all the truth of God is precious. May you reject none, but prize all, and be led by the Spirit to receive it and search into it, and never be warped by any *part* of it or by creature opinion, that your faith may "not stand in the wisdom of men, but in the power of God." "Sanctify the Lord of Hosts Himself, and let *Him* be your fear, and let *Him* be your dread." Oh, may He make you a clear witness for His truth, and may that truth make you free from every error and false way. May the blessed Spirit correct all error in each of us, and grant that in His light we may see light.

I gather plainly from the Scriptures that all the wicked are to be warned, the thirsty to be invited to the waters, the hungry to the feast, those who have no money to the wine and milk, and, then, the large, broad, sweet word in Revelation is "Whosoever *will*, let him take the water of life freely." Beyond this I think you could not go, because all would not be willing. "It is God which worketh in you to will and to do of his good pleasure." You cannot enlarge your invitations too much to those who are willing, and you cannot err on the other side by keeping within the limit of Scripture warrant. Do not press this or any other point slightly ; many, by so doing, have "daubed the wall with untempered mortar." Do not go for counsel to human authority, even the highest, but seek on your knees, to have these things made plain to you. It is a solemn thing to stand as a watchman between the living and the dead. As you have written freely, I do so too. We have no thought of contention, but write affectionately in search of the truth; I, in prospect of eternity, you (if spared,) with the prospect of telling to dying fellow-sinners the way of salvation. Surely each of us has peculiar need to be sober and watch unto prayer ; and, perhaps, you sometimes feel "who is sufficient for these things?" But your sufficiency is of God, by whom alone the stripling David delivered the lamb out of the paw of the lion and the bear. May that same God send you to proclaim deliverance to many a lamb of the Saviour's flock whom the roaring lion is seeking to devour.

. . . . Ah, my brother, the Canaanite will to the end be still in the land, and we shall often groan, being burdened; but we must seek that these Canaanites may be more and more put under tribute [1] by the power of the

1 Joshua xvii. 13.

cross, and the blood of Jesus received by faith.   You know
the original inhabitants of Canaan are taken for a type of
the evils of our nature, and the great sin of Israel was
being too friendly with them.   Does not this tell home
upon our experience ?   Is there not at times a parleying
with besetting sins and inward evils, which have often cast
us down wounded ?   The indwelling of sin will remain
while we are in the body ; but if our souls are lively and
healthy, we shall be seeking for its power to be more and
more subdued ; not by our own efforts, but by faith in
Jesus.   If we feed this serpent, it will bite us in return; if
we give liberty to these Canaanites, they shall be pricks and
thorns to us.   Numb. xxxiii. 55, Josh. xxiii. 12, 13, with
some other like passages, have been in this sense very instructive to me.   Oh ! I am an evil creature, I have been
overcome by inward evil again and again, and have often
been too friendly with the natives of my old heart.   This
makes me now fear anything that ministers to them ; this
makes me shun even "the doubtful territory," because I am
sure that *there* they may get encouragement to lift up their
head.   In fact, my dear brother, I am so weak, so sinful,
that I am never safe away from the cross of Christ.   There
we not only learn the crucifixion of the world, but the
crucifixion of self ; and as the evil that is in us stirs and
strives, we can only have victory by His cross and by His
blood, which cleanseth from all sin.   I think none can have
been more tried with inward evil than I have; but, even
after a defeat, the Captain of the Lord's host has shewn me
that all my victory is *in* Him and *by* Him; so that, while
abased in mine own eyes, and loathing myself in the dust,
I have understood, to His praise, that in the highest sense

"ẟher warfare is accomplished, her iniquity is pardoned, for she hath received of the Lord's hands double for all her sins." Cheer up, therefore, press on towards the prize, tarry not in all the plain; your Lord has promised that "sin *shall not* have dominion over you," but He has also said, "he that soweth to his flesh, shall of the flesh reap corruption," and "the backslider in heart shall be filled with his own ways." Of both these I know the bitterness, and their best remedy is living by faith on Jesus, who has put away all our sin by the sacrifice of Himself. The Lord strengthen you in the conflict. The beloved apostle says, "I have written to you, young men, because ye are strong, and the word of God abideth in you, and ye have overcome the wicked one;" and Paul says, "Young men exhort to be sober-minded." . . .

This is a land of clouds and of storms, but they send us afresh to the hiding-place.

> " Hide me, O my Saviour, hide,
>   Till the storms of life be past;
>   Safe into the haven guide,
>   Oh receive my soul at last."

Sweet to the weary one will be that message, "The Master is come, and calleth for thee." And, now, farewell; "the conies are but a feeble folk, yet make they their houses in the rocks." May we do so too; there is a spring in the rock which flows sweetly for all the inhabitants. May you drink thereof and afresh lift up your head with joy. The Lord enrich you with covenant favour, and grant you such revelations of a precious Jesus as shall eclipse all beside.— Believe me yours, &c., R. B.

LXXXIV.

The exercise of faith.

TO MRS TURNER.

HIGH PAVEMENT, NOTTINGHAM,
November 27, 1855.

MY BELOVED FRIEND IN JESUS, "Think it not strange concerning the fiery trial which is to try you, as though some strange thing happened unto you," but be comforted in knowing that the Lord's gold is always tried with fire, and that the trial often comes in a time and way least expected; like him of old who said, "When I looked for good, then evil came unto me; and when I waited for light, then came darkness. I went mourning without the sun: I stood up, and I cried in the congregation." And thus it seems to have been with you in the change of ministry, which must have been very trying; but

> " God is His own interpreter,
> And He will make it plain."

Still wait on Him in wrestling prayer, and ere long the dark cloud will burst in blessings on your head. The Lord often puts a death upon means and ministers, because we are so prone to "look *to* them, instead of *through* them." "Power belongeth unto God;" and the most suitable and efficient ministry is only a blessing as He makes it so. In order that we may learn this experimentally, and be taught to live in simple dependence upon Himself, He will sometimes cause the Brook of Ordinances to dry up for a season, by which I mean we shall feel no power in them, and the minister whom we have found most profitable shall bring no message from the Lord to our souls. I have been in this case, my dear friend, and have had to bless the Lord for it afterwards; for although very painful, yet the blessed Spirit does thereby teach us to profit, and bring us to say with David, "My soul, wait thou only upon God, for my expectation is from him."

I am grieved to hear that you are suffering serious bodily affliction; but if in it you find Jesus, it will indeed be to you a cup of blessing, as I have fully proved; for as the bitter waters of Marah were made sweet by the healing tree which Moses cast into them, even so the most bitter affliction is healed of its bitterness when by faith we apprehend a precious Jesus as the Tree of Life, whose leaves are for the healing of the nations. I think I told you how much I have enjoyed these words, "who healeth all thy diseases," as regards myself; not that my body is healed of the disease, or is ever likely to be, but the disease itself is healed of all that would savour of wrath, curse, or bitterness; it is all sent in love, though disagreeable to the flesh; and the spirit seeing so much, so very much mercy in it, can feelingly and joyfully say, "It is well." This, however, is only "by the working of his mighty power," for when I was first fully confirmed as to the nature of the malady, gloom overhung my mind, and I could not for some time feel as I desired. I have sometimes thought it was like the first day—evening and morning—not the brightness first, but the shade. My soul did groan unto the Lord for a blessing in it, but I could not for some time spread out my case before Him, or "fill my mouth with arguments." Yet He hears "the voice of our weeping," and our groaning is not hid from Him; yea,

it "enters into his ears." He knows what it means, and
that we would say and feel if we could, "Thy will, not
mine, be done."

We may groan and sigh, and think we cannot pray, but
that groan and that sigh are prayer in His account, and He
often answers them, as this unworthy heart can testify; for
though in one part of this affliction my mind was enveloped
in cloud, yet ere long the blessed Sun of Righteousness did
arise with healing in His wings. Then was sorrow turned
into joy before Him, and gloom and darkness fled away at
His presence. O beloved, He can take off the keen edge
from everything to which our frame is subject, and turn the
curse into a blessing, yea, turn the water of affliction into
the wine of consolation. I have been led quite unintention-
ally to speak thus of myself; but perhaps those things flow
most freely which we have ourselves tasted and handled;
and as you are now a "companion in tribulation," may the
blessed Spirit breathe into your soul some word of comfort
or encouragement, that by His power you may be strengthened with might in the inner man unto all patience and
long-suffering, with joyfulness.

May I be allowed to say that whatever be the nature of
your affliction you will find it weakening to look at it; but,
looking unto Jesus, you will have, moment by moment,
incomings of strength and support—not a stock in hand, but
just as you need it. When Peter looked at the waves, he
soon began to fear and to sink, but while he looked at his
Master, though they were still boisterous, yet all was well.
So I find it, and so will you. When looking at this or that
painful thing it is quite too much for us, but when looking
unto Jesus, and leaving all to Him, we are borne through

the trial, and the very mountains become a plain ; yea, and the floods which we thought would overwhelm us are made to divide that we may pass safely through.

May the Lord increase our faith, and cause us to live in the fullest privilege of those deep words, " Ye are not your own ;" and may He be pleased so to nourish your faith by His word and Spirit that you shall find how sweet it is

> " To lie passive in His hands,
> And know no will but His."

Then you will say, " This is the Lord's doing, and it is marvellous in our eyes." Whatever your present state may be, my heart would say to you, " Is anything too hard for the Lord ?" Nothing ! He can support and deliver ; He can make you joyful *in* the affliction, and then bring you with joy *out* of it. If it be His holy will, may He soon command deliverance for you, saying, " I am the Lord that healeth thee."

I trust your soul is more at rest in Jesus. Oh ! may He bring you fully into that liberty wherewith He makes His people free, which is such a liberty as the debtor has when his surety has paid all he owed ; such a liberty as the prisoner has when he is told that the law has now nothing against him. " Who shall lay anything to the charge of God's elect ? It is God that justifieth : who is he that condemneth ? It is Christ that died, yea, rather that is risen again, who is ever at the right hand of God, who also maketh intercession for us." [1]

But, say you, am I the character here spoken of ? Read Rom. vii. There the character is described to whom belongs the " no condemnation " of Rom. viii., and I do think yours

[1] Rom. viii. 33, 34.

is there described ; but as long as we look to our evidences for comfort we shall be full of disquiet, for we discover such weakness in our faith, such wavering in our hope, such coldness in our love, yea, such shortcoming in everything, that we cannot find here any rest for the sole of our foot as regards spiritual confidence; it must be all in Christ; "He is the rock, and his work is perfect," while our works are all broken and faulty. Oh ! may the blessed Spirit set your feet upon this Rock, and establish your goings there. May He enable you to make the venture of faith, just as you are, with wants and woes, sins and fears.

> "Venture on Him, venture wholly !
> Let no other trust intrude."

And it is not only one venture, but many. The life of faith is continued venturing afresh, finding no more in self to encourage us at the last than at the first, remembering in the midst of all discouragements how " David encouraged himself in the Lord his God." And that is just what faith does. By reason of the flood of corruptions within and tribulation without, the poor soul can find no place of rest, but, by faith, she flies to the Ark, and the Lord pulls her in.

I commend you to that precious Jesus who still "receiveth sinners, and eateth with them."—And, wishing you every covenant blessing, remain in His warm love your unworthy but affectionate friend, RUTH BRYAN.

LXXXV.

"Healing leaves for the sorrows of the way."

"They have taken away my Lord, and I know not where they have laid Him."

TO MRS TURNER.

High Pavement,
Nottingham, *May* 5, 1856.

MY BELOVED FRIEND, The above was the sorrowful plaint of one who had known the presence of Jesus, and now felt His absence; who had enjoyed His company, and now mourned the loss of it. All the world was nothing to her without the Lord; she came to indulge her love and grief by adding "sweet spices" to the myrrh and aloes which were already wrapped with His precious body: but even that body was gone, this last solace was denied her; and, oh! what a sinking, saddened heart she had, when, weeping and wondering, she looked again into the sepulchre. Methinks it was a hopeless look; she had already seen that the holy body was not there, but she would look once more at the very spot where it was laid. And what was her joy when she was greeted by His living voice calling her by name! She expected not to hear that voice again, she had no thought of beholding a risen Redeemer; but He had said, "I will see you again, and your heart shall rejoice," and His words were now sweetly fulfilled in this seeking soul, who, having much forgiven, loved Him much.

But perhaps you will wonder what all this has to do with you. Why, my beloved, I have heard from our dear Mrs

S

N—— that you are depressed, and so I have been thinking that, perhaps, like poor Mary, you are feeling as if you had lost your Lord. Then, when He appears to stand afar off, all looks gloomy, afflictions are more painful, trials more perplexing, and even mercies look less cheering. The poet has truly said—

> " I can do all things, and can bear
> All sufferings, if my Lord be there;
> Sweet pleasures mingle with the pains,
> While His left hand my head sustains.
>
> " But if my Lord be once withdrawn,
> And I attempt to work alone;
> When new temptations spring and rise,
> I prove how great my weakness is."

We are so prone to commit these two great evils—departing from the Fountain of living waters, and hewing out to ourselves broken cisterns that can hold no water. And our wise and gracious Lord will let us, for a season, reap the fruit of our doings, in order to make our folly hateful to us, but He will not always chide nor cast off for ever. He will return unto us with mercies, and with healing in His wings. He is the good Samaritan, and if we have spiritually fallen among thieves, who have stripped us of our garments of praise, and robbed us of the joys of His salvation, and wounded us till we feel half dead; though He may first let us prove that all "self-helps" and creature helps are vain, yet at length He will be sure " to come that way," and minister to our needy case, saying, " I am the Lord that healeth thee."

But if this be not your case, and that rather in sovereignty He has been pleased to withdraw His blessed presence, saying, " It is expedient for you that I go away," and you, like

Mary, are sorrowing; yet, dear friend, you do not sorrow without hope. He has not only said, "I go away," but also, "I come again unto you;" and by the absence of sensible enjoyments for a season, He means you to learn more of that life of faith which is honouring to Him and strengthening to the soul. He says by the prophet, "Who is among you that feareth the Lord, that obeyeth the voice of His servant, that walketh in darkness, and hath no light, [or bright shining?] let him trust in the name of the Lord, and stay upon his God." So whatever be your case, there is a remedy in Jesus, which the blessed Spirit will bring home and apply, causing you to sing that dear wilderness song, "He restoreth my soul."

Have you wandered? The good Shepherd will seek you out, and bring you back.[1] Have you sought help from creatures? He will disappoint you there, and give you all in Himself.[2] Have you sinned? Your advocate pleads for you, and His precious blood cleanses you from all sin.[3] Has your Beloved withdrawn Himself? Arise, and seek Him in the Word, in the ordinances of His house, and in your closet; then ere long He will be found of you, and you shall joyfully say, "I found Him whom my soul loveth." It is not in vain to seek Him, to wait on Him, and to wait for Him; all of which the blessed Spirit will enable you to do. But should you be tried with an increase of bodily affliction, your blessed Lord is the Physician of value who can reach and touch that case also, wherefore do not pore over it, but take it to Him with whom all things are possible; yea, He can even bring you a step higher than all that has been said, enabling you to rejoice in His will,

[1] Ezek. xxxiv. 11, 12. [2] Hosea ii. 7, 14, 15. [3] 1 John i. 7, ii. 1.

when most contrary to the flesh, and to live daily in the spirit of that deep sentence, " Thy will be done." Oh, that is a blessed state! then is the mind kept in perfect peace, being stayed on Him. May the Lord bring us to it, by His own power, and for His own glory!

I have been very weak and ill, but am just reviving again for a season. " My times are in Thy hands," and whether it be health or sickness, if Jesus be but glorified, it shall be well. We are His dear-bought purchase. Oh, what a price has He paid for us! And will He suffer sin, or Satan, or any circumstances of body or mind, to separate us from Him, and rob Him of His right? No, never, never, He loves us too well; in all things we shall eventually be more than conquerors through Him that loveth us. Cheer up, beloved friend; He may suffer us to wade deep in our own corruptions, He may bring us through fire and through water of temptation and tribulation, but He will bring us out into the wealthy place, and we shall see His face with joy. " Faithful is He that calleth you, who also will do it." We have you often in remembrance; and I shall be happy if, before this reaches you, the gloom you have felt be past, and you are filled with praise and thanksgiving to Him who alone is worthy. Seek for close walking and much communion; and may you daily " count all things but loss, for the excellency of the knowledge of Christ Jesus our Lord."

May every covenant blessing be with you. Kind love from your poor unworthy friend and fellow-pilgrim,

RUTH BRYAN.

LXXXVI.

Comfortable words for a sorrowing spirit."

" Why weepest thou? Whom seekest thou?"

TO MRS TURNER.

HIGH PAVEMENT,
NOTTINGHAM, *August* 13, 1856.

MY DEAR MRS TURNER, Once again I take up my pen to greet you in the dear name of Him who was anointed to heal the broken-hearted, to preach deliverance to the captives, to set at liberty them that are bruised, and to comfort them that mourn ; that those which mourn may be exalted to safety.

I understand that at this time your harp is on the willows, that you are a woman of a sorrowful spirit, and one of them that mourn. I know not what is the cause of your being at present cast down, but your heavenly Father knows, and He has promised that He will not suffer you to be tempted above that you are able to bear, and that, with every temptation, He will make a way to escape. " Faithful is He that calleth you, who also will do it." You know David said, " When my spirit was overwhelmed within me, then Thou knewest my path," implying that he did not know it himself; and Job said, " But He knoweth the way which I take : when He hath tried me, I shall come forth as gold." And when was this ? Why, it was just when he went forward and backward, to the right hand and to the left, in search of Him, but he could not find Him ; yet he believed that the Lord knew all, and would bring him out of that hot furnace even as gold. Ah, say you, "but I am not gold." Well, beloved, that may be so to your view, because the dross is rising up, and you can see and feel nothing else; but the great Refiner sees differently, and I quite believe that it will be proved that "better is the end of a thing than the beginning thereof."

Many of the Lord's people have come into very dark and intricate paths of experience, but never were they left or forsaken, although many have often feared it, saying, as David, "I shall one day perish by the hand of Saul." But did he perish? No; neither shall you; the Lord would not have shewed you such things if He had meant to destroy you. It is to humble you and prove you, that He may do you good in your latter end; and when He has shewn you a little of what is in your heart, He will shew you something of what is in His heart, even "thoughts of peace, and not of evil, to give you an expected end." He will then reveal the everlasting love which has been fixed upon you from all eternity, and is now drawing you to Himself. Yea, you shall see such love flowing from your Father's heart in the precious gift of His beloved Son, whom He delivered up to the sword of justice and to the curse of the law for your sake, that though you find within nothing but abomination, and without nothing but sin and shortcoming, though you feel yourself full of wounds and bruises and putrefying sores, yet shall you experience that with His stripes you are healed, in His blood you are cleansed, and in His righteousness you are justified.

Hear what He says, "O Israel, thou hast destroyed thyself; but in me is thine help." You may be now learning something of the depths of your malady, but it will only enhance the blessing of the cure. "The deep of your misery calls unto the deep of His mercy," and it shall not call in vain. Satan, the devouring lion, may be roaring against you, he may open his mouth at you, but the Lord will not leave you in his power; the good Shepherd will deliver you even though you feel broken and wounded.[1] Whatever the enemy touches, he shall not touch your life, for that is "hid with Christ in God." O my dear friend, I know his fearful power! there was a time when I felt as if I was in his mouth, but he was not permitted to close it upon me; the Lord graciously delivered me, and I live to encourage others to hope in His mercy. I have also known what it is to travel through the wretched wilderness of my own heart, and learn something of its corruptions—feeling hard, cold, barren, prayerless, and everything else that is hateful. It was like that dreary land mentioned in Jer. ii. 6, and it felt as solitary as if none else could be there— "they wandered in the wilderness in a solitary way." But One eye was watching, though unseen; One arm was supporting, though unfelt; and at length the Sun of righteousness arose upon my sorrowful soul, and, "turned the shadow of death into the morning." Then I wanted to fly away from these lowlands of sorrow, and be at rest in His bosom for ever, but He said, "Go back and tell thy friends and neighbours how great things the Lord hath done for thee, and hath had compassion upon thee." Many years have passed since then, but I have not yet spoken half enough of His wondrous love; and so I now say to you, He hath delivered, He doth deliver, and in Him we trust that He will yet deliver. You cannot be more gloomy, helpless, hopeless,

[1] Amos iii. 12.

and unbelieving than I was, and "He who hath delivered me from so great a death" will deliver you also. "His hand is not shortened, that it cannot save; neither His ear heavy, that it cannot hear;" and if your iniquities have separated between you and your God, the precious blood of Jesus cleanseth them all away, who Himself says, "Look unto me, and be ye saved." The bitten Israelites were not healed by looking at their wounds, but at the brazen serpent, which was a type of Christ; and so while you are poring over your sins and yourself you will only sink lower. "Looking unto Jesus" is the way of deliverance. "They looked unto Him, and were lightened; and their faces were not ashamed."

Perhaps you say, "But I cannot, He is hid from my view." Well, my beloved, if you cannot look at Jesus yet, seek to be looking towards Him, as Jonah ii. 4, and it shall not be in vain. Whatever be your case, this is the way of relief, and from this way Satan will mightily struggle to keep you, knowing that thereby he will be overcome. The cross and blood of Jesus are more than a match for him; and when the vilest or weakest sinner shelters there, his fiery darts are quenched, and the prey is delivered. May the blessed Spirit enable you to look forth with the eye of faith to the Lamb slain, and to come away from self and all besides to Jesus. "Unto whom coming as unto a living stone." Oh, come away, come, come to Jesus! "He will in no wise cast you out." "The Spirit and the Bride say, Come," and by the Father's drawings you shall have power so to do; for "He giveth power to the faint, and to them that have no might He increaseth strength."

Oh that I could so speak of the worthy Lamb as to set your heart on fire with love to Him and longing after Him, that you might keep following Him like those blind men, who, when told to hold their peace, cried out the more a great deal, "Jesus, thou son of David, have mercy on us!" He granted their request, and He will grant yours; His delays are not denials. It has been well said, "If Christ seem to keep His door closed against you, it is not to shut you out, but only to make you knock the louder." Oh, we do our precious Jesus great wrong in our hard thoughts of Him, because He does not answer immediately! "Lord, increase our faith." Adieu, dear friend. The Lord bless you, and in His own time strengthen, stablish, and settle you.—With kind love in our adorable Emmanuel, I remain, though most unworthy, yours affectionately,

RUTH BRYAN.

Psalm xii. 5.

LXXXVII.

A foretaste of "the glory that excelleth."

TO MISS C.

May 24, 1838.

MY DEAREST ANNE, Join me, I beseech you, in praising and adoring that precious Jesus, who has done so much for such an unworthy worm as I am. The language of my heart is, "What shall I render?" for again have I been favoured with draughts of heavenly joy and bliss unutterable. Again has the high and lofty One that inhabiteth eternity revealed Himself to me in the person of Jesus, by the power of the Spirit. Oh yes, the bright beams of uncreated glory have again shone upon my soul in the face of my Beloved, in whose life-giving countenance their radiant effulgence is so softened that mortals may in spirit behold, admire, and love. O my dear friend, I cannot tell you the holy joy with which I have again tasted, nay, drunk of the cup of salvation, being washed in blood, robed in righteousness, and crowned with love; so that I have basked in the sunshine of my Redeemer's presence, and bathed in the ocean of bliss unutterable, finding all human language inadequate to sound forth His praise. I have exultingly called upon the glorified spirits (in whose society I felt myself) to aid my feeble strains, and teach me nobler sounds; and with triumph I have solicited the angelic hosts to strike their immortal lyres, and louder sound His praise whose name is love, for mercy revealed to vile ungrateful me.

Oh for more gratitude to my precious Saviour, my Lord, my life, my all, through whose streaming veins these blessings come to me! I am lost in astonishment at His amazing condescension, and view with adoring wonder the heights, lengths, breadths, and depths of love, passing knowledge. When I ask why *I* should be thus loved and blessed, I am confounded. The cause is beyond my reach, but the effects blessedly flow into my soul. I know you will, you do rejoice with me. Oh to remember that we have an eternity to spend together in the full-orbed presence of God, our own God, where sin will never interrupt, but we shall unceasingly serve and love Him as we ought, and sing, " Unto Him that loved us, and washed us from our sins in His own blood," the Lord God and the Lamb, be glory for ever and ever. men. Hallelujah! May the Lord vouchsafe to each of us more and more foretastes of the glory which is to be revealed, till we hear the soul-thrilling words, "Arise, my love, my fair one, and come away." "Even so, come, Lord Jesus."

I meant this to have been a note of thanks for your kindness, but that must be another time, for Jesus's fragrant name, full of sweetness, has absorbed my soul, and now none, none but Jesus. O Thou adorable Prince of Life, draw us closer and closer to Thyself, fill us more and more with Thy undeserved and overwhelming love, till it shall please Thee to grant us in one long everlasting embrace to lose our sorrow and our sins.

I write with a trembling hand, but an overflowing heart. I know you understand my language, and therefore speak freely, though unable to utter a thousandth part of my Redeemer's grace and my happiness. Adieu, my much-loved friend.—Accept the sincere love of your unworthy

RUTH.

LXXXVIII.

Christ the Author and Finisher of faith.

TO MISS C.

May 1845.

MY DEAR ANNE, I am truly grieved to see you so cast down, and wonder why it is; but your heavenly Father knows all. May He glorify Himself, and comfort you. He hath delivered, He doth deliver, and we trust in Him that He will yet deliver. May He increase your faith, and keep

it in constant exercise; for "this is the victory that overcometh the world, even our faith," (1 John v. 4.) Taking the
shield of faith, all the fiery darts of the wicked one are
quenched. Through faith the ancient worthies did wonders,
and even weak women have been gloriously triumphant.
Faith says, "Hath He said, and shall He not do it?"[1]
Though all be dark and contrary, I will trust and not be
afraid. May this be your feeling; and whether it be a bear
or a lion, or an uncircumcised Philistine, that is come out
against you, meeting them in the name of the Lord of hosts,
they must be overcome, and you will have to sing of Jesus.
He hath slain His tens of thousands.

Perhaps you will think I am too much indulged just now
to be able to write suitably to one bound in affliction and
iron. I freely confess my inability, and just write to sympathise. The path of life is ever above to the wise, to save
from the snares of hell beneath, and therefore I point upward. Christ is the way of life, light, and liberty. Power still
belongs unto God; but when in a low place myself, I did
even then love to hear of the way of faith, though I could
not get at it; and, now that the Lord has given me faith as
a grain of mustard seed, I am doubly fond of that way, and
if I had a thousand souls black as hell I would trust them all
to the love, blood, and righteousness of Emmanuel, yea, trust
them to His honour too, for He says, " Him that cometh to
me I will in no wise cast out."[2] If but the most weak or
wicked that ever came were to be rejected, what would He
do unto His great name, " faithful and true?" Oh, it shall
never have such a stain upon it, let unbelief say what it may!
" He will regard the prayer of the destitute, and not despise

[1] Num. xxiii. 19.   [2] John vi. 37.

their prayer,"[1] though He may not seem to reply when they expect it. "Wait on the Lord; be of good courage, and He shall strengthen thine heart: wait, I say, on the Lord."[2]

Dear Anne, I know not your present malady, but I know Christ is the remedy for it. O all-healing, all-loving, all-absorbing Christ, be Thou revealed in manifested power, or give faith to trust Thee in apparent absence and distance, for Thou art worthy to be trusted through the very worst. I wish you a speedy and blessed deliverance, and power from the Lord to rejoice, not in it, but in the Deliverer, to whom be endless praises evermore. Amen.

I did not mean to write so much, but I have got to that cruse and barrel which never waste, so no ink or paper can suffice. There is more in Christ for empty souls than pen or tongue of men or angels can tell. May you have free access, and eat and drink, and forget your poverty, being taken up with His riches, fulness, and glory, in whom dwelleth all the fulness of the Godhead bodily.

The Lord comfort you, and establish your heart with grace. Adieu.—Yours affectionately, in our Beloved One,

HIS GLEANER.

LXXXIX.

The precious trial of faith.

TO MISS C.

January 1, 1848.

BELOVED FRIEND, I wish you joy in the Lord, peace in believing, and, as we commonly say, a happy new year. I

[1] Ps. cii. 17.　　　　[2] Ps. xxvii. 14.

was sorry, my dear Anne, to hear you had been so poorly, and your sister also. You will be glad to nurse her, and she will do the same for you, so the benefit will be mutual. I trust you will both soon recover. Through mercy we are much as usual, but sickness abounds on all sides, and many saints have fallen asleep. We seem to be in a great hospital, so many loved ones are sick; but Jesus walks the wards where His own loved ones lie, and whether He wills that they die or live, He saith unto the righteous, it shall be well with them.

Though there are times when we have no sensible feeling of enjoyment, yet, if really hanging upon Christ, there must be safety. The more simple faith is, the less will it be shaken by the removal of comfortable feelings or apparent absence of effects and fruits; and I humbly believe the Lord is pleased at times to let us feel the lack of these things, to discover to us that we were taking somewhat of our satisfaction from the fruits of faith instead of wholly from the object of faith. Well may it be said to us, herein thou hast done foolishly; for since all the fruits of righteousness are by Christ Jesus, the more we would abound in them the more we must have to do with Him by faith, and be the more cleared from everything else. This clearing process, as effected by the Lord, is very painful to us. But it is good to be emptied, and thereby prove whether Christ is all our salvation and all our desire. Though this trial should convince us that our eye is not single, we need not fear, but, however humbling, be thankful for the discovery, and make use of it as a plea to the Lord to go forward, even though further abasement should follow. We must abide the fire, and be more anxious for purification than for relief from pain. For what is the perfection of refining? Not only to have the gold pure, but for the refiner to see himself in it; and you know, for one face to be fully seen in another, more than brightness is needed to reflect it, there must be a direct position of feature to feature, and the least turning aside to another object will prevent the full development of the countenance. So you see, when the fire has produced the intended effect, the subject of it is not to be taken up with the purity produced, but rather to be absorbed with Him who managed the process, and, beholding Him with open face, be changed into the same image from glory to glory, even as by the Spirit of the Lord.

May we come experimentally to know these mysteries, and have faith to trust our best Beloved, not through our frames and feelings, but with them seeking more and more that He may be glorified. Oh, this is a conquering point! for when His honour is our object, our selfish aims are scattered, and we glory only in the cross of our Lord Jesus Christ, willing to die with Him that He may be our only life. Therefore, though there may seem to be a death on our prospects and joys and feelings, as well as on our fruits, the word is, "Fear not, only believe. I am the resurrection and the life." Being one with Him, we may safely follow Him whithersoever He leads, and, looking unto Him alone, we shall do so triumphantly.—Yours ever,

HIS GLEANER.

XC.

Glowing anticipations of the joy of heaven.

TO MISS C.

The School,
Ockbrooke, *Aug.* 21, 1849.

Dear Friend, Not in exile, but at school; a very dull but happy scholar, with such love upon love and line upon line from such a blessed Teacher, who saith, "I am the Lord thy God which teacheth thee to profit, which leadeth thee by the way that thou shouldest go." Oh, this is a sacred place! I am receiving many private lessons bearing immediately upon my own experience, conflicts, and mistakes, in which the Lord my God fainteth not, neither is weary. I listen for Him, I listen to Him, and marvel greatly, concluding most certainly that there never was such an unworthy creature so favoured. I think one result of every new lesson is, "Behold, I am vile;" "I abhor myself, and repent in dust and ashes," seeing much wrong in all the past, and desiring afresh to forsake all and follow Jesus only.

My earnest cry now is for guidance, to have any home where the Lord will bless me, and I may not be corroded with worldly care. The most humble place, with a quiet mind and the Lord's presence, seems just what I want—to serve Him in lowliness on earth till the welcome hour when He shall say, "Enter thou into the joy of thy Lord." Indeed it must be without a "Well done, good and faithful servant." It is with me all mercy and no merit.

May the Lord give us still to commune freely in that love which passeth knowledge, and changeth not. Oh, the blissful heights, and depths, and lengths, and breadths which are ever here to be enjoyed. Love is the dear element in which I delight to live. I long to be unloosed from mortality, and get absorbingly into its pleasurable abyss and fulness of joy, but till then must seek above all things to live in love—I mean in that sense in which it is said, "God is love; and he that dwelleth in love dwelleth in God, and God in him."[1] All that would interrupt or interfere with this must I cast away, counting all things but dross that I may win Christ and wear Christ, and be found in Him, and find Him in me. He is the manifestation that God is love; He is the love of God in living power and revelation. Oh that saints would leave the many things which are behind, and press on towards simplicity and love.

> "'Tis love that makes our cheerful feet
> In swift obedience move."
>
> . . . .
>
> " This is the grace that lives and sings
> When faith and hope shall cease ;
> 'Tis this shall strike our joyful strings
> In the sweet realms of bliss."

Oh to breathe only and ever in the pure, sweet element of holiness and love ! That will be congenial with the inner man, which will then no longer be the *hidden* man ; for we shall be all outside. I mean there will be nothing in us or about us obscure or concealed. Body and spirit will be pure transparent light, as you know I once saw in a glorious dream such as mortal words can never fully describe. *That* glory is brighter than the noonday sun, fairer than the moon, and quite too dazzling for mortal sight. Oh that we could disperse these mists of flesh and sense, and our freed

[1] 1 John iv. 16.

T

spirits range those fields of light of which the Lord God and the Lamb are the brightness and glory. Oh to see as we are seen, to know as we are known, to understand each other fully without needing the dull imperfect medium of words. That would indeed be living all on fire, and glowing as we would wish.

What you say of loving the patriarchs, prophets, and apostles reminded me of 1 John iii. 14: "We know that we have passed from death unto life, because we love the brethren." Truly, love will flow to all the members of the living family if we are begotten of God in a new life, and methinks the most so to those who have most of love, because there will be most of Him. Oh, indeed, a glorious throng of glorified ones await the consummation, and are saying, "Thy kingdom come." How they welcome each dear pilgrim who puts off the travelling dress, and comes to rest with them, till that morning without clouds, when all the redeemed shall at once put on the full court robes, except those few who already have them, and who are like an earnest handful of the rich ripe harvest. What high company awaits us! It is almost past belief for poor uncomely me. I want enlarging to take in the wonder more thoroughly.

Ah, my beloved friend, all will end well at last, though the conflict is now often severe; but after a toilsome night, and nothing caught, the morning often brings deliverance —a net full of fishes, and a meal prepared.[1] Oh, turn in, Thou Beloved, and tarry with us, for the evening shades draw on. Come, Thou risen Lord, and sup with us, and we with Thee. Stay till the night of this world's woe be past, then take us up where suns never rise and set, but

[1] John xxi. 6, 17.

Thou art endless day. Quite spoilt for earth, we must have much of Thee, till we shall come where Thou art all in all. I would have dear saints on fire with His love, vying who can love Him most whom none can love enough. To Him I affectionately commend you for keeping and teaching, and am in Him yours warmly, RUTH.

Eph. iii. 17-19.

XCI.

The fresh venture upon Christ of a doubting soul.

TO MISS C.

MY DEAREST ANNE, My heart yearns over you, and much do I long that you may be comforted. Jesus can and will relieve your aching heart. What is it, my beloved friend, which distresses you? Is it the absence of Jesus? Ah! *that* is a sorrowful condition; but He loves you just as much as when you leaned on His bosom, and He *will* come again and embrace you, making you ashamed of the jealousies you now feel; for surely it is not knowing a friend to trust him only so far as we can see him. Oh, then, may the Spirit enable you even in the dark to trust in the Lord and stay upon our God.

Is it sin breaks your heart? The blood of Jesus cleanses from *all* sin (I am a living witness of it); from heart and life sin, indulged and repeated—sins of ingratitude and carelessness, sins against light and knowledge, and a thousand others. Do not, therefore, be cast down: since I have found mercy, none need despair. Venture with all your guilt upon Christ; you know He has borne the curse due to it, and He will restore peace to your conscience.

But, perhaps, you have been looking over your evidences, and by reason of the mist which now envelops you they appear so dim that you question whether they are genuine. I have found it sometimes well to give Satan a little ground here: throw evidences away, and suppose what he says is true, that we have been deceived, and then fly to Christ just as we are, without one plea, hanging simply upon His blood and righteousness as a helpless sinner, determined, that if we perish, it shall be in venturing upon Him. Thus shall we prove whether it is true that He can and will save to the uttermost *all* who come unto God by Him. You cannot think what relief I have had in this way.

But, whatever be your case, the remedy is in Christ. May it soon be feelingly applied. I feel ashamed to give you these lispings, for you were in the way of believing long before I was, but we both remember the child who said to its mother, when she wept for her husband, "Is Jesus Christ dead?" Whereby her inordinate grief was reproved. So may my simple strains, by the Spirit's power, touch the discordant note in your soul, and if not, you must pardon and accept the attempt in proof of the love and sympathy of your unworthy but attached   RUTH.

XCII.

*The faithfulness of our heavenly Boaz towards a heart
He is alluring to Himself.*

TO MISS C.

MY DEAR ANNE, We read this morning the 1st and 2d chapters of Ruth, and the thought forcibly struck me that

you are like my namesake when she was but a gleaner in
the field of Boaz. He was then her near kinsman, and had
the right to redeem, but the time was not come. He said
nothing about relationship, but just encouraged her tö glean
in his field, abide by his maidens, and sit beside his reapers,
partaking of their fare. Thus it is with you; you have
picked up ears and gleaned handfuls in the field; you have
fed with the maidens and servants, and have been surprised
that such bounty should be vouchsafed unto you; and
though now you are longing for higher privilege and closer
communion, yet forget not to be thankful for such things
as you have, for He hath said, " I will never leave thee nor
forsake thee." He says also, as Boaz did, chapter ii. 8, and
your humble friend would say, as Naomi did, verse 22, keep
on in the field till he says to thee, Come up higher; for in
truth "the man"[1] will not be in rest until he have finished
the thing in open consummation of union, ancient as eternity.

He may try your faith and patience, and He has a right
to do so, for whether they be little or much He is the
author of them; but be not discouraged; His time is best,
though yours seems always ready. He does feed and up-
hold you, and keeps your soul alive in famine sometimes,
and these are but a part of His ways. When He brings you
openly to His home and His heart, and feasts you at a
plentiful board of wine well refined, and fat things full of
marrow, His love will not be greater than it is now.

Oh, believe well of Him, however ill things may seem
to sense and reason. These are evil counsellors, and they,
with Satan, do often bring us to dishonour our best Friend,
and judge Him by feeble sense. If one soul perish hang-

[1] 1 Tim. ii. 5.

ing on Him and pleading His blood and righteousness, the Rock of Ages would have become shifting sand; and what would He do with His great name? It would be tarnished indeed—which will not, cannot be. Rest, beloved, upon the blood and righteousness of Jesus, and the faithfulness of Jehovah, when you have neither feeling nor fertility in yourself to encourage you.—Adieu. With love and longing for your soul's health, I am your fellow-gleaner,

RUTH.

XCIII.

The efficacy of the precious blood of Jesus.

TO MISS C.

3 MELVILLE PLACE, FILEY,
Sept. 25, 1857.

DEAREST ANNE, I must greet you once more from this place in the name of Jesus. I hope you are recovering, and are having all afflictions sweetened by the love of the " Man of sorrows," who was so well acquainted with grief. I have felt some sweetness in looking up for your brother. May the Lord manifest Himself to his soul. If he is a blood-bought jewel, he shall not be missing in the day of account. The great salvation is not of merit but of mercy; so none need despair because of crimson sins : the rich blood of my precious Saviour makes them white as snow. This I can well witness, for none could be worse. What a glorious company will there be on the Mount Zion above of blood-washed sinners, once so black, then so white; once so far off, then so near; once so full of fear and trembling, then so safe for ever and ever. How shall we praise the worthy Lamb who brought us there at the cost of His own heart's blood ! Oh, that poor doubting souls had more conception of the virtue and efficacy of that blood which *has* cleansed and *will* cleanse millions and millions of black sinners, and made them fit company for God and the Lamb. How it would encourage them to come to that fountain opened for sin and for unclean- ness, which is free to every longing soul who is crying, " Wash me, Saviour, or I die!" Would that I had more conceptions of the freeness and fulness of the finished salva- tion, and that this contracted heart were enlarged to appre- hend more of the love of the Saviour to poor needy sinners. What an amazing object our Father has given us to behold by faith, even His crucified Son, who was the brightness of His glory and the express image of His person. Yet for poor sinners was His visage marred more than any man's. His meat and drink was to do the will and work of His Father; yet "it pleased the Lord to bruise Him," and thus marred, and bruised, and crucified, He says to bruised reeds, " Look unto me, and be ye saved "—unto Me, bleeding, agonizing, made a curse for your sin. Look unto Me on the Cross, to be healed of your diseases, and forgiven your iniquity ; none ever looked in vain.

Oh that our eyes and hearts may be fixed here ; then shall we be constrained to sing and give thanks. " Unto you, therefore, which believe, He is precious."[1] Not which *have* believed, but in the present tense. Oh, to live believing by the power of the blessed Spirit, who takes of the things of Christ and shews them to the soul, drawing it out towards

[1] 1 Peter ii. 7.

this adorable Man, who is more precious than the gold of Ophir. Soon will clouds and vails be done away, and we shall see Him as He is with open face.—Believe me, yours very affectionately, Ruth.

Jonah ii. 7.

XCIV.

Praise in recording the Lord's dealings of love and faithfulness.

TO MISS C.

Ockbrook, *March* 30, 1849.

Dearest Anne, I thank you for your kind execution of my troublesome commissions. . . . You know how sweet to my heart is communion of saints; but the Lord does not forget His "sparrow alone." Again and again He comes, laying me lower in the dust, and while I behold His glory I wonder not at the inspired pen so multiplying words—" A far more exceeding and eternal weight of glory." Mark, it is now in measure apprehended, while we look not at the things which are seen, but at the things which are not seen, and which are eternal.

How wonderful that the Lord should withdraw me from things seen, to bring near, very near, that weight of glory which you know had begun to beam upon me with such brightness and power that I verily thought I could not and should not live. I truly feel that if I do, it will be as real a coming back as Hezekiah's was, so many things seemed to portend going home. The mercies of my blessed affliction it is impossible to recount. Oh, that as the Lord is sowing bountifully, He may not reap sparingly, but Himself be the increase. You know how I have trembled at 2 Chron. xxxii. 25: "But Hezekiah rendered not again according to the benefit done unto him; for his heart was lifted up: therefore there was wrath upon him, and upon Judah and Jerusalem." We have such a Christ that we little think how far His glories and His matchless love surpass what we have ever yet conceived. We do not make half enough of Him, heaven's brightest gem, and richest treasure. Oh, that the precious Comforter may reveal Him more and more, that we may count all things else but dung and dross.

When I read your note I thought I saw one cause of your ailment in your mental conflict, which I sensitively feel but cannot relieve. I must still keep telling you of our dear, dear Lord; for though it may seem to be in vain, I do not know through which lattice He may please to shew Himself. He works variously and wondrously. Do not think, because of the howling storm and tempest, that He is not with you; the stormy wind fulfils His word, and the threatening waves obey His bidding. The keen winds of winter accomplish His will, and the apparent barrenness of that season has its use. So there may be a time too when our souls seem to lie barren; but the Lord is doing something with the ground; and when it is prepared, He will in the right season cause greenness and growth to enliven it again. Be encouraged then, trust Him through the process. It is not needful you should understand it; keep venturing your soul, with all its wants and woes, upon the blood and righteousness of Jehovah-Jesus. You may safely risk all here; and if the

Spirit so enable you, you cannot be lost, feel what you may. Excuse all this in love from a slow learner. Adieu.—With affectionate love in Jesus, yours ever, RUTH.

1 Peter v. 10.

The primrose from my own dear garden smiles still upon me while I am writing.

XCV.

The vicarious sufferings of Christ the end of the law.

TO MISS C.

OCKBROOK, *May* 22, 1849.

MY DEAREST ANNE, Dost thou believe on the Son of God? Dost thou live believing? Is the very life and death, person and work of Jesus, the daily feast of thy soul? Art thou eating His flesh, and drinking His blood? For thus we shall dwell in Him, and He in us. Oh, it is healthy, lively living to be eating and drinking *Life.* Christ is our life, and the blood is the life, and this is the food which our Father has wonderfully given us. Let us see to it, beloved one, that we are seeking spiritual health and strength in no other way than by the continual, daily feeding on Christ. It is a present act—" eateth " and " drinketh."

Truly, I am seeking for constant renewals in a life of simple faith by the power of the Holy Ghost. When thus anointed, there is to us an ever fresh, ever full, sweetness in heaven's precious Lamb, an everlasting bloom of beauty on this rich, ripe grape; and though often pressed into our cup, yet the juice remains undiminished. "Eat, O friends; drink, yea, drink abundantly, O beloved," is His invitation who says, "I am come that they might have life, and that they might have it more abundantly." To accomplish this, He had death abundantly indeed; for all of the sting, the curse, and the wrath, which death and hell would have presented to His chosen, did He drink up. Oh! what a cup was this to be received in love from a Father's hand. Thus came our life.

Hearken, beloved, to these words: "Send Lazarus, that he may dip the tip of his finger in water, and cool my tongue; for I am tormented in this flame."[1] That thirst, that heat, that torment I must have endured for ever, had not Jesus Himself borne it, when for me under its heat He said, "I thirst." Oh, what scorching did that precious Lamb suffer, when water was denied Him and vinegar given. This was unutterable love. Muse and marvel, O my soul! I like in meditation to go over the very things which our Beloved went through, not viewing them only as a whole, but seeking to the Holy Comforter to unfold and shew out every act separately, what it was to Him, what it would have been to me—the very reality of it. Truly, I could not have been plucked as a brand out of the fire, unless some other had stood the burning for me; and then clearly follows the sure escape. For if my accepted Surety, with my sin upon Him,[2] stood the burning till all my sin was consumed, (which He did, for He made an end of sins,) upon what, then, in me are the fires of justice and wrath now to kindle? Their fuel is gone in the soul that believes in Jesus, for if He was

[1] Luke xvi. 24.   [2] Isa. liii. 6.

made sin for me, who can or will make that sin over to me again ? Jehovah will not, others cannot.

Oh, this precious truth! it is gospel wine to my poor soul. I hope you, dear Anne, will drink it with me, and feel refreshed. I do love a thorough salvation, and my conscience has been so law-stricken that it never dare be satisfied with one which could not look at that law with open face. Here comes the experimental benefit of having much to do with Jesus; for look at Him where or how we will, He fits the law exactly. Yea, He outshines it, holy as it is, and, viewed in His transparent heart and life, it seems to gain new brilliancy and glory. What then? Why, when this Christ is ours, and we are "found in Him," then law and justice wear a continual smile, and we must smile too, when, looking right on to the end of the law, we find Jesus there, its full satisfaction and our righteousness. Thus, too, we stop not short of perfection, but meet a holy law with a holy Jesus, rendering unto God the things that are God's. I sincerely hope, my dear friend, you will be happily constrained to smile away all your tears, finding yourself with most unworthy me in the blessed fold of this so great salvation, and in the blessed embrace of everlasting love. Are you tired of my same subject, dearest? I think I have hardly begun to learn it yet, for the Comforter still preaches in my soul. I greet you in the fresh fragrance of our Beloved, and His good ointments. To Him I commend thee : may He bless and comfort thee in Himself.—I am, thy warmly-affectionate   RUTH.

XCVI.

Fainting pilgrims encouraged by a testimony concerning Jesus.

TO MISS C.

OCKBROOK, *Aug.* 2, 1849.

DEAREST ANNE; It does melt my heart, while I write, to feel that, receiving all in Him, we can say under all, "It is well." O precious Saviour, what do we not possess in having Thee? All things are ours, for use and benefit. Ministers, the world, life, death, things present, things to come, all are ours in Thee, for Thy glory and our need, but Thyself our portion, our glory and joy. All praise to our Father, who hath entailed such blessings upon us in time and eternity: neither earth nor hell can cut them off from us, or keep us out of them. We do at times get beclouded, so that all seems obscure, and we do not apprehend or enjoy our privileges; but when the fog is cleared away, we find our immovable blessedness secure as ever in our unchanging Head. I wish you, then, beloved, abiding faith, enduring faith, and yielding faith, in whatever case you may be, though I should rejoice to hear of your health in body as well as soul. Faith is a grace ordained of God for taking possession of Christ and eternal life in Him; and you know from the Book of records, that "we which have believed do enter into rest."[1] Therefore, let us rejoice that by faith we may be in heaven, I had almost said before our time, but I

[1] Heb. iv. 3.

mean before we put off this tabernacle. Christ is our heaven, and He is in our souls both the hope and the fore-taste of glory. This I can honestly and experimentally affirm; and since I have been permitted to tread the very threshold of eternity, and in Beulah's lovely land clearly to see the glory, and eat of the celestial fruits, surely I ought, like Joshua and Caleb, the more strenuously to encourage fainting pilgrims with the solemn assurance, that what is before us is well worth waiting for, running for, fighting for, dying for. So let us cheer each other, and seek grace cheerfully to be about our Father's business.

I thank you for your sympathy in my late disappointment of having to come back, and again put on my sandals and take up my staff. . . . . There must be a ripeness for glory, as well as a ripeness in glory; wherefore I would be patient, and no longer foolishly urge my Father to pluck unripe fruit. I find no better way of losing myself and my sorrows than by getting absorbed in Him who has borne them, and no surer way of sinking under them than by poring over them. To this latter work Satan is a great prompter, knowing that there he has plenty to work upon. How blessedly safe, when he points us to self, to point him to Jesus. He cannot stand that, but we can stand by it, as did those now safe landed who "overcame him by the blood of the Lamb." I can never think we dishonour our blessed Surety by frequent reference to Him and His finished work. Rather do we thereby magnify the Lord and His work, which men behold. If His works of creation are to be extolled, how much more the work of redemption, which living men behold. Oh, for an enlarged heart to walk in Him who is the law's fulfilment, and thus by faith meet its demands with full weight and measure. Doubly, trebly precious does our Lord become as we thus walk in Him, in whom we find such fulness, that we need not once turn with regret to our own poverty. How blessed for self to be thus put out of the way. Do not you see that it is the law of faith which excludes boasting, except in the Lord ? for in the Lord shall one say, have I righteousness and strength. That saying is in accordance with our Father's doing, for He hath made Him to be unto us " Wisdom, righteousness, sanctification, and redemption." This truth received by faith is food to nourish the soul unto eternal life ; and thus we become strong in the Lord and in the power of His might. Truly, if the second Adam fulness be not an overmatch for the first Adam emptiness, we may pine and mourn ; but if it be so, which Scripture and experience prove, then let the inhabitants of the Rock sing, let them shout from the tops of the mountains, and let the children of Zion be joyful in their King. Thus gospel wine is strong and reviving : it cheers my heart, and I long that many should drink and be refreshed.—With love, yours warmly, RUTH.

Ps. xxxiv. 8.

XCVII.

Gospel wine to cheer the warrior.

TO MISS C.

Sept. 9, 1859.

DEAREST ANNE, . . . It seems to have been the Divine will that the children of Israel should learn war, and that those who saw it not at the entering into Canaan should be taught it by the nations which were left unsubdued.[1] Of course these nations would be often striving to invade the possessions and lessen the power of this favoured people. Then they must fight for their privileges ; and from the records of their battles we plainly see how, while trusting simply in the Lord, a mere handful of them overcame thousands of their foes ; not their own sword or their own bow, but His right hand and His holy arm brought them the victory. Doubtless all was typical of the experience of the spiritual Israel. They have nations of lusts and evils within, headed by that great and fearful captain Unbelief ; and nations of snares, allurements, trials, and cares without, while Satan is the grand commander of the whole. Yet has he only a limited power, being himself under the control of the mighty Captain of Salvation, who always binds him in his attacks with this restriction, "Hitherto shalt thou come, but no further." However, as the spiritual as well as the literal Israel must learn war, you need not wonder that the armies of the aliens often beset you, and that the men of your own house rise up against you.

Remember those who by faith put to flight the armies of the aliens, and remember David, who said, " Although my house be not so with God, yet hath he made with me an everlasting covenant, ordered in all things, and sure : for this is all my salvation, and all my desire, although he make it not to grow." [2] May you, by grace, follow the faith of these ancient worthies, "considering the end of their conversation : Jesus Christ, the same yesterday, and to-day, and for ever."[3] Be in nothing terrified by your adversaries, since your

[1] Judges iii. 1, 2.   [2] 2 Sam. xxiii. 5.   [3] Heb. xiii. 7, 8.

Redeemer is mighty, the Lord of Hosts is His name. What blessed promises are made to the overcomers; but how could these promises belong to us if we knew nothing of foes and fighting? These foes are overcome by the blood of the Lamb, " not by might, nor by power, but by my Spirit, saith the Lord of Hosts."[1]

You mention the sinking state of my health. I am very weak, but may not be so near Home as you sometimes think. Oh, may our precious Jesus so reveal Himself that sorrow may be turned into joy by His presence, and the best wine be kept till the last, so that then both the living and the dying may lift up their eyes and see no one but Jesus only. At times I think I may not be the first of our circle to sleep in Jesus. However, it shall be well, and each shall prove, " My grace is sufficient for thee." I wish that there may be much joy in the Lord, and songs of praises at my departure. He is so gracious to me, a solid rock, now that this tabernacle is trembling to the dust; a rock also that yieldeth honey ; where bread of life is given, and waters of salvation are sure. " Let the inhabitants of the rock sing, let them shout from the top of the mountains." Isaiah xii. is a blessed song when put into the heart by the Divine Comforter. The Lord prepare us for life or death, and make us willing for either. Wrapt up in our precious Jesus, we are safe for both. Oh, seek, seek absorption in Him, and with Him; so shall the restless desires of the flesh be kept in silence by His power.[2]

Let us finish with praise, for it becometh the redeemed to be thankful. " Blessed be the Lord, who daily loadeth us with benefits, even the God of our salvation." " Glory

[1] Zech. iv. 6.   [2] Hab. ii. 20.

to God in the highest, and on earth peace, goodwill toward men." [1] May the goodwill of Him that dwelt in the Bush rest upon you, dear Anne.—And with kind love in Him, believe me, your ever-affectionate   RUTH.

XCVIII.

The difficulty of total self-surrender.

" He knoweth the way that I take; when he hath tried me I shall come forth as gold."—Job xxiii. 10.

"The fining pot is for silver, and the furnace for gold ; but the Lord trieth the hearts."—Prov. xvii. 3.

"Whose fire is in Zion and his furnace in Jerusalem."—Isa. xxxi. 9.

Mal. iii. 3, 4.   Psa. ciii. 9.   1 Cor. x. 13.

TO MRS H.

NOTTINGHAM, *Nov.* 24, 1847.

BELOVED IN THE LORD, COMPANION IN TRIBULATION, AND IN THE KINGDOM AND PATIENCE OF JESUS CHRIST, Often have I thought of writing to you, and now I seem emboldened to indulge myself a little by allowing my willing spirit to blend with yours in sympathy of joy, and sorrow, and in sweet converse of Jesus.

In Him, then, my beloved Amelia, accept my first greeting upon paper, and my sincere desire that He may still lead you on in the divine life as evidently as heretofore He has; though it must still be to the rooting up and putting down of all that is of the flesh, for He has determined that no flesh shall glory in His presence. We easily assent to

[1] Luke ii. 14.

this in words, but the Lord will have more than theoretical knowledge in His school, He will bring all who sit at His feet to the practical experience of the words they utter and the lessons they learn. This I have lately been discovering more than ever before; having, in times of glowing manifestation, said, in sincerity of heart, many warm things which the Lord has latterly, by afflictive dispensations, put to the test, and I have found that it is one thing to say, "Lord, if it be thou, bid me come to thee on the water," and then to step out firmly in faith; and it is another to walk on firmly and confidingly when the wind is roaring, and the waves are raging. It is one thing to feel Jesus so precious that we in faith give up our all to Him and His service; it is another for Him to claim what we have so given, as His own right; and, according to our resignment, to take away the different parts of our earthly all, and so to prove whether Himself is indeed ALL to us, or whether we only say so.

I have found Leviticus xxvii. 28 very sweet and strengthening since the Lord has been putting in His claim; for I saw that I had devoted what I have and am to the Lord in love, and that now He has called upon me to pay my vows. My happiness would be in going forward in His strength in faith; and my weakness and distraction would be in conferring with flesh and blood, seeking to hold back what I had vowed. The Lord keep thee, beloved, single-eyed and simple-hearted, willing to give up the "Isaac" whom thou lovest[1] (whatever that may be) at His bidding, then you shall neither suffer lack nor loss.

My mouth is still further open to you, and my heart is enlarged because your spirit is so singularly in unison with

[1] Gen. xxii. 2.

my own in waiting only upon God. It is the safe and the right way, though very contrary to the flesh, which is always in a hurry for deliverance, seeking its own things by any means; but the new man seeks the things which are Jesus Christ's, and wants deliverance in Him and according to His will, and would rather honour Him by waiting, than have the flesh eased by a lighter cross or a smoother path.

Again, beloved friend, my very soul rejoices that the dear Revealer of secrets is making known to you the "blessedness of the man to whom the Lord will not impute sin." Mark, "will not impute." These words have sounded through my soul by the Spirit's power with more melody than earth's softest, sweetest sounds could ever produce. They raise us high above the creature in its doings or misdoings, and give us to see our deliverance from condemnation, solely, in and through Him, the precious Lamb of God, our Surety. He was condemned for our vile, black sin, which He has put for ever away by the sacrifice of Himself, so that when the iniquity is sought for upon us, it shall not be found. "Who shall lay anything to the charge of God's elect? It is God that justifieth. Who is he that condemneth? It is Christ that died, yea, rather, that is risen again."—With love in our precious Well-Beloved, I am, dear Amelia, your affectionate   RUTH.

XCIX.

The joy of union and communion with Christ.

"Hearken, O daughter, and consider, and incline thine ear ; forget also thine own people, and thy father's house ; so shall the king greatly desire thy beauty : for he is thy Lord ; and worship thou him."—Psa. xlv. 10, 11.

"The king hath brought me into his chambers."—Song i. 4.

"Thou shalt no more be termed Forsaken ; neither shall thy land any more be termed Desolate : but thou shalt be called Hephzi-bah, (my delight,) and thy land Beulah, (married :) for the Lord delighteth in thee, and thy land shall be married."—Isa. lxii. 4.

Rev. xix. 7, 8.

"And this is the name whereby He shall be called, THE LORD our right-eousness."—Jer. xxxiii. 16.

Col. ii. 10.

TO MRS H.

SABBATH MORNING, *Feb.* 26, 1848.

ALL HAIL! MY PRECIOUS SISTER, I greet you with a sincere heart; welcome to the unspeakable delights of union with the King of kings, the most high and mighty Prince, Emmanuel, the Lord of Hosts, the King of Glory! Your song of love has made my heart as an open fountain, so that I have wept abundantly, in joy unfeigned, to find another love-stricken soul who, separated from all besides, shall know the blissfulness of absorption in the Beloved. Surely this Well-Beloved hath " put in his hand by the hole of the door," and my bowels are moved for Him and for you; so that I must respond, though in feeble strains, to love's own language, which my heart knows right well, triumphantly exclaiming,, " It is the voice of my Beloved, He is " white and ruddy, the chiefest among ten thousand,"

"Yea, he is altogether lovely."[1]   He has borne away my heart and my heart's affections ; and, now, love and the Beloved are my most delightful theme.

Sabbath night.—I had not time, my dearest Amelia, to pour out all my heart's fulness this morning, and whether there will be a renewal of it is known to Him who openeth and no man shutteth, who shutteth and no man openeth, who can turn water into wine, and poverty into plenty. This has been a blissful day to me, heaven begun, and glory antedated.   At times you have been very near me, and per- haps, if I knew *more* of spirit blending with spirit, and soul communing with soul, we might have enjoyed it more fully. I wish to wait quietly upon the Lord for the further unfold- ing of His blissful secrets, and revealing of His glorious Person.   And here my heart bounds with delight, for it is the Person of Christ that ravishes my soul, and has made me a willing captive to His matchless charms—

> "All human beauties, all divine,
> In my Beloved meet and shine."

Perfect humanity, ineffable divinity, one glorious Person, our all-lovely Emmanuel. The union between this matchless One and ourselves is double : we are joined to Him by one Spirit, so that when born of the Spirit we partake of His nature, and He for very love took a body like our own. "Forasmuch as the children are partakers of flesh and blood, he also himself likewise took part of the same," and thus "we are members of his body, of his flesh, and of his bones," and it is blessedly written, "They are no more twain, but one flesh."   "This is a great mystery, but I speak con- cerning Christ and the Church."

[1] Song v. 10, 16.

This morning I had not heard your letter to dear Anne. She has this evening read it to me. It is delicious to my spiritual taste, savoury meat, such as my soul loves. The Lord thy God brought it unto thee and me, to Him therefore be all the glory. Fear not the loss of joyous sensations, my very dear friend; your precious Husband and His love will be ever the same, and you will come in sweet reciprocal love to such devotedness to Himself, that you will, as it were, lay down His smile, and His shine, and His kiss, and His benefits at His dear feet, and seek His glory above them, and say, Honour Thyself by me, rather than please me with these. When you have thus left them *for* Him, you will find them most richly and continuously *in* Him. To take Christ for His own sake is a secret worth worlds, and has in it that other secret, " rejoicing in the Lord always." I know not whether I am clear to you, but must finish.

Accept warm love from the warmed heart of your dearly-affectionate RUTH, the happy gleaner.

P.S. Monday Morning.—I should tell you, my beloved Amelia, that I have had rich enjoyment in dear Madame Guyon. I do not think her views quite correct in some points; but in others I have been astonished to find her speak my very secrets, known only between the beloved and my soul. She was a kindred spirit, and drank deeply of Love's pure stream; yea, she at length lived at the Fountain-head. After going quite through, I regaled myself with delight here and there amongst her precious things. At times I was enraptured to find one in mortality pouring forth such pure strains of divine love, till at length one evening, while thus engaged, it was as if the Beloved of my soul gently beckoned me away from her, saying, Come to Me, and receive it first hand. You will be sure the invitation was welcome. I immediately closed the book, and have not opened it since; for "His lips are like lilies, dropping sweet smelling myrrh;" "the law of his mouth is better to me than thousands of gold and silver," and to hear of Himself from Himself is better than any instrumentality whatever. Do you know, beloved friend, this is the way the Lord has ever dealt with me, He Himself has been my dear instructor; most frequently without any creature. Gal. i. 12, is my very own verse, "For I neither received it of man, neither was I taught it, but by the revelation of Jesus Christ." He has powerfully spoken to me, too, from 2 Sam. ix. 7, "Thou shalt eat bread at my table continually." How blessed to sit at the King's table, to see Him, to hear Him, to learn of Him. Oh! indeed, I would rather be a doorkeeper in the house of my God, than dwell and fare sumptuously in the tents of wickedness. My heart says, "Let thine handmaid be a servant to wash the feet of the servants of my Lord."

I have thought of you in your last bereavement; you now know a little of my anguish—the lonely bed, the lonely meal, the vacant chair, &c.; but Jesus makes up for all these, does He not? To His dear heart of love, and arm of power, I now commend you, and in Him rest in bonds indissoluble. —Your ever-affectionate   RUTH.

C.

Deep draughts drawn with joy from the wells of salvation.

" Eat, O friends ; drink, yea, drink abundantly, O beloved."—Song v. 1.
" I am come that they might have life, and that they might have it more
　　abundantly."—John x. 10.
" There is a river, the streams whereof shall make glad the city of God,
　　the holy place of the tabernacles of the most High."—Psalm xlvi. 4.
" Thou visitest the earth, and waterest it : thou greatly enrichest it with
　　the river of God, which is full of water."—Psalm lxv. 9.

TO MRS H.

Ockbrook, 1849.

My dear Amelia, And so your earth seems at this time
to be watered and enriched, for " we have this treasure in
earthen vessels, that the excellency of the power may be
of God, and not of us." [1] And you need not fear to drink
largely, for after all your tiny draughts the "river of God"
will be still full of water. It is a "pure river of water of
life, clear as crystal, proceeding out of the throne of God
and of the Lamb." Neither should you fear to go forward
into its blissful depths, for they are from the ankles to the
knees, from the knees to the loins, and when these are gone
through they are waters to swim in.[2] If you are become a
swimmer, hear the glad tidings ; it is a river that cannot be
passed over. Therefore fear not, but live in life and dwell
in love till the God of love rebuke thee, whose own sweet
promise is, "Therefore with joy shall ye draw water out of
the wells of salvation." [3] In this new-creation world there
is not only a flowing into the new creature, (for the new

[1] 2 Cor. iv. 7.　　　　[2] Ezek. xlvii. 3-5.　　　　[3] Isa. xii. 3.

wine of the spiritual kingdom is put into the new bottles,) but there is also a flowing out, for, saith He who is the beginning of this creation of God,[1] " He that believeth on me, out of his belly shall flow rivers of living water." [2]

As for your gladsome notes under love's thrilling power, they are according to the direction : " Let the inhabitants of the rock sing, let them shout from the top of the mountains." [3] If all on earth seem too dull to respond to your strains, methinks they will find an echo in the very rock itself. For it is said of Him who is our rock, " He will save, he will rejoice over thee with joy. He will rest in his love. He will joy over thee with singing." [4] Surely we, who are the children and partakers of such mighty love, must rejoice also as its precious fulness inundates our souls with a full tide of ecstasy.

Ah, my dear Amelia, the precious love of our glorious " Well-Beloved " is indeed overpowering. I wonder not at your raptures, and do much rejoice that in this cold region there are yet a few who are glowing in that heavenly fire which God himself hath kindled and will never extinguish. I attempt not to pour into your already full soul, but just pen these feeble lines lest I should appear indifferent, which indeed I am not. I delight to listen to your song of love, and rejoice in your joy, the substance of which I well understand. It is " Christ in us the hope of glory." Ah, and the foretaste of glory too ! The Lord make and keep us faithful to Himself.

You well know that I also am at school. I have been in the very suburbs of the Celestial City, and have seen the

[1] Rev. iii. 14.
[2] John vii. 38.
[3] Isa. xlii. 11
[4] Zeph. iii. 17.

King in His beauty, and thought the everlasting doors were opening to receive my happy soul; but returning bodily strength convinces me that my wilderness work and warfare are not ended. I think the lesson now before me is, that we must be a constant sacrifice to Him who was so rich and willing a sacrifice for us, that all our wishing and willing must give place to a dissolving into the divine will, and our constant prayer be, "Father, glorify thy name." Many things tend to make me feel that henceforth I must live an earthly life, not in any wise "seeking mine own things, but the things which are Jesus Christ's;" doing which, the flesh must be constantly sacrificed. Having willingly laid it upon God's altar in spite of its own struggling, may He keep me from ever withdrawing it or conferring with it again, remembering that "no man having put his hand to the plough and looking back is fit for the kingdom of God." Oh, in very deed I believe I must be more than ever a stranger and pilgrim on this earth. I have deeply loved my happy home and sweet domestic endearments; but my Lord has broken up the one, and taken me from the other; and, having thus at His command left the shore, I must not wish to regain it, but ever embrace Him as my glorious "all in all," worthy of a thousand hearts and lives if I had them to give. Plead, oh, plead, that I may "stand perfect and complete in all the will of God;" for I must say, "Not as though I had already attained, either were already perfect," "but, forgetting those things which are behind, and reaching forth unto those things which are before, I press toward the mark."

I can but write to you with a heart kindled in the blissful flames of love divine, having had much, very much forgiven, and feeling that I can never love half enough, for I owed ten thousand talents, and the rich blood of my Beloved cancelled all the mighty sum. Now the rich love of the same dear heart flows into mine with more power and sweetness than words can tell. The Lord be with your spirit, and your spirit confidingly and rejoicingly with the Lord.—So desires, with much love, your warmly-affectionate, but unworthy RUTH.

CI.

The Spirit's teaching.

TO MRS H.

OCKBROOK, 1849.

MY OWN SWEET AMELIA, Surely your words are pleasant words to my soul, because they flow in sweet accordance with the pure law of liberty and love; which is, that "in all things Christ shall have the pre-eminence," yea, that He shall be all, and we nothing. Our Teacher must be one, the teaching is so in unison; and how blessed, my dear Amelia, that flesh and blood hath not revealed this unto us, but our Father which is in heaven, whom it hath pleased to reveal His Son in us, and also to give Him unto us as our precious heavenly Bridegroom. The glories of His person, and ravishments of His love are not for a carnal eye or stranger bosom, but only for her of whom He says, "My dove, my undefiled, is but one; she is the only one of her mother, she is the choice one of her that bare her." [1]

My heart rejoices that you are feeling the worth and weight of souls for whom our precious Lord travailed in

[1] Song vi. 9.

sweat and blood. It may be your high privilege to be His instrument in awakening some from the dreadful sleep of death in sin. My heart longs that this be done more than words can tell, and also that living ones be aroused to a sense of their high privileges in Christ Jesus, Who is too little known and too little sought after. Surely, my very dear Amelia, we, who through grace have a glimpse of these glories and taste of this blessedness, should be right earnest in telling the good tidings to those of the king's house within,[1] who yet believe not the joys of a present salvation. Though they listen to us with jealousy, we have the witness in ourselves, and can say honestly, "That which we have seen and heard declare we unto you."[2] We would testify *to* man when the Lord calls us, but we seek not testimony *from* man ; it were an insult to the Divine majesty, when we have already His testimony in our conscience.

Adieu, my very dear friend ; the Lord keep thee all His own.—In His precious love which flowed out in richest blood, I am your warmly-affectionate, RUTH.

CII.

The Lord is everything.

TO MRS H.

OCKBROOK, *Sept.* 1849.

MY VERY DEAR AMELIA, I sit at my window, and look towards Castle Donnington, and though it is just now too

---

[1] 2 Kings vii. 9-11.   [2] 1 John i. 3, 4.

hazy to discern it as I often do, yet my heart rejoices that there lives one who warmly loves my Jesus, and whose soul thrills affectionately towards unworthy me in Him and in His sweet love, and for His dear sake alone. It is this, my dear Amelia, which gives your love such a warm reception in my poor heart, as none merely for my own sake could receive. Your letter caused tears of love, to Him Who is so very near and precious in all our conflicts and sorrows. Ah! my dear friend, how does our vigilant foe lie in wait to spoil us of our " Resting-place," and to cast us down from Christ, our Excellency. How does he work upon our natural sensibilities, and our present circumstances, to produce first disquiet, then discontent, and then urge us, if possible, to some carnal mode of relief! But the Lord "will keep the feet of His saints," " He suffereth not our feet to be moved." Therefore, " in your patience possess ye your soul." Abiding in Him, ' there shall not a hair of your head perish," and possessing Him, ye cannot lack anything.

Remember, your life is consecrated to the Lord, and in whatever circumstances you must seek and serve *Him only.* Already have you proved that His *reward* is with Him, and a rich one too, nothing less than Himself in present possession, and delights in Him beyond expression. Ah! and His work is before Him, and He will do it, nor shall any let or hinder; but He will "let patience have its perfect work, that ye may be perfect and entire, wanting nothing."

On Thursday I had the pleasure of an interview with your beloved friend, and Mr and Mrs J. H——. The conversation of Mr H——was, I think, solidly edifying to the poor gleaner. When they were gone, my soul was in a most blessed state of Sabbatism, and I could only weep tears of the most serene and peaceful joy, willing to be baptized into the death, as well as crowned with the glory of my Lord, my Life, my ALL. You speak of "things new and old;" thus it was with Mr H——, he spoke of some things new to me, and entered into others which my soul loves, and which it was taught by the Lord alone, without the intervention of any human instrument. As usual, my heart failed a good deal at the thought of meeting a stranger, and I also thought he would be so allegorical that I should not understand him, but it was not so. I suppose he accommodated his mode to my usage and simplicity. I am quite convinced, that where there is the one true life there will be union, whatever be the difference in outward form. I fear dear Mrs B—— did not share our profit, as she had to go and see some one at the school, and such distraction of the mind lessens real bene-fit. I think, too, in our meetings for spiritual communion, the more there is of closeness of thought, and the less of indifferent subjects, the better—" Little foxes spoil the vines."

I expect to leave this sacred retreat next week, and return to my little Bethel Home—Gen. xxxv. 3, seems to be the word on my mind on this subject. May it also be as verse 9. May the Lord bless you, my beloved, and " keep thee in all thy ways ;" and give us both to live in sweet simplicity, "rejoicing in Christ Jesus, and having no confidence in the flesh." I must send you Deut. xxx. 20, it is so very sweet to me. Our "Christ is our life;" to Him may we cleave, that in Him, the good Lamb, we may dwell, and willingly let the flesh go to the cross and death He has appointed for it. Gal. ii. 20, vi. 14.

" And now, I commend you to God, who is able to build

you up, and to give you an inheritance amongst all them that are sanctified." Excuse this poor letter.—Accept warm love in our best Beloved, and believe me in Him, our bond of union, your ever-affectionate RUTH.

CIII.

The inward witness.

TO MRS H.

HIGH PAVEMENT.
NOTTINGHAM, *Oct.* 6, 1849.

MY OWN DEAR AMELIA, " Stand fast in the liberty wherewith Christ hath made you free, and be not entangled again with the yoke of bondage." The more liberty in Christ, the less in self and creatures ; the more in them, the less in Him. They comport not together; one will destroy the other ; and if we are really living in the liberty of love and privileges of union, we shall hold and use all creatures, and creature good, only in the Beloved, and for His glory. In so far as He is our all, selfish ends and aims will be lost. Just as the rod of Aaron swallowed up the rods of the magicians of Pharaoh, so will all those powers which were once instruments of unrighteousness in self-love, be swallowed up in Christ, by Whose power in us they will be used as instruments of righteousness unto God.

How little, my beloved friend, is this liberty of love known in the present day, and how soon are we counted mystic if we speak of its delights ; but having the precious secret within, we are in that sense independent of human opinions.

We feel the love burn, we hear the Beloved speak, and we know the oil flows, because our souls are afresh and afresh anointed therewith, and because of which anointing, every yoke of bondage is destroyed.[1] We are no longer the "servants of men;" but being amenable at a higher bar, to that alone we appeal for judgment in every case, and by that decision we abide, let who will condemn or cast us out as evil. Oh, it is precious that we are "free born," and not in bondage to any man : " The Lord is our lawgiver, the Lord is our king; he will save us." " Some trust in chariots, and some in horses; but we will trust in the name of the Lord our God,"—and we shall not trust in vain; " though faith, even the smallest, shall surely be tried." I know it, for I prove it constantly.

I have met with some circumstantial contrarieties to try faith, which make me cry for more grace. Sometimes providences seem to contradict promises, that there may be a death put upon our fleshly expectations, and the blessing be enjoyed in the Lord's way and at the Lord's time. Do not our souls exclaim, " How unsearchable are His judgments, and His ways past finding out?" Well, dearest friend, all is well. The Lord is leading me, a poor, blind creature, by a way I knew not, according to a precious sermon I heard the last Sabbath at Ockbrook, from Isa. xlii. 16, which just described what I was coming into. But my Beloved has sweetly whispered, "I am with thee, trust Me in the dark."

I wonder how you are travelling on. I was happy to receive your last sweet note, and to learn that you were again disentangled by Love's own power; may you be preserved by the same power with single eye, simple faith, and

[1] Isa. x. 27.

love pure and fervent. Fail not to write to me when you feel the prompting thereto, though this letter deserves no reply.

And now, my dear Amelia, may your garments be always white, and your head lack no ointment. Keep yourself pure by abiding in Him who is your purity. To His warm love I commend you. He is our bond of union, and since He changeth not it cannot be broken. Adieu in the sweet love of our heavenly Friend and best Beloved.—Ever yours affectionately, His gleaner, RUTH.

CIV.

Counsels to hearken to the voice of the good Shepherd only.

TO MRS H.

NOTTINGHAM, *Feb.* 20, 1850.

MY LOVED ONE IN OUR BELOVED, AND FOR HIS PRECIOUS SAKE, In His own sweet love I salute you in spirit, and in our oneness in Him desire to commune of Him, joyfully forgetting ourselves and each other, that He alone may be remembered. May He be the glow between us, His living love being the fire of our fervour. Truly we want no false fire of the flesh, for all such will go out in utter darkness; we want no sparks of our own kindling, for He says of such, "This shall ye have at mine hand, ye shall lie down in sorrow." God himself has kindled his own fire of love in our souls, and in the renewings of it by His Spirit we flow out to each other in His praise. Oh, blessed privilege, not to know or be known after the flesh, but "all for the lifting of Jesus on high," that He may increase and we decrease !

Very sweet is the flow of your love-strain, my dear Amelia. It is sweet for His sake who is to His bride what no earthly language can ever fully express ; for when we have said all we can, the fullest and sweetest remains untold. Each bosom must know for itself the secrets of love, or they are not known at all ; and where really enjoyed, they will flow from soul to soul in something more powerful than words. I feel it, beloved friend, it is inexpressible—one life, one love, one Beloved, one blissful eternity, in which we shall know as we are known, and see as we are seen. What, what shall I render that I, so unworthy, should be the object of such love ? "If a man would give all the substance of his house for love, it would utterly be contemned." [1] Oh, it comes free, or I had never known it ; and most freely, without creature effort, does it flow back to its source and flow out to those kindred souls who are enkindled by its sacred fire. Truly I am formed *by* love, *for* love. To the God of love, who is love, be all the praise ! "This people have I formed for myself, they shall shew forth my praise." O our precious Christ, surely we will welcome the fiery coals of Thy jealousy, the vehement flame of which shall burn out from our hearts every name, every image, but Thine own, for only then can our inner man be satisfied, "when we awake up in Thy likeness." Oh, then, set us "as a seal upon Thy heart, as a seal upon Thine arm" for ever.

It seems the will of our Father that you and I, dear Amelia, should walk for a season in much circumstantial contrariety, and perhaps just as we seem ready to cast the

[1] Cant. viii. 6.

anchor or touch the shore, we are unexpectedly sent out again into a fresh storm. So it has been with me, but all is well. There is no perishing with Christ on board; "the winds and waves obey Him," and the storm blows up or blows over, precisely according to His loving will. This morning our family reading was Matt. xii., and at verse 20 my soul melted, and your spirit seemed blended in its softness and its triumph. Yea, it seemed for you: "A bruised reed shall He not break, and smoking flax shall He not quench, till He send forth judgment unto victory." "Judgment unto victory,"—it needs no comment; I could say much, but words will only impoverish. I cast this bread upon the waters of your soul and of your circumstances; if you are fed by it in all its fulness, it will not only invigorate now, but be found after many days. May He who kindled the flame of our friendship be pleased constantly to take off all that is of the creature, that it may burn free and bright to His glory alone, and that we may live in each other's hearts without leaving any the less room for Him "who filleth all in all." O holy, lovely Saviour, keep Thy poorest, vilest worm in her true nothingness, in all her and Thy beloved ones, and just make her only help them to love Thee more. Take this loving Amelia and consecrate the union of our hearts, in oneness with Thee, to Thine especial service and Thy glory; ever keep us clear of each other,—ah, and of all others,—that communion may be free and blissful in Thee, of Thee, with Thee, and for Thee. Amen.

Now, my beloved friend, one word more. The work of grace in my soul never would be systemised, and never could I square it to any model which creatures have presented, even the very best of them. I have had just to give

up all into the forming hands of my Beloved, and be willing
to be what I call a "nondescript." I am too high for some,
and too low for others, and exactly like none, except as we
both are in Christ. I do not say it will be thus with you,
but, if it should, you will not be alone; and I must say it is
truly glorious to go on with Jesus only." Many would cut
us off and cast us out, but He says, "Because I live, ye shall
live also." Though now hidden in the *déshabille* of this
mortal state, yet when "He who is our life shall appear,
then shall we also appear with Him in glory." And though
not understood by many of our "mother's children," yet do
we rejoice to be naked and open to the eyes of Him with
whom we have to do.

As for our leading in experience, when we try to keep in
any line chalked out to us by others, we only get bewilderment; for one builds up, and another pulls down, and the
confusion becomes more confused. So, at least, I have
found. My first real establishing, after years of tossing,
came exactly as Gal. i. 12, and I just believe that in the
same way only will the teaching go on. I speak not to
bring you into my line of things, but just to encourage your
heart, if your teaching seem not fully to conform to that of
any of your fellows. It is vain to pare off or piece on, to
please those we most esteem; each stone has its place in the
spiritual buildings, and each member its office in the body;
the preparation for which, is best understood by Him who
worketh all things after the counsel of His own will. We
need not fear, if He only knows what He is doing with us,
and what is to be the issue,—but love will still confide.

And now, my dear friend, methinks I have lost both you
and myself in the absorbing glories of Him who is the only

"altogether lovely." Ah, He has borne away my poor heart in triumph, but He has left His own in its place. Happy exchange! Heartless for earth I would henceforth remain that I may be heart-full of Him. Whatever wise ones or great ones prescribe, be it mine to live in sweet simplicity in the element of love, which truly is most congenial to my soul. Here I breathe freely, live joyfully, and not only take every cup from my Beloved's own hand, but drink it for His own sake, not because of what is or is not in it.

Now, a warm adieu from the veriest worm, who has, by divine light, life, and power, been made a living monument of sovereign, saving grace.—In the endearment of undecaying love, your most unworthy, but warmly affectionate,

RUTH.

CV.

The unchangeableness of Christ in the midst of a changing world.

TO MRS. H.

HIGH PAVEMENT, *May* 1850.

MY MUCH-LOVED AMELIA, You will have wondered at my long silence, and that I should have allowed two precious letters to remain so long unanswered. Indeed I would have written; but when He shutteth none can open, and when He bindeth none can walk at large. "Even so, Father, for so it seemeth good in thy sight." "Good is the will of the Lord concerning me." "Not my will, but Thine be done."

Peace be unto you, my loved Amelia, and the love of

the Father, Son, and Holy Ghost. May the one holy Lord God of Israel dwell richly in your heart. It rejoiced me greatly to hear that the anointed One[1] had proclaimed "liberty to the captive," and that your disentangled soul was again rejoicing in its best Beloved. "Stand fast therefore in the liberty wherewith Christ hath made thee free, and be not entangled again with the yoke of [creature] bondage;"[2] lest He say, "Let her alone; she hath loved idols, after idols let her go." Instead of this, I the rather hope that you are still looking out of the "Dove's eyes," which are pure eyes, and do ever reject every attraction but the rightful one. Your letter upon the "Dove's eyes" was very precious, and that such a Beloved should condescend to be ravished[3] with such a spouse is marvellous indeed; but, as you rightly observe, "it is His own loveliness reflected when she gazes steadfastly upon Him."

O my dear Amelia, for a steady, undiverted look of our Beloved! How do the contrarieties of the wilderness, working upon this corrupt flesh, seem to come between us and Him! In our experience there is an eclipse of His brightness who is our beauty; though still through all He loves, "and hates to put away." Praise Him, my poor, unstable soul, that He changes not,[4] and therefore I am not consumed. Ah, no! Divine love prevents the consuming of its object in any other fire than its own, but in those fires is only a making meet to be more absorbed in its inexpressible blissfulness. This poor heart has had many a tossing lately, but it feels the security of love which, amidst all, does insure and assure that the union is eternal, and that no things of time shall dissever it.

[1] Isa. lxi. 1.   [2] Gal. v. 1.   [3] Song iv. 9.   [4] Mal. iii. 6.

" My everlasting song is this,—
　Jesus is mine, and I am His."

Many of His dealings I do not understand, and I often feel
myself a poor, weary pilgrim, but His love and His bosom
are the home of my new heart; and there it reposes in
safety, while the tempest howls around and the storm beats
upon the outer man. I do not mean you to think I have
been in great trials, but I have had many little contrarieties in the path, and much exercise of soul.

I am more and more convinced the way upward is one
of tribulation, and the high heads and trifling hearts of
most professors look as if they were not in it. But honestly
we say,

" Above their highest mirth,
　Our saddest hours we prize ;
　For though our cup seems mix'd with gall,
　There's something secret sweetens all ;"

but the worst and roughest of our heavenward path is infinitely preferable to the best a worldling knows. And how
came unworthy we into the secret ? Oh, love would have
it so,—love would have His own, and made us " willing in
the day of His power." " Not unto us, not unto us, but
unto Thy name be the glory." So says my heart, as it freely
ascribes all "to the praise of the glory of His grace, wherein
He hath made us accepted in the Beloved." And though
my flesh wants an easy path, my spirit often feels the blessed
benefit of the cross, and blesses Him who lovingly endured
it with the curse for my unworthy sake.

I was thankful to find your mind so abstracted from
earthly things when you last wrote, and I hope it continues
by the Spirit's power to forsake all for Christ. You will
find more than all in Him, the glories of whose person out-

matches all beside. And now, dear Amelia, I commend you in body, soul, and circumstances to Him whose love first united us, and who will remain amid all fluctuations. "Jesus Christ, the same yesterday, to-day, and for ever," our Beloved, our Friend, our ALL IN ALL. His blessing be ever your enriching.—With dear love, believe me *in Him* your affectionate RUTH.

CVI.

The Lord refreshing His people with the river of His pleasures.

TO MRS H.

HIGH PAVEMENT, *June* 2, 1850.

MANY thanks for your precious letter, it is like Song i. 12. "The time is short: it remaineth, that both they that have wives [or husbands] be as though they had none."

"Hearken, O daughter, and consider, and incline thine ear; forget also thine own people, and thy father's house; so shall the King greatly desire thy beauty: for he is thy Lord, and worship thou him."

"I am my beloved's, and his desire is towards me." Oh, the wonder!

"He is the chiefest among ten thousand." "His mouth is most sweet; yea, he is altogether lovely." "Thou, [O beloved,] art [infinitely] fairer than the children of men; grace is poured into thy lips." "As the apple-tree among the trees of the wood, so is my beloved among the sons. I sat down under his shadow with great delight, and his fruit was sweet to my taste."

It is marvellous, my dearest Amelia, that our beloved spiritual Bridegroom should again draw near and ravish your heart with His inexpressible love and loveliness at this especial time. Surely everything is beautiful in its season, and these visits of love are peculiarly beautiful now, sweetly intimating that your earthly bonds must be loosened and your heavenly ones drawn closer, just seeming to say, "Thou shalt be for Me," "and thou shalt not be for another; so will I also be for thee." The Lord knows what are His own purposes concerning you, but He is not bestowing these favours for naught. He will make us know that His spiritual gifts are neither to play with nor for display, but for the edification of His household. It may be as you think, that ere long He will call you to active service; but this will not be with wisdom of words, lest the cross of Christ should be of none effect, but in your own utter weakness, that the excellency of the power may be manifestly of God, and not of the creature. May He be with you and with your mouth, causing you to utter knowledge clearly, not fouling the pure stream with anything of the flesh. Well may it be said, "Who is sufficient for these things?" and joyfully may it be answered, "Our sufficiency is of God."

I could not but write to you to-day, humbly adoring Him who has made us one, not only in union, but in communion. Surely I rejoice in your joy, and with you rejoice in the Lord our righteousness. The last fortnight the Lord has been pleased to favour me with endearing communion. He has come down on my soul like rain on the mown grass, and granted me such glimpses of His all loveliness as have

ravished my heart, and made the new song of praise burst
forth with fresh ardour from my enraptured soul. Oh, He
is so worthy, so worthy, that the highest, sweetest strains we
reach disappoint us, and we feel that we *would* praise Him
but *cannot!* The 12th chapter of Isaiah has been one of my
melodies, and with joy indeed have I drawn and drunk water
"out of the wells of salvation." Bless the Lord, O our souls.
It is very marvellous; I feel it so; and, while longing for
more, I wonder I have so much; but He has blessed, and
none can reverse it. "There is no enchantment against
Jacob, neither is there any divination against Israel." He
has brought us to dwell in that mountain where He has
"commanded the blessing, even life for evermore." "Because
I live, ye shall live also." Not I, but Christ liveth in
me." What ease, what release it is when He is our all!

To Him I commend you in love. "Now unto Him that
is able to do exceeding abundantly above all that we ask or
think, according to the power that worketh in us, unto Him
be glory in the Church by Christ Jesus throughout all ages,
world without end. Amen." Adieu.—In tender love ever
yours in our best Beloved, RUTH.

CVII.

Christ worthy of the soul's highest love.

TO MRS H.

BETHEL COTTAGE, *Jan.* 12, 1851.

MY VERY DEAR AMELIA, "Where art thou?" and what
art thou doing? Art thou a widow indeed trusting in God,

and continuing in supplication and prayers, serving Him
with fastings and prayers night and day in Christ, the
true temple? 1 Tim. v. 5; Luke ii. 37.

Released from the creature yoke, is Jesus the heavenly
Bridegroom now your all? As saith the prophet, "Thy
Maker is thine husband; The Lord of hosts is his name."
Say, my beloved, is His name as ointment poured forth to
your soul? Are you satisfied with Him, happy in Him,
restless without Him? Are creatures and things without
Christ in them, like the empty sepulchre to mourning Mary,
who had lost her Lord, and would accept no substitute?
It was His love united us, and made communion sweet; it
is in that love I now inquire, "Is it well with thee?" How
are the fruits of the valley? Does the vine flourish, and
the tender grape appear, and the pomegranate bud forth?
Is it seed-time or harvest with you? Are you reaping
the precious fruits, or having long patience for them, and
watching for the early and for the latter rain?

I am just myself an empty sinner, living in and on a full
Saviour, "who loved me, and gave Himself for me." I am
crucified with Him. He lives in me; "the life I live in the
flesh is by the faith of the Son of God." I find His service
perfect freedom, and sweetly prove that "the way of the
Lord is strength to the upright." Unto you that believe
He is precious." Ah, indeed no words can express how precious our glorious Emmanuel is to the gleaner's heart. "I
am poor and needy, but the Lord thinketh upon me;" and
He has said in my soul for this new year 1851, "Ye are not
your own, ye are bought with a price." It felt very, very
solemn; and then a short time after that word followed,
"Thou art mine," which was very sweet and melting. Oh,

to glorify Him in body and spirit, which are His—"bought and paid for," the price His own rich blood! Amazing! Was ever love like this? Ah, *never!* He is the Prince of lovers, the best of all beloveds; worthy, worthy is our lovely Lord the Lamb! Of all on earth I surely am most indebted to Him, and owe Him an eternity of praise. Isa. lxiii. 7.

Now, my loved one, I affectionately commend you to "Him that is able to keep you from falling, and to present you faultless before the presence of His glory with exceeding joy."—And, in our precious Jesus, remain yours very lovingly,   RUTH.

CVIII.

The blind led by a way they know not.

TO MRS H.

HIGH PAVEMENT, *July* 16, 1852.

"I will bring the blind by a way that they knew not; I will lead them in paths that they have not known : I will make darkness light before them, and crooked things straight. These things will I do unto them, and not forsake them."

"And He took the blind man by the hand, and led him out of the town," and when away from all, He gave him sight in a most gradual and sovereign manner, see Mark viii. 23-25. The blind man could not see where Jesus was leading him; he must confide entirely in Him; neither could he know why He should lead him along in darkness, when

he had asked to be restored to sight.   If he reasoned, the
thought would be, "Why not give it me at once?"   But
"my thoughts are not your thoughts, neither are your ways
my ways, saith the Lord."   Deliverance seldom comes in
the way we look for it; for "who hath directed the Spirit
of the Lord, or, being his counsellor, hath taught him."
Isa. xl. 13.

Ah, my dear Amelia, has not the Lord frustrated our
purposes over and over again?   I cannot tell you with what
majesty that last-quoted passage has often come to my mind,
with v. 14, "With whom took He counsel?"   Not with
puny, sinful worms.   He will counsel *for* them, but not
with them : "My counsel shall stand, and I will do all My
pleasure."   Yet "fear not, thou worm Jacob, I will help
thee,"—help thee to stand still and see My salvation, or
help thee to walk on in the dark in a rough and unknown
path, just as my wisdom sees fit.   Spiritual eyesight is not
given to look at the outward path, but to look at our Guide;
not to look before us at the way we are going to travel, but
to look only at Him who will guide us safely through all,
who will Himself be our way *in* the way, but not our way
out of it.   Oh, to be kept abiding in Him, and constantly
looking unto Him!   It is most safe and blessed, but very
contrary to flesh and blood.

How I do like Jer. xvii. 5-10, it is so descriptive of the
blessedness of trusting in the Lord alone, and the sterility
and disappointment of all creature confidence.   I know not
your present difficulties, nor need I know them, for I could
not bring you out of them ; but I do bless the Lord He has
brought you into the very best posture of soul—looking to
Him alone.   Tell your sorrows and secrets to this thy

Friend, watch His eye, obey His bidding, and go not to carnal and lower means for relief. You will find it turn to good account, if you are helped to wait it out and watch it out, not as carnal Saul, to wait till a set time, and then if relief tarry endeavour to extricate yourself.[1] I write the things that I do know, my loved Amelia, having at some times smarted for the haste of the flesh, and at others inherited great blessing by waiting for the Lord, even in very trying circumstances and amidst many counter voices ; but "in keeping of His commandments there is great reward." —Adieu in our heavenly Bridegroom, and in His undying love.   RUTH.

CIX.

Deliverance granted IN, *not* FROM *affliction.*

TO MRS H.

HIGH PAVEMENT, *July* 14, 1853.

MY LOVED AMELIA, Again the Lord is proving to me the blessedness of taking up the cross, and also how much I shrink from it. I seek deliverance *from* the cross, but find my Lord has put deliverance *in* it ; and if I could writhe myself away from it, I should miss the blessing ; but when by His enablings it is fairly taken up, there is indeed a new song put into my mouth, even praise to His name. The soul at such times seems to triumph in Christ, something like Paul when reconciled to the thorn in the flesh. Indeed I feel it good to be laid low, and kept low at the feet of my precious Lord, though He is bringing it about in ways

[1] 1 Sam. xiii. 8, 15.

most unexpected and undesired. I am much longing for humility, and He is laying open to me my pride by the very smart I feel in being made nothing; truly His ways are wonderful, far above mine, and His thoughts also. His goings towards me and before me are very stately, and worthy of a God who giveth none account of His matters, but worketh all things after the counsel of His own will, and all things for good to those that love Him, and are the called according to His purpose.

May the Lord preserve all your goings, and hold you in His paths, that your footsteps slip not. To Him I commend you; may He fulfil in you all the good pleasure of His goodness, and the work of faith with power. Farewell in our Beloved.—Ever thine with much affection, RUTH.

CX.

The happiness of those that endure.

TO MRS H.

October 17, 1855.

MY OWN DEAREST AMELIA, I cannot refrain from saying how very welcome and suitable were some things in your letter this morning. I was deeply writhing under a sense of my useless, worthless, unprofitable life. Think, then, what balm to hear afresh that the savour of His good ointments had been caused to flow through my heart and pen to those hearts dear to Him. And by other seasonable passages in the letters, I was afresh strengthened to endure in things which were then pressing. Oh that word "endure," what has it been to me by the Spirit's power! I have often said, it is worthy to be written in letters of gold. But it is written in better than gold, even in living characters, by the finger of God, in the fleshy table of the heart. And the blessing is richly found at the end of it, " He that shall *endure* to the end the same shall be saved." This was one of my winter lessons when in the furnace. Not alluding only to eternal salvation, but also the many salvations we need in the pathway to glory ; in most dispensations there is a time to endure ; it may be while sowing in tears, or it may be while suffering with patience; but as we are enabled to abide in the trial with God, the reaping in joy and the crown of rejoicing does certainly follow.

My heart rejoices with you in the Lord. Oh, what wonders of His love have I been proving, though many a rough wind from the wilderness has been blowing; but in wilderness dispensations He causes rivers to flow forth, and streams in the desert.—Hoping soon to speak face to face, I remain, with tender love, your ever-affectionate RUTH.

CXI.

" I will guide thee with mine eye."

TO MRS H.

HIGH PAVEMENT, *Nov.* 29, 1855.

MY EVER-DEAR AMELIA, How truly have we both proved that when "the Lord shutteth none can open, and when he opens none can shut." I trust the present opening in your case will eventually prove of real benefit to your bodily health, and also that you may have as manifestly the Lord's

Y

presence and instructions as (to His glory I am constrained to confess) I have had, in going from my own home, quite as unexpectedly as you. He leads us about to instruct us, as it is written, "He led him about, he instructed him, he kept him as the apple of his eye."

In the summer I had the kind offer of being in the country for a few weeks quite close to Nottingham, but I declined ; in fact, I could not go, my mind was barred against it. The same benefit was then offered to a dear friend, who directly accepted it, and was just longing and pining for country air. She went, and it was a benefit to her in several ways; thus the shutting up to me was an opening to her. Afterwards another kind friend just outside the town invited me, but I felt quite unfit to be away from home, and declined. Soon after another friend, who is herself in weakness, much urged me to spend two nights with her, as she was going to be quite alone. Again I started back, both on account of my own feelings, and also because of the manifest inconsistency of refusing two friends but accepting a third, all just close to Nottingham, but oh, my friend, how powerfully did the Lord say, "*Go,*" by a tide of Scripture flowing into my soul to that effect, and also answering every objection as it rose. What could I do but obey ? It was the obedience of faith, for sight and sense were in many ways against it. I went, as the weakest child, in much fear and trembling, though assured it was the right way, and oh! what a blessing we had. It was indeed a season of refreshing from the presence of the Lord, and His poor gleaner came back with her heart full of Divine blessing, which had been commanded "of purpose" for her, though it fell not from the hand of any reaper.[1]

[1] Ruth ii. 16.

Truly, " the way of the Lord is strength to the upright ;"
" his voice is full of majesty ;" it overcomes the soul,
and gives to its timid questions an answer of assurance
which none can gainsay or resist. " Where the word of a
king is there is power;" and when I was wondering " why
accept this and refuse the other ?" He said, " My people
shall be willing in the day of my power." Since the above, I
have, by the same Divine leading, spent a fortnight with the
friends to whom I gave the second refusal, and truly have
seen the Lord's goings in that house in answer to prayer,
and also felt the power of Satan striving against the spirit
of power. Whom resist steadfast in the faith; and truly in
the conflict the Spirit did strengthen my soul with that in-
valuable word "ENDURE," and enduring (by His power) to
the end, there was salvation. " Yea, in all these things we
are more than conquerors through Him that loved us." Thus
in my bodily weakness I have been called out when I had
thought to retire, and spend my few remaining days in a
quiet pavilion with my Beloved; but, however, to his honour
I must say, " He hath done all things well," and "His paths
drop fatness ; they drop upon the pastures of the wilderness," and then we, His "little hills, rejoice on every side."

I am now very poorly, and also much bowed under a deep
relative trial, in which I am anxiously watching for the
guiding cloud, and listening for the directing voice. I seldom
sail long on a smooth sea, but often do I see the Lord's
wonders in the deep, and bring up many a pearl from thence.
I am a poor weak creature, and often fear when I enter into
the cloud, and cry in the storm, " Save me, O God, for the
waters are come in unto my soul." Then He doth deliver
the poor and the needy when he crieth; He hath delivered,

He doth deliver, and we trust that He will yet deliver. I am weak and tried, but one of those feeble folk whose dwelling is in the rock.[1]—Dear love, from your warmly-affectionate RUTH.

CXII.

The triumphant security of God's people.

HIGH PAVEMENT, *November* 10, 1857.

MY EVER-DEAR FRIEND, Where art thou ? On the battle-field, or on the watch-tower, or compassed about with songs of deliverance ? You are in daily remembrance, and your precious child also, though your letters have remained so long unanswered. I cannot tell you how much they have been enjoyed and prized by myself and others. While affection-ately feeling for your painful position, I cannot but rejoice at the divine teachings vouchsafed therein. As we are not our own, we have no right of choice how we shall be led, or by what means instructed. "He led him about, he instructed him, he kept him as the apple of his eye;" "kept" by the power of God through faith unto salvation, and "kept" in most wonderful cases and places; "kept" in the flood and in the flame; "kept" in the light and in the dark; "kept" in plenty and in poverty; "kept" in the seven-times-heated furnace and in the den of lions; and "kept" safely through all; "kept" also when the Divine Keeper seems to give advantage to our enemies—"Thou broughtest us into the net; thou laidest affliction upon our loins; thou hast caused men to ride over our heads; we went through fire and through water;" but "Thou broughtest us out into a wealthy

[1] Prov. xxx. 26.

place." Oh! this is precious leading and keeping, to bring us out from self and creatures into Christ our wealthy place, for in Him we shall be safe from fear of evil, shall be satisfied in the days of famine, and shall not be afraid in the year of drought. Abiding in Him, all the schemes of our foes shall be disappointed. Haman may plot and erect a gallows too, but his wicked device shall fall upon his own head. He shall be constrained to proclaim the honour of the Lord's servant, and then die by the very means he had prepared for him. Balak may hire Balaam to curse Israel, but he shall be compelled to bless them, for there is no enchantment against Jacob, nor divination against Israel. God hath blessed them, and Balaam cannot reverse it. The blessing will flow through Him, and to them, against Balaam's will; he can neither share it nor stop it. "Thou preparedst a table before me in the presence of mine enemies," or, Thou makest them prepare a table, and then flee away and leave their plenty for Thy starving people. So did the Syrians for Israel, and the poor outcast lepers were honoured to discover it, and get the first of the feast. When this meat from the eater was brought into the city, then was unbelief trodden down in the gate, and the Lord alone exalted in that day; His promise being fulfilled, and His people delivered, when to sense and reason there seemed no way of escape, (2 Kings vii.)

Oh! my dear, happy is he or she that hath the God of Jacob for their refuge, and whose hope the Lord is. "He is the Rock; His work is perfect." "Let the inhabitants of the rock sing; let them shout from the top of the mountains," for there is both protection and supply. "His place of defence shall be the munitions of rocks; bread shall be given him ; his waters shall be sure;"—sure indeed, for they drink of that spiritual rock which follows them, which rock is Christ; and "they thirsted not when He led them through the deserts." Though Amalek came out against them, he could not prevail. "No weapon that is formed against thee shall prosper; and every tongue that shall rise against thee in judgment, thou shalt condemn. This is the heritage of the servants of the Lord; and their righteousness is of me, saith the Lord." "This man shall be the peace when the Assyrian cometh into our land." "The Assyrians, thy neighbours, great of flesh,"—to look at them would destroy peace, but to look at the glorious man Christ Jesus keeps peace. "Thou wilt keep him in perfect peace whose mind is stayed on Thee, because he trusteth in Thee."

I do indeed rejoice with you on account of your beloved daughter, whom the Lord has graciously given you, in a dearer tie than that of nature; I hope to write her a line or two, though I feel very incompetent to do so. The Lord has been most gracious to me. He keeps me feeling my poverty, weakness, and inability; but makes His grace sufficient for me in a wonderful way, endearing a precious Christ more and more. My heart overflows with adoring gratitude for such a portion. The Lord is the portion of my inheritance, and of my cup, and he is a daily portion, as the manna was to Israel. "Give us this day our daily bread." "I am the bread of life;" "he that eateth me, even he shall live by me;"—and so feeding on Him, we shall grow up into Him in all things, and grow out of all besides. "The Lord bless thee and keep thee," and make a plain path, because of thine enemies. With tender love, yours ever most affectionately in the Beloved, RUTH.

CXIII.

The Lord's service perfect freedom.

TO MRS H.

1857.

MY OWN DEAR AMELIA, It was sweet to meet in His name, whose love is our bond of union, and who is Himself the sweetness of our communion. How stately have been His steps towards each of us! how has He drawn us away from all others, to reveal Himself more fully and gloriously! But, oh, that He should have looked upon so vile a one as myself with love and favour! Oh, that He should have brought me "under the rod, into the bond of the new covenant; " this is a marvel in my eyes! How well do the provisions of that new covenant suit *my* soul: "I will not turn away from them to do them good; but I will put my fear into their hearts that they shall not depart from me." Blessed Redeemer, let me ever be set as a seal upon Thine arm, as a seal upon Thine heart, for love is strong as death, and jealousy is cruel as the grave; and be Thou daily sealed anew in my warmest love, that our delights may be ever new and mutual.

I must now thank you for the precious epistle so full of heavenly teaching. You have indeed repaid my long silence with a rich outpouring, which must have cost much time; but I believe as it is refreshing and instructive in reading, so it would be also in writing, and that you would prove the Lord's service perfect freedom. His reward is with

Him whether in doing or suffering, according to His will. With me you have no doubt proved that it is better to labour and endure in His will, than to rest in our own, and thus I doubt not your long epistle was more enriching than exhausting. I rejoice in its Divine lessons, hoping to ponder them in my heart.

That the Lord sent you living truth through me, to nourish His own life in you, is a favour of which I am most unworthy : "Not unto us, not unto us, but unto Thy name, give glory." Where there is a pot of oil in the house,[1] it will be poured out into empty vessels at the command of our great prophet,—but, like the poor widow's cruise, there shall be no wasting by such using.[2]

I rejoice that you have been having communion with our Beloved, and feeding on the Tree of Life ; nothing else can nourish the inner man or satisfy living faith. This is the true bread, of which if a man eat, he shall live for ever. "He that cometh to me shall never hunger ; and he that believeth on me shall never thirst." I love to mark the present tense of Scripture which teaches the continuousness of a life of faith ;—it is not said, He that has come, and has believed, but cometh, believeth, &c., and even to the end "the just shall live by faith."

Fare you well, my loved one,—every blessing be with you, and the Lord lead you in a plain path because of your enemies.—With tender love, your ever-affectionate

RUTH.

---

[1] 2 Kings iv. 2-4.   [2] 1 Kings xvii. 16.

CXIV.

Sweet fruit gathered from a bitter root.

TO MRS H.

High Pavement, *August* 1857.

My dearest Amelia, " Whatsoever a man soweth, that shall he also reap " : he that soweth to the wind shall reap the whirlwind; he that soweth to the flesh shall reap corruption; he that soweth to the Spirit shall of the Spirit reap life everlasting. " Oh that they were wise, that they understood this, that they would consider their latter end !" in every dispensation, for " better is the end of a thing than the beginning thereof;" or it is worse. Of the tried and afflicted man of God who was persecuted by his neighbours, we read —" The Lord blessed the latter end of Job more than his beginning;" of the man whom Satan voluntary left for a season, we read—" The last end of that man is worse than the first." Faith often sows in tears ; but he that thus goeth forth and weepeth, " bearing precious seed, shall doubtless come again with rejoicing, bringing his sheaves with him." In this our precious Christ hath the pre-eminence. He was the man of sorrows and acquainted with grief. He sowed the seed of the kingdom in tears when He wept over Jerusalem ; but ere long He will joyfully see of the travail of His soul and be satisfied, when He shall say, " Here am I, and the children whom Thou hast given me." Thus also it often is with His members ; they sow and water and watch with tears, but reap in joy, while the carnal man sows with laughter and reaps disappointment. These things we have both known by experience, for when, having begun in the Spirit, a deceived heart hath turned us aside to the flesh, we had to feed on ashes, and the things which our soul refused to touch have become our daily sorrowful meat.

I have no judgment in your present case, "the judgment is God's;" inasmuch as you have sown to the Spirit in —— , travailing for his soul, you will reap life; but if in anywise there was mixed a sowing to the flesh, in that measure a harvest of corruption must be the result, which, however, shall issue in new destruction to the flesh, and new instruction to the spirit, by Him who is wonderful in counsel and mighty in working, and who turneth the shadow of death into the morning. It seems —— is sowing to the flesh indeed, but if the life be there, the Lord will separate the precious from the vile, will lead him with weeping and with supplication, and it may be you will rejoice together, not in each other, but in the Lord, who has said, "They shall not be ashamed who wait for me." You would, indeed, dear friend, bitterly feel the change in one whom you had nourished as a son in the gospel. However, by the grace of God which is in you, you will commit yourself fully to the Lord to execute judgment for you, while you still watch for his soul as they that must give account, desiring that his wood, hay, and stubble may be burnt up, and be saved even so as by fire. May it be given you to stand still and see the salvation of God, proving that the battle is the Lord's who will in very wonderful ways fight against the flesh and its schemes, and disappoint its enterprises, but will even in all these things make the new man more than conqueror through Him that loveth us. May your flesh have a new death, and your spirit enjoy more glowingly the crown of life, through this sharp exercise, and may the Lord bring out of the snare of the devil him who seems now led captive by him.

You are doubtless compassing the walls by faith through keeping silence till the day He shall bid you shout as Joshua vi. 10, and "lift up thy voice," to "shew my people their transgression, and the house of Jacob their sin." [1] The Lord make you faithful to His word, both in silence and in utterance, and enable you to care only for His honour, leaving your own entirely in His hands, since He has said, "He that toucheth you toucheth the apple of his eye." Moreover, dear friend, this dark dispensation will be "as a cloud with rain," if, by His power, it bring about a fresh lifting up of yourself from all creatures, to see no man save "Jesus only." "Was I ever a barren wilderness, to Israel a land of drought?" No, never. He is our straight way through crooked circumstances, and our pleasant way through the vexations of self and others. He keeps us alive in time of famine, for He is our plenty in the midst of poverty.

The things which I taste and handle declare I unto you, for deep abasings and continued emptiness are my experience. When I would gather ought but Him, most kind, most tender is it of Him to scatter it; indeed I have cause to praise Him for heights and for depths, for in both He has dealt wondrously for His holy name's sake.

I am glad to hear of your affairs, for though you be as a "lily among thorns," yet they shall not really harm you. Our Beloved was crowned with thorns, thus shewing that He had gained the victory over them for His bride, and

[1] Isaiah lviii. 1.

now He just teaches her with the briers and thorns of the wilderness. Many of your teachings and quotations are very sweet to me. I have had the same view of love which passeth knowledge, "for knowledge puffeth up, but charity edifieth."

I rejoice to hear that your beloved A—— M—— is a comfort to you, and much more that she is brought under the easy yoke and light burden of our blessed Saviour. May she be whole-hearted with Him and for Him, making no reserves; then will she largely foretaste that blessedness in Him which the natural eye hath not seen, or ear heard, but He hath revealed it unto us by His Spirit. Kind love to her.

The Lord bless you, make His way plain before you, and grant that your cruse and barrel be daily renewed as your needs require. "Your heavenly Father knoweth that ye have need of these things." May your erring friend be restored.[1] Power belongeth unto God, and His kingdom is not in word, but in power. May a new day of power come to his soul, for Thy people shall be willing in the day of Thy power. Fare thee well; may thy place of defence be the munitions of rocks, where thy bread shall be given, and thy water shall be sure.—With affectionate love in our one Beloved, yours ever in Him.   RUTH.

[1] James v. 19, 20.

CXV.

Christ the portion of His people.

" O God, command deliverances for Jacob." "Strengthen, O God, that which Thou hast wrought for us," "for Thou also hast wrought all our works in us."

" I will bring the blind by a way which they knew not ; I will lead them in paths they have not known ; I will make darkness light before them and crooked things straight ; these things will I do unto them and not forsake them." "The cup which my Father hath given me shall I not drink it ?"

TO MRS H.

HIGH PAVEMENT, *May* 20, 1858.

MY EVER-DEAR AMELIA, Yes, thou shalt drink it and praise the Lord. He wisely appoints and times every cup, and all is love. Bitters are strengthening, sweets are comforting, and through all He will sustain the hidden life with the hidden manna, of which, if a man eat, he shall live for ever. It was said of the Paschal Lamb, "with bitter herbs ye shall eat it," which remains true to this day, as I experimentally prove, but find it truly

> " Sweet to lie passive in His hands,
> And know no will but His."

When I attempt to *judge* His dealings I get into bewilderment and confusion ;—when I attempt to choose my own ways I make endless mistakes, and at length fall at His feet abased at my own foolishness. The government shall be upon His shoulders, and of the increase of His government and peace there shall be no end. Therefore "I will go in the strength of the Lord God; I will make mention of Thy righteousness, even of Thine only."

I have been passing through many deep trials since I last communicated with you, my dear friend, all proving that the Lord's thoughts are not our thoughts, nor His ways our ways. My thoughts are vain, and I hate them; but "how precious are Thy thoughts unto me, O God! how great is the sum of them!" if I could reckon them up in order they are more than can be numbered. "I know the thoughts that I think toward you, saith the Lord; thoughts of peace, and not of evil, to give you an expected end."

Many thanks for dear H—— M——'s letter. It is precious. It is indeed an indulgence to you both to dwell together in the Lord; but you are holding all ready to resign at His word, knowing that He only is your sure dwelling-place and companion for ever. Oh! sweet privilege, to hold all in Him, and for Him, and so live on Him, that we shall not be impoverished if all else be withdrawn.

> " There nought is in the creature found,
> 　　But may be found in Thee ;
> 　I must have all things and abound,
> 　　While Christ is all to me."

" I am thine inheritance," says our loving Lord; and as we live by faith, we find that we have a treasure in the heavens which faileth not. Brooks dry up, cisterns become broken, but the all-fulness treasured in Jesus is inexhaustible; and in the greatest outward straits we may be living in plenty and rejoicing in Him, as Hab. iii. 17, 18.

What need I have to cry, "Lord, increase my faith!" We are not straitened in Him but in our own bowels; too often are they straitened; then we can only rejoice in His gifts: but when enlarged into Himself we can rejoice in Him whether He bestow or withhold, spiritually or temporally. He is our peaceable habitation, our own dwelling, and quiet resting place, for so far as we live in His will, we are insured from disappointment, and are not afraid of evil tidings, our heart being fixed, trusting in the Lord. " Thou wilt keep him in perfect peace whose mind is stayed on Thee, because he trusteth in Thee." "The eyes of the Lord run to and fro throughout the whole earth, to shew himself strong in the behalf of them whose heart is perfect towards Him." Faith can "be still" with such a refuge and helper. He who has given all up has nothing to lose; and he who has found all in God has nothing out of Him to desire. Thus Mary sits still in the house till she receives the stirring message, " The Master is come, and calleth for thee;" and she also sits still at the feet of Jesus, feeding on Him, while busy Martha is preparing for Him. How plain that He was Mary's ALL, and that she realized that He had entertainment enough in Himself without any of her additions; she therefore leaves Martha to serve alone, while she feeds on her Lord, and He delights in her, and the satisfaction is mutual. May Mary's place and Mary's portion be yours and mine for ever; but it is only His own almighty power that can hold us to it. The flesh would ever be moving and meddling, for truly the professing Church in this day is a city full of stirs; and many of the living family are tossing to and fro in the general tumult, while their spiritual complainings are many, and amount to this, " While I was busy here and there, He was gone." Oh! keep us, gracious Lord, abiding in Thee, whilst others go and come.

Now, my beloved friend, I have many desires towards you.

Having just left off writing to take tea, I read over it Isaiah xxxv. with much sweetness, and if the Lord open it to your faith as He has to mine, you will not lack this day's bread, and with to-morrow will come its portion also. "Take no thought for the morrow; sufficient for the day is the evil thereof;" and "as thy days so shall thy strength be,""for the Lord God is thy strength, and He will make thy feet like hinds feet. Even upon the mountains of difficulty, He maketh a way for His ransomed to pass over; yea, He is the way in which thou shalt run and not be weary, walk and not faint; He is the straight way through crooked circumstances. "I will cause them to walk by the rivers of waters, in a straight way wherein they shall not stumble."

Now, beloved, I commend you to Him who "is able to keep you from falling, and to present you faultless before the presence of His glory, with exceeding joy." To Him alone be glory by us, and in all that befalls us, in this wilderness journey, for we are not our own, bnt are bought with a price, that we should be to the praise of His glory, who hath made us accepted in the Beloved.—In Him, our bond of union indissoluble, yours, with fervent love,   RUTH.

CXVI.

Faith's grasp of things unseen.

TO MRS H.

June 1858.

MY DEAREST FRIEND, Warmest thanks for your last letter. I judge you are in straits and trials. May the Lord strengthen your faith, so that you may be reconciled to all His ways and dealings. When fully reconciled we can walk lovingly with Him, even while He walks contrary to our flesh and its idols. Oh to follow Him fully, as Joshua and Caleb did, who held fast to His faithfulness amidst all the cavilings and improbabilities of flesh and blood, and even though the people talked of stoning them. They were quite sensible of their own weakness and the strength of their enemies, but what of all this? Faith did not look to creature arms or might, but stood on firmer ground. "If the Lord delight in us, then he will bring us into this land, and give it us; a land which floweth with milk and honey." Surely Christ is our good land; and though unbelief and Satan rage, and carnal reason cavil, the children of the promise shall possess their possessions. "I am thine inheritance, saith the Lord." In Him all things are ours, not to glory in or rest in, but to seek the things of Christ in them, and His glory by them. "Let no man glory in men, for all things are yours."[1] Oh, this precious grace of faith, may the Lord nourish and cherish it. Yea, faith is strong in old age to claim the fulfilment of the promise; and, having seen many wars and wonders of the Lord, it puts in the plea for every inch of ground for which the word has gone forth. See Joshua xiv. 9-11, yea, read the whole chapter, for it is very rich, and also Numbers xiii. and xiv. Oh for more Joshuas and Calebs! for truly "no good thing will he withhold from them that walk uprightly," which is to walk in Him, not in the flesh.

Affectionate love to your precious child. Dear girl, she bears the yoke in her youth as I also did, but have praised

[1] 1 Cor. iii. 20-23.

z

the Lord for it many times. His yoke is easy, and His burden light; it is the endeavour to evade it which is the misery. His cross is lined with love, however rugged and unsightly the outside may appear to carnal reason. Praise Him, O my soul, and praise Him, O ye cross-bearing companions. See what your forerunner did. He, bearing His cross, went forth.[1] Fear not to follow the Lamb, wheresoever and howsoever He leadeth. In each footprint he has left a blessing. "The Lord is with you while ye be with Him,"[2] and if He be for us we need not fear what flesh can do unto us.—With much love in our lovely and loving Lord the Lamb, your own ever-affectionate

RUTH.

CXVII.

Sweet lessons in the valley of Humiliation.

TO MRS H.

June 1858.

MY VERY DEAR FRIEND, I hope you are still kept steadily following onward in the way of faith. Oh, how sweet to live in momentary dependence upon Him, and independence of all beside; then are we satisfied with His fulness, however low creature streamlets may run. Do I not long to be more fully and always in this way of faith? Yes, verily; though, alas! I am too often turned aside by carnal reason, my old and powerful foe.

Oh, my dear Amelia, I think none of the Lord's children are

[1] 1 John xix. 17.　　　　[2] 2 Chron. xv. 2.

so slow to learn and so easily beguiled in some things, from the simplicity which is in Christ. I cannot boast of any attainments. I am laid low in the dust, and very, very poor; yet I have a rich Beloved, who scorns not my lowliness, and only keeps me short in hand that I may not be able to do without Him, and that I may glory in nothing but Himself, in whom I can never glory too much. It is good to be in the "valley of humiliation," the air is congenial to the new man, and very salutary, though not pleasing to this proud heart. Moreover, there we have much of the company of Prince Immanuel, who chose that spot for His earthly residence ; for "He made Himself of no reputation, and took upon Him the form of a servant, and being found in fashion as a man, He humbled Himself, and became obedient unto death, even the death of the Cross." Oh, it was a mighty stoop of love. I marvel and adore, desiring to follow the Lamb whithersoever He leadeth.

I heard a little of His wondrous ways towards you from dear Mrs B——. It is wonderful how He sends His benefits in such a way as to cut off all glorying in the flesh. You shall not be delighting in His benefits, but absorbed in Himself. Against this the enemy fights hard, presenting various things to divert from that safe and secret place into which he has no access. While delighting in gifts he can touch us, but, when wrapt up in the Giver, he is defeated, Psalm xci.

Fare you well. Affectionate love to your dear self, dear child, and dear Mrs B——, from yours ever warmly,

RUTH.

CXVIII.

Written within two months of her death.

Suffering no interruption to the believer's joy.

TO MRS H.

THE BANKS OF JORDAN, *May* 1860.

MY BELOVED AMELIA, Many thanks for your note. The Lord bless you and reveal Himself to you, and through you, more and more.

I rejoiced in Him, my best Friend, in the love of espousals, and now prove that rejoicing was not in vain, what He is in the banqueting-house He is in the furnace, all we need ; and the low chastened praises of suffering times are dear to Him as the more gladsome songs of bridal days. He was my theme then, my glory and joy—He is so still. He was my companion then, when drinking of the spiced wine—He is so now while receiving the vinegar. He has had it before me, and is my brother born for adversity, and precious companion in tribulation. I would glorify Him in the fires and praise Him to the last. Thou shalt do it, for Thou art my life, and Thou art my praise, O my Beloved !

You will take these imperfect lines in token of love in Him which decayeth not with withering mortality. I am feeble and sore broken in the flesh, but the spirit is untouched, " our life is hid with Christ in God," and no disease or death can find it.

Farewell, in the undying love of our changeless Lord, yours ever most affectionately, RUTH.

"Which things perish in the using," is strongly stamped on all below.

CXIX.

Lessons in the furnace.

TO MRS H.

" He hath done all things well."

June 7, 1860.

I was grieved to hear of your affliction, my beloved Amelia, and the more because I doubt it was brought on by over-walking that day you were here. But while with affectionate sympathy I feel for your suffering, I know most fully that it was not by chance or in vain, for

" Not a single shaft can hit,
   Till the God of love sees fit;"

and each one shall hit the right place, and accomplish His purpose. Oh ! it is so sweet and quieting to know that Divine purpose runs through every event of our lives—"let fall some of the handfuls of purpose for her," not only handfuls of pleasant mercies, but also of afflictions and trials at the appointed season, while His will runs as a straight line through every crooked circumstance, and our dissolving into that will, shall be our peace amidst it all. I hope you are now restored to your usual health. Thanks for your note and Mr H——'s, in both which I found a suitable word. I ought to have acknowledged them sooner, but I have been much worse. I am now reviving again, but very weak, having at times very deep exhaustions, at others much suffering. It is marvellous how I am kept in this state, but I know it is all right. If my gracious Lord will but be glorified thereby, I shall rejoice.

I have had the exercise of not seeing or hearing my Beloved, which was an additional trial under increased affliction, but at length He instructed me thereby from 1 Peter i. 7, and I felt the trial had been profitable and strengthening. I am now favoured with more conscious nearness, which alleviates bodily suffering.

Excuse all defects, I am very feeble. I have not written it all at once, and find it difficult to write, my arm being so contracted; but never mind, "the lame take the prey," and sit at the King's table, so all is well. Adieu, my loved Amelia. The storms of life will soon be over, the fetters of flesh will fall off, and the freed spirit reach its own element of holiness and love.—With dear love in our lovely and loving Lord, I rest in Him, your very affectionate

RUTH.

SANSON AND COMPANY, PRINTERS, EDINBURGH.

Printed in the United States
63071LVS00001B/1-54